INTEGRATED
EXPERIENTIAL COACHING

INTEGRATED
EXPERIENTIAL COACHING
Becoming an Executive Coach

Lloyd Chapman

With contributing author Sunny Stout Rostron

KARNAC

First published in 2010 by
Karnac Books Ltd
118 Finchley Road
London NW3 5HT

British Library Cataloguing in Publication Data

A C.I.P. for this book is available from the British Library

ISBN-13: 978-1-85575-739-4

Typeset by Vikatan Publishing Solutions (P) Ltd., Chennai, India

www.karnacbooks.com

CONTENTS

LIST OF TABLES   xi

LIST OF FIGURES   xiii

FOREWORD   xv

ACKNOWLEDGEMENTS   xix

ABOUT THE AUTHOR   xxi

INTRODUCTION   xxiii

CHAPTER ONE
Reflections on my personal journey   1

   Introduction   1
   My coaching journey   2
   Conclusion   12

CHAPTER TWO
The meta-philosophical framework   15

Introduction   15
Wilber's Integral Model   20
Wilber's principles   24
  Reality is composed of holons   24
  Capacities of holons   25
  Holons emerge   26
  Holons emerge holarchically   26
  Cognitive power and task complexity   28
  Holons include but transcend their predecessors   30
  Depth and span   31
  Evolution and transformation   32
  Stratified systems theory and complexity of information   34
Wilber's developmental process in the individual   36
  The prepersonal   40
  The personal   41
  The transpersonal   42
  Development is not a simple linear progression   47
  Individual and cultural progress   49
  A more integrative approach   52
  Critique of Wilber   53
  Integrative growth and development   60
An alternative integrated model   61
Kolb's Experiential Learning Model   65
  The Learning Styles Inventory (LSI)   68
  Experiential learning and development   73
  Kolb's developmental stages   75
Integrating the models of Wilber and Kolb   77
Summary   80

CHAPTER THREE
The methodological framework   81

Introduction   81
Phenomenology   82
  Subjective versus objective reality   83

Phenomenology's fundamental issues   84
The phenomenological method   86
    The Epoche process   88
    Phenomenological reduction   90
    Imaginative variation   92
    Synthesis of meaning and essences   93
Integrating transcendental phenomenology
    with the Integrated Experiential Coaching Model   93
Mastery   96
    The Dabbler, Obsessive and Hacker   97
    Valid knowledge   100
Learning conversations   103
Stages in the coaching relationship   114
    Stage 1: Establish contact   115
    Stage 2: Present current situation   116
    Stage 3: Explore current situation   117
    Stage 4: Choose foci   118
    Stage 5: Implement the working
        Learning Conversation   119
    Stage 6: Closure and review   119
Case study: How the Integrated Experiential
    Coaching Model is applied   120
Summary   123

CHAPTER FOUR
The business framework   125

Applying the Integrated Experiential
    Coaching Model in business   125
Strategy formulation and implementation   126
    The Balanced Scorecard   127
    The design problem   131
Structuring and designing the organization   136
    Managerial complexity   138
    Individual competencies   139
    Intrapsychic versus person-environment mix   151
Executive coaching defined   158
Summary   158

CHAPTER FIVE
Applying and researching the integrated
    Experiential Coaching Model   161

Introduction   161
Ethical and legal considerations   162
Implementation of the coaching process
    and the Integrated Experiential Coaching Model   165
Research design   168
    My role as researcher in terms of the design
    and conduct of the project   172
Research methodology   172
    Participants – co-researchers   172
    Data-gathering method   173
Data analysis and processing   174
    The Epoche process   174
    Phenomenological reduction   175
    Imaginative variation   176
    Synthesis of meaning and essences   177
Research findings   185
The Quaker Persuasion Model   190
The Corporate Leadership Council   194
Mintzberg's eight propositions   202
Limitations in doing the research   209

CHAPTER SIX
The integrated experiential coaching
    model in a team context   211

Concrete experience   212
Reflective observation   213
Abstract conceptualization   213
    Storytelling   216
Active experimentation   217
    Follow-on coaching interventions   217
Conclusion   218

CHAPTER SEVEN
The impact of stress on learning   219
Lloyd Chapman and Sunny Stout Rostron

Stress and the management of complexity –
   by Lloyd Chapman   219
   Stress and biofeedback   221
The Ten Components of a Thinking Environment® –
   by Sunny Stout Rostron   226
   Attention   230
   Equality   232
   Ease   233
   Appreciation   235
   Encouragement   236
   Feelings   237
   Information   239
   Diversity   240
   Incisive questions   244
   Place   245
   Existentialism and the thinking environment   245
   Learning from experience and
      emotional literacy   246
   Conclusion – by Lloyd Chapman   247

CHAPTER EIGHT
Personal reflections and implications
   of the coaching journey   249

Implications of the coaching journey
   for me as a person   249
Final reflections on learning   253

CHAPTER NINE
Conclusion   261

   Concrete experience   265
   Reflective observation   266
   Abstract conceptualization   267
   Active experimentation   268
   Conclusion   268

BIBLIOGRAPHY   269

INDEX   275

LIST OF TABLES

TABLE 1
Dialogue versus debate 8

TABLE 2
Wilber's 17 stages of individual development 37

TABLE 3
The basic structures of consciousness and the ages
at which they emerge during development 38

TABLE 4
The spectrum of stages, pathologies, and methods of treatment 45

TABLE 5
The three stages of individual and cultural development 50

TABLE 6
The bipolar structure of the psyche 53

TABLE 7
Wilber's stages of development in relation to Kolb's stages 78

TABLE 8
A simple category system of personal learning myths 111

TABLE 9
A dichotomy of power and control in learning   143

TABLE 10
Reflection-on-action and reflection-in-action   145

TABLE 11
Differentiating coaching from therapy   149

TABLE 12
Key elements of the Systems and Psychodynamics Model   154

TABLE 13
Research methodologies that were considered and rejected   169

TABLE 14
Executives' preferred option for developmental intervention   195

LIST OF FIGURES

FIGURE 1
Wilber's four-quadrant Integral Model   20

FIGURE 2
Measures of truth   22

FIGURE 3
Evolution of consciousness   24

FIGURE 4
Spectrum of consciousness   44

FIGURE 5
The Integral Psychograph as a holarchy   47

FIGURE 6
Organizational interventions in Wilber's model   58

FIGURE 7
Kolb's experiential learning model   67

FIGURE 8
The Experiential Learning theory of growth and development 74

FIGURE 9
Integrated Experiential Coaching Model   79

FIGURE 10
Integrated Experiential Coaching Model expanded   94

FIGURE 11
The maturity phases of the Integrated Experiential
Coaching Model   95

FIGURE 12
The Mastery Curve and its enemies   97

FIGURE 13
Learning conversations   103

FIGURE 14
Personal Learning Contract (PLC)   104

FIGURE 15
Integrated Experiential Coaching Model skills   108

FIGURE 16
Stages in the coaching relationship   115

FIGURE 17
The context of executive coaching   126

FIGURE 18
The underlying structure of organizational layers   134

FIGURE 19
Designing the internal processes of the organization   137

FIGURE 20
Designing the architecture of the organization   138

FIGURE 21
Evolution of managerial skills   142

FIGURE 22
Stages in the coaching relationship   165

FIGURE 23
Low returns on coaching effort   196

FIGURE 24
Heart rate variability pattern showing frustration or anger   223

FIGURE 25
Heart rate variability pattern showing sincere appreciation   225

FOREWORD

Coaching is growing across the globe as a viable and useful intervention to help executives deal with the complexity they face day-to-day. In response to this increased demand, many coaches have presented their "model" of coaching to the world of business, and a number of these have made it into print. Few are based on a rigorous development process or have provided the reader with an insight into their development.

We wanted to offer to the readers of our professional coaching series the opportunity to engage with a practitioner who had been through a journey of learning built on their experience, the litera-ture and research. In doing so, the aim was not to declare that this was the model that should be used. Rather, in common with the call in the *Dublin Declaration on Coaching* of the Global Convention on Coaching (GCC, 2008), we see practitioner-led research into coach-ing practice as a key part of the knowledge base for emerging pro-fessionalism within the field. Finding the right practitioner to do this was never going to be easy, but we were delighted when Lloyd Chapman accepted our invitation to attempt this task.

He brings a wealth of experience in business, and as an executive coach has worked at the leading edge of coaching initiatives. He has also committed himself to a scientist-practitioner framework, in which he believes that research is fundamental to practice, and practice in turn informs research.

So we asked him to share with us his journey through his own development as a coach, and to offer that as a way to help others do the same—not to come to the same conclusions, but to make the journey for themselves. We believe he has succeeded in creating the first truly integrated executive coaching model which brings together understanding from the worlds of learning, business and psychology. It is not, as the reader will become aware, an easy journey (this is not a book for the faint-hearted), but for those who stay with it we believe it will be one worth making.

What is the journey on which you, our readers, are about to embark?

Lloyd starts with his own journey to becoming a coach. He takes the view that who we are is part of the offer we make to clients, and influences the way we practise. So his invitation to the reader is to take that journey with him, by noting what occurs to you as he outlines how he arrived at the point of being a coach. He suggests you attempt a similar exercise in charting your progress to the coach you are now, noticing what occurs to you as you do so.

He then takes you through an interesting exploration of the theoretical territory. He asks: "Can the prospective coach make their model explicit? What philosophy, theory, application and experience underpin the coach's work? Has their work been researched; if not, what evidence do they have to substantiate their claims about their work?"

He shares the process of how he developed the Integrated Experiential Coaching Model within the scientist-practitioner framework. He uses a number of theoretical ideas, but draws in particular upon the work of Ken Wilber, A.H. Almaas, and David Kolb. This in itself represents new syntheses. However, he then goes on to build a methodological exploration using the transcendental phenomenology of Moustakas (1994), Schumacher's (1978) four fields of knowledge, and Harri-Augstein and Thomas's (1991) learning conversations. As a result, he proposes that coaching is about facilitating integrated experiential learning in individuals in order to enhance personal growth and development. If he had stopped there, he would have made a valuable and original contribution. However, he goes further, and explores how the Integrated Experiential Coaching Model can be applied "in the messy and complex world of managerial leadership". He incorporates strategy using the work of Kaplan and Norton (1996), Galbraith, Downey and Kates (2002), and Rehm (1997). This is further enhanced through work on individual leadership competencies (Jaques and Clement, 1997), and the work of Oshry (1999) and Kilburg (2000). He argues that behavioural problems manifested by individuals within an organization could be intrapsychic, or due to systemic organizational design problems, or even the result of a combination of both.

He concludes that an effective executive coaching intervention should be able to deal with each of these possibilities to enhance both individual and organisational growth and development. His synthesis produces a comprehensive and elegant theoretical framework for executive coaching.

The journey continues with a detailed account of his experimental work in the use, further development and refinement of the model. The reader will see the development in action, and it is rare to find this process elucidated in such detail. These sections will repay careful reading. Applications in team coaching and stress follow. He concludes with recommendations for the reader's development of your own model of practice, and thus the book returns to its beginning – the journey to be the coach you want to be.

The book meets the need we identified for a clear and rigorous account by an experienced coach of the development of their model within the scientist-practitioner framework. As such it makes a contribution to the call from the Global Convention on Coaching for practitioners to make their work available for scrutiny by others. For our readers we believe it will provide inspiration to continue with your own journeys, and a wealth of ideas you can experiment with and apply to the benefit of your clients.

Professor David Lane
Series Editor
Professional Development Foundation and
International Centre for the Study of Coaching,
Middlesex University.

ACKNOWLEDGEMENTS

The writing of this book would never have happened if it was not for the persistence of Professor David Lane, who has been encouraging me to write this book since 2006. At times I think he had more faith in me than I had in myself. Eventually his persistence has paid off, and the book has been written. I am also thankful to David for arranging a publisher for this book, and for his guidance and recommendations.

To my colleague Nick Wilkins who edited, re-edited and proof-read. What I appreciate most is his attention to detail, and the speed with which he did the work. If it was not for him, it might have taken another year for this book to have been completed.

To my colleague Sunny Stout Rostron for her continuous encouragement, for authoring the section on the Ten Components of a Thinking Environment® in Chapter seven, and for assisting with the editing. Like David, Sunny kept on at me to publish.

Lastly to my wife Pamela, my daughter Ashley, and my son Sheldon, for putting up with my absences and grumpiness over the length of this project. I hope that I am able to make up the time that I have not spent with them while I was working on this book.

ABOUT THE AUTHOR

Lloyd Chapman is an executive coach, organizational architect and certified personal fitness trainer. He has 22 years' business experience in leading, managing and implementing strategy, large-scale organizational change, mergers and acquisitions, business process re-engineering, and workflow implementations and various other IT-related projects. He is a founding director of the Manthano Institute of Learning (Pty) Ltd, a consortium of executive coaches delivering integral, experiential coaching grounded in work-based learning and research.

Lloyd completed a Doctorate in Professional Studies in Executive Coaching through Middlesex University and the National Centre for Work-Based Learning in the United Kingdom. (He was the first person in the world to qualify with a DProf in Executive Coaching). He holds an MBA degree and degrees in marketing, theology and a diploma in personal fitness training.

He has been a guest lecturer at the Graduate School of Business of the University of Cape Town, the University of Stellenbosch Business School, and the Department of Industrial Psychology of the University of South Africa. His post-doctoral research interest is the issue of how high levels of stress affect an executive's heart rate variability, which in turn inhibits optimal cortical (logical) functioning.

Lloyd is fortunate enough to live in Cape Town, South Africa with his wife, daughter and son.

INTRODUCTION

If you are hoping that this is another book which will provide you with a five- or seven-step coaching model, please put it down, as you would be wasting your money. This book is not aimed at the novice coach, it is aimed at those coaches who have extensive experience and would like to anchor their practice on a theoretically-grounded, evidence-based scientist-practitioner model. Senior executives and human resources management practitioners who have an interest in using and sourcing executive coaches will find this book helpful, in that it will give them an idea of the kinds of question they should be asking of prospective coaches. Can the prospective coach make their model explicit? What philosophy, theory, application and experience underpins the coach's work? Has their work been researched; if not, what evidence do they have to substantiate their claims about their work?

This book is an experiential account of my journey towards becoming an executive coach. So why write my story, and why do I think that my story can make a contribution to the discipline of coaching? In July 2008 a number of coaches from around the world met at the Global Coaching Convention (GCC) in Dublin to discuss the development and professionalization of coaching. The GCC's

Working Group on a Research Agenda for Development of the Field noted in the Research Appendix to the *Dublin Declaration on Coaching* that "Research is critical to the development of the emerging profession of coaching", that "Every practitioner has the responsibility of doing research in their own practice", and that "Practitioner and academic research are considered to be of equal value to the coaching community and its developing body of knowledge" (GCC, 2008:11).

In supporting that notion, however, I was immediately confronted with a dilemma. And the dilemma was simply this: there are so many coaching books in the market. Books on coaching models, what coaching is, and what it is not. But nowhere could I find a book which explained how a coach could develop their own practice and coaching model within the scientist-practitioner framework. And if we want to develop the emerging profession of coaching within that framework, there needs to be examples of what it means to be a scientist-practitioner, and how to develop one's own model and practice within that framework.

This book is a response to that need. This is my story of how I developed and researched my own coaching model and practice within the scientist-practitioner framework, which ultimately led to the first Doctorate in Professional Studies in Executive Coaching completed through the National Centre for Work-Based Learning at Middlesex University, London. It is not an attempt to present the definitive model on coaching; it is rather my model that I developed for my coaching practice, and that was born out of my experience; it is congruent with who I am. The more fundamental aim of the book is, however, to share a thought process with you that will enable you, the reader, to hopefully develop your own coaching model and practice within the scientist-practitioner framework.

In their book *The Modern Scientist-Practitioner: A Guide to Practice in Psychology*, David Lane and Sarah Corrie (2006) argue the case for reformulating what it means to be a modern scientist-practitioner within the profession of psychology. I believe that their reformulated scientist-practitioner model is a very good basis on which to establish and define the profession of executive coaching. They suggest that the scientist-practitioner organizes their reasoning skills around three domains, namely purpose, perspective and process (Lane and Corrie, 2006:48–49):

1. **Purpose**. They believe that in undertaking any psychological enquiry it is vitally important to be clear about the journey's fundamental purpose. What is it that the practitioner and client are hoping to achieve? In other words, what are the outputs or results that the client wants to achieve? In defining a clear purpose, clear boundaries can also be established. It helps to define with whom the therapist will and will not work, and when it will be important or necessary to refer the client to another professional.

2. **Perspective**. They point out that part of the agreed purpose would include being able to define what the therapist brings to the encounter. This would include all the practitioner's models, values, beliefs, knowledge and philosophies, as well as a sense of their competence limitations. I would go so far as to say that this would include the metaphysical models and assumptions that the person holds.

3. **Process**. Having defined the purpose and perspective that underpin the work, it then becomes possible to structure a process to undertake the work. So what method or tools can be used to help achieve the desired purpose within the constraints of the specified perspective?

Lane and Corrie's (2006) three perspectives for the scientist-practitioner are very similar to, if not the same as, Mouton's (2001:137–142) "three worlds" framework for research, comprising:

1. **World 1**. The world of everyday life and lay knowledge. This is the world of ordinary social and physical reality. This is where we spend most of our lives and we use lay knowledge, i.e. common sense, experiential knowledge, wisdom, insight and practical know-how, to solve problems and gain insight into everyday tasks and problems. It is here that social and practical problems arise that require interventions, action, programmes or therapy. Lane and Corrie's (2006) "purpose" will be formulated in, and to address problems encountered in, World 1.

2. **World 2**. The world of science and scientific research. Scientists select phenomena from World 1 and turn them into objects of scientific inquiry. "Whereas in everyday life we search for knowledge that will help us cope better with the challenges and demands of each day (a very pragmatic interest), the aim of

science is to generate truthful (valid and reliable) descriptions, models and theories of the world" (Mouton, 2001:138). This has to do with the research process in terms of its problem statement, design, methodology and conclusions. This of course takes place within certain defined theories, models, typologies, concepts and definitions. World 2 is the context of Lane and Corrie's (2006) process domain.

3. **World 3**. The world of meta-science. This is the world in which we reflect on the reasons and justifications for certain actions. More importantly, it is the world of critical reflection, deciding which theory, indicators, measurements, and research design to choose. Over time this has led to various meta-disciplines, theories and paradigms, including paradigms in the philosophy of science and in research methodologies. This is the perspective domain covered by Lane and Corrie (2006), a critical component which I believe is often neglected by coaching practitioners. In fact, I would not stop at the world of meta-science; I am in full agreement with E.F. Schumacher, the economist and Rhodes Scholar, that it should include the metaphysical:

> Education cannot help us as long as it accords no place to meta-physics. Whether the subjects taught are subjects of science or of the humanities, if the teaching does not lead to a clarification of metaphysics, that is to say, of our fundamental convictions, it cannot educate a man and, consequently, cannot be of real value to society ... What is at fault is not specialization, but the lack of depth with which the subjects are usually presented, and the absence of metaphysical awareness. The sciences are being taught without any awareness of the presuppositions of science, of the meaning and significance of scientific laws, and of the place occupied by the natural sciences within the whole cosmos of human thought. The result is that the presuppositions of science are normally mistaken for its findings. Economics is being taught without any awareness of the view of human nature that underlies present-day economic theory. In fact, many economists are themselves unaware of the fact that such a view is implicit in their teaching and that nearly all their theories would have to change if that view changed (Schumacher, 1989:98–99).

If coaching is to develop into a fully-fledged profession, I believe that it is critical for us as coaches to develop our critical reflection skills and apply them to the world of meta-science, metaphysics and meta-theories as it pertains to coaching. Therefore, I am in total agreement with Lane and Corrie (2006) that scientist-practitioners must be able to make their perspectives explicit. Only if we make them explicit can they be held up for critical reflection.

In this book I will share the process of how I developed and continue to develop the Integrated Experiential Coaching Model within the scientist-practitioner framework. Part of the process is to make the Integrated Experiential Coaching Model explicit so that it can be held up for critical reflection. It is my sincere hope that it can contribute to the dialogue of what it means to be a scientist-practitioner within the evolving and emerging profession of coaching. In order to make the model explicit I will use David Kolb's (1984) Experiential Learning Model.

Chapter one: Reflections on my personal journey

Chapter one is a personal account of my own concrete experience and reflective observation on that experience. It is my story of how I stumbled into the field of coaching. Like so many coaches I have met, I did not plan to become a coach; it was an evolutionary journey. The chapter outlines the way in which I came to develop an interest in coaching, and the theories that contributed to that interest.

Chapter two: The meta-philosophical framework

Chapters two to four deal with the philosophies and theories that underpin the Integrated Experiential Coaching Model; in other words, these are the abstract conceptualization chapters. In Chapter two, I explore three meta-theories that have influenced, and are an integral part of, the Integrated Experiential Coaching Model. The first meta-theory is the Integral Model of Ken Wilber. I want to make it clear from the outset that I believe Wilber's theory is **a** theory and not **the** theory. I have, however, found it to be a very useful conceptual framework within which to think and do my work.

The second meta-theory that is explored very briefly in Chapter two is the Diamond Approach developed by A.H. Almaas. Once again,

I do little justice to the depth and excellence of his work. But in the context of this book, it is necessary only to make the reader aware of Almaas's work. I would highly recommend his work to any person exploring a more integrative approach to life.

The last meta-theory explored in Chapter two is the Experiential Learning Theory of David Kolb. The more I work with his theory, the more respect I gain for the depth involved therein. Sadly, I believe that many people use Kolb's work very superficially. Finally, I end Chapter two with the integration of Wilber (1995) and Kolb (1984); and this new synthesis is the Integrated Experiential Coaching Model.

Chapter three: The methodological framework

Having a theory with no methodology is of no value to anyone, and so Chapter three deals with the methodological framework. The chapter uses the transcendental phenomenology of Moustakas (1994), Schumacher's (1978) four fields of knowledge, and Harri-Augstein and Thomas's (1991) learning conversations, to further enhance the Integrated Experiential Coaching Model. The Model proposes that coaching is about facilitating integrated experiential learning in individuals in order to enhance personal growth and development. It is "integrated" in that it caters for Schumacher's four fields of knowledge, and for Wilber's Integral Model which analyzes personal development through various levels of consciousness, especially in the personal and transpersonal levels. It is "experiential" in that it uses Kolb's Experiential Learning Model as the injunction or paradigm, and uses Harri-Augstein and Thomas's concept of Learning Conversations as the primary learning tool.

Chapter four: The business framework

In Chapter four I explore how the Integrated Experiential Coaching Model can be applied in the messy and complex world of managerial leadership. The chapter takes the theoretical Integrated Experiential Coaching Model, and adds a business context to it. This is done by incorporating strategy formulation via the Balanced Scorecard of Kaplan and Norton (1996), and organizational design principles with reference to the work of Galbraith, Downey and Kates

(2002) and Rehm (1997). All of this has to happen within a world of managerial complexity which can overwhelm executives.

Having set the business context, Chapter four then explores the individual leadership competencies of Jaques and Clement (1997), and how those competencies could help an executive cope with managerial complexity. What becomes clear is that within the business context, coaching is not therapy. Using the work of Peltier (2001), a clear distinction is made between coaching and therapy.

Lastly, referring to the work of Oshry (1999) and Kilburg (2000) it is shown that behavioural problems manifested by individuals within an organization could be intrapsychic, or due to systemic organizational design problems, or even the result of a combination of both. Hence it is argued that an executive coaching intervention should be aimed at working with cognitive potential, values, knowledge, skills and wisdom within the system in which the individual operates. In the Integrated Experiential Coaching Model, executive coaching is therefore about facilitating integrated experiential learning in individuals in order to enhance personal growth and development with the aim of improving individual and organizational performance. It is not therapy.

Chapter five: Applying and researching the integrated experiential coaching model

In Chapter five I move into the active experimentation part of experiential learning. This chapter briefly presents the findings of my doctoral research, which involved applying and researching the outcomes of coaching within the context of the Integrated Experiential Coaching Model. I then go on to explore how the Integrated Experiential Coaching Model has strong similarities to the "Friendly Disentangling" method or persuasion model developed by the Quakers. In 2003 the Corporate Leadership Council in the US published a report titled *Maximizing Returns on Professional Executive Coaching*. The report stemmed from research that the Corporate Leadership Council had undertaken at the request of its members into the effectiveness of Executive Coaching as a development intervention. I explore how the Integrated Experiential Coaching Model and the research findings relate to the five identified challenges identified by the Corporate Leadership Council.

In his book *Managers Not MBAs*, Henry Mintzberg (2004) challenges the conventional notion that the MBA degree develops managers. Following his critique of the MBA programmes, Mintzberg (2004) suggests a different approach to developing managers based on eight propositions. Although he expounds the propositions in the context of university training, I believe that they are applicable to coaching as well. In the last part of Chapter five, I explore these eight propositions, and see whether or not the Integrated Experiential Coaching Model and my doctoral research findings can be related to them.

Chapter six: The integrated experiential coaching model in a team context

Chapters six and seven deal with ongoing refinements to the Integrated Experiential Coaching model as a result of continuous critical thinking based on new evidence gathered from practice and my own ongoing experiential learning journey. Chapter six explores how the Integrated Experiential Coaching Model can be applied within a team coaching intervention.

Chapter seven: The impact of stress on learning

Chapter seven discusses the impact that stress can have on a manager's ability to learn, which in turn has a direct impact on the individual's ability to manage complexity. The chapter then explores feasible ways of dealing with and managing stress effectively.

Chapter eight: Personal reflections and implications of the coaching journey

Chapter eight concludes the experiential learning cycle, and I once again reflect on my own experiential coaching journey. This time, however, the reflection is on the development, application, research, and continuous refinement of the Integrated Experiential Coaching Model.

Chapter nine: Conclusion

In conclusion, I give some recommendations on a process that can be followed in order to develop your own coaching model and methodology within the context of the experiential learning cycle.

CHAPTER ONE

Reflections on my personal journey

Introduction

Given that the scientist-practitioner model is a dynamic process, I believe that it is important to start this book with a brief overview of how I stumbled into the field of coaching. I never planned to become an executive coach. I think that, like so many other coaches, I developed into a coach through a process of unfolding experiences. This is my story. But why share my story, and what relevance does it have for you as a coach? As scientist-practitioners our practice is grounded in our work and in our experience. We ply our trade in Mouton's (2001) "World 1", the world of ordinary social and physical reality. It is here in the world that we encounter practical problems that require interventions, action and programmes. In an attempt to find practical solutions to those problems, we tend to draw on our own experience, reflect, do research and look for theories that can help us to make sense of the reality we are confronted with. When we find theories that help throw some light on the issue, we tend to experiment with them to see if they work for us. In so doing we move into "World 3", in which we reflect on the reasons and justifications for certain actions. More importantly it is the world of critical reflection, deciding which theory, indicators, measurement and actions we need to choose.

One way to make sense of this entire process is to reflect on our own lives, through telling our story. As we tell our story, we are forced to reflect on our own experience and the events that shape that experience. We reflect on how we responded to those events, the people and the theories that helped us to make sense of those experiences. We do not become coaches in a vacuum, or overnight; it is an unfolding evolutionary process.

As you read the story of my journey I would encourage you to be aware of your responses and reactions to what you read. For it is not uncommon that as we listen or read another person's story, certain memories and connections can be triggered that will help you remember aspects of your own journey. Take note of them, journal about them, or write them down. Reflect on your own experience as thoughts and memories are triggered. Remember the connections, people, theories and experiences that contributed to your own journey as a coach. Use my story as an example to remember your own. Use it as an example of how to reflect on your own experience. In the end it is not my story that is important but your own. For in your own experience and story you will discover the **Purpose**, whereby clear boundaries can also be established for your work as a coach. That will help you to define with whom you will and will not work, and when it will be important or necessary to refer the client to another professional. You will discover the **Perspective** that underpins your work. This will include all the models, values, beliefs, knowledge and philosophies that have influenced you, as well as a sense of their limitations. This will ultimately help you to define and structure a **process** to undertake the work you do. In other words, what method or tools can be used to help achieve the desired purpose within the constraints of the specified perspective?

My coaching journey

I started my working career as a minister of religion after completing my Theological studies in 1984. During my probation year I decided to leave the ministry and enter into the world of business. My interest in business arose through my interaction with executives during that probation year. I had the fortunate privilege of working with executives in a number of settings. The interactions from which I learnt the most, however, occurred when I ministered to executives dying of cancer or having had double or triple heart bypass operations. It gave me a perspective on life that has never left me. It also developed a strong empathy within me for these leaders of industry. Most people only see executive's successful sides; I got to know them when they were at their most vulnerable. Despite their outward success and enormous wealth, in the end it actually meant nothing. The awareness that life is more important than our work has never left me.

On completing my National Service I worked in a bank for three months and then joined the Investments Division of a large life assurance company. Initially I provided administration support to the portfolio managers, and later I worked in marketing. Here my function was to analyze unit trust performance, and write all the marketing material. The five years in the Investments Division taught me a great deal about financial markets and their complexities. I gained a good working knowledge of economics and the impact it has on various industries and the financial markets. It taught me to look at business in a more holistic way, and I gained a working knowledge of macro- and microeconomics.

During this time, my ability to do quantitative research and my analytical skills grew exponentially. I therefore decided to do my MBA dissertation on "The viability of index funds for the Republic of South Africa". With hindsight I can now see that my MBA dissertation was the first piece of concrete experiential learning I had ever undertaken. Unfortunately, as with most Masters degrees the abstract conceptualization was limited to learning existing theories and applying them to a new context.

In 1992, having just completed my MBA, I joined another life assurance company. The late-1990s were a very interesting time in South Africa. The African National Congress (ANC) had been unbanned in 1990, the first democratic elections in the history of the country had taken place in 1994, and the country was a political miracle. The same could not be said of the business environment. Prior to the 1994 elections many industries had grown and survived in a protected environment. This was especially true in the case of the financial services industry. The most protected of all were the life assurance companies, which had grown and thrived in an environment of exchange controls, high inflation, with effectively no competition, and they controlled the unit trust industry.

The net result was too many life assurance companies in the market. Given that they effectively had no competition, they were running very expensive operations. The overarching strategy for the industry was "new business at all costs". Quality service did not exist. These institutions were at the mercy of the intermediaries. The intermediary was king, not the client.

Given the changes that were occurring in the country, there was a realization that the company had to be transformed or it would not survive. It was in this environment that the General Manager of Administration invited me to come and work for him. At the time, Peter Senge's (1990) concept of the "learning organization", and Michael Hammer and James Champy's (1993) theory of "business process re-enginering", were the topics of discussion in the boardrooms of South Africa.

The General Manager of Operations knew that the company was running an expensive operation, and he wanted to re-engineer the administration processes. I had introduced him to a systems dynamic computer simulation package called iThink®, and suggested that we use the package to simulate our business processes before we make any changes to the business.

As a result, we opted to first build the processes in a computer simulation environment and do all our what-if analysis in that environment. I was given responsibility for this project, to do the analysis, involve everybody and build the model. For the first time in the company's history there was an actual understanding as to how complex the new business process within a life company was.

Until we had built this model, one of the assumptions was that if we implemented an electronic workflow system we could get rid of all our regional underwriters and save the company a great deal of money. What we learnt was that our assumptions were incorrect, and that we would have a huge bottleneck in the process if we kept only our head office underwriters. It was impossible for them to cope with the new workload. As a result, a number of regional underwriters were relocated to head office. Once they were in place we started to implement the re-engineered process.

Due to the success of the project, I was placed in charge of the workflow project. Strategically this was a critical project, in that workflow could improve our cost ratios substantially. There were only two life companies in South Africa at the time that had decided to implement workflow on a national basis. All the remaining companies had opted to implement workflow in a centralized head office environment. Due to the postal service in South Africa being very ineffective and unreliable, workflow was seen as being critical to improving customer service. Needless to say, a technology project of this magnitude would be very complex.

The first thing I did was to attend a project management course. The second thing I did was to model the complexity of the project in iThink®. Once again I had to work with all levels and functions within the organization. This was one of the steepest learning curves in my life. The thing about workflow is that it cuts across the entire business. This was really the point in my life where I started to think in terms of processes instead of functions. Workflow breaks down all functional boundaries. The other thing about workflow is that it is a very complex environment, in that it interacts with every single computer system within the company. This is where my analytical and synthesizing abilities grew in leaps and bounds. I had to analyze which systems were involved, how they worked, and the interdependencies between them. Finally, all this had to be synthesized into a workable model. It was during this process that I learnt to apply systems thinking to solve a practical business problem.

When I had completed the model we realized that our current network was not going to cope with the demands the workflow system would place on it. We did a number of tests and then realized we had to replace our entire network. A new network was implemented.

My team then set about building the workflow system. Within 18 months the first phase of the workflow project was implemented. This was my first experience of managing a large, complex project which was of strategic importance to the company.

I was then given the responsibility for developing an Internet strategy for the company, which my team and I did. We were the first life assurance company in South Africa to give our clients and brokers access to their information via the Internet. In fact, when Bill Gates visited South Africa he used the company website as an example of what was possible using the Microsoft® environment.

By late 1996 the company had developed some very sophisticated IT systems and infrastructure. We had become very proficient in the client server environment. The problem, and the frustration, was that we had built sophisticated systems but we were finding it difficult to get people to use the systems optimally. We had changed the infrastructure and excelled, but we had totally ignored the change management side of the project. The technical side was excellent, but the social and cultural change was nonexistent. This is where I learnt that technology does not provide a company with a strategic competitive advantage. Technology is only an enabler. The strategic advantage of a company is its people; it is the ability of the people to learn faster than their competitors.

In September 1996 the Managing Director invited me to become the company strategist reporting directly to him. Eventually, the General Manager of Administration convinced me to take the job, on the grounds that it was a good platform from which to start influencing cultural change within the organization. In October 1996, at the age of 33, I was appointed company strategist and secretary to the Executive Committee.

By early 1997 the Executive realized that we did not have the skills or knowledge to manage large-scale change interventions. As a result, a consulting firm was contracted to help us transform the culture of the company. Cultural surveys had revealed a very autocratic and disempowered culture. The Executive felt that if the company was to survive in the new environment they had to start empowering their staff.

The project involved the entire company in strategy formulation and implementation. The process was basically a combination of Future Search Methodologies and Participative Redesign workshops, known as the "Transformation Process". Future Search Methodologies were conceived during the 1960s by Emery and Trist at the Tavistock Institute, and further developed and popularized during the 1980s by Marvin Weisborg. Participative Redesign was adapted by Bob Rehm in the mid-1990s.

As company strategist I worked very closely with the consultants from the beginning. However, the ownership of the project rested with the Managing Director. The process effectively started with the Managing Director doing a personal future search and setting the direction for the company. An executive future search would continue once the strategy was co-created. This was followed by a search involving the entire management team, who further co-created the strategy. At the same time, a process began in which people within the organization elected representatives who would attend a national future search conference. In July 1997 the national conference took place, the first of its type in South Africa, in which 80 people from every level within the organization were present to co-create the company's strategy.

Thereafter, each executive would cascade the process through his or her entire division. These workshops would then be followed up with re-design workshops where self-managed teams were introduced. By this time, it become apparent that the process was more complex than anybody had anticipated.

I began to realize that many of the executives and senior management were overwhelmed by the complexity involved with such a large-scale change initiative. I found myself spending more and more of my time coaching the executives on a one-on-one basis. It was then that I started to read the work of Ken Wilber. In Wilber I found an author that provided me with a more holistic framework for my thinking. It had slowly dawned on me that systems thinking was not as holistic as I had originally thought. Wilber introduced me to the concept of levels of consciousness, and that there is a worldview associated with each level. Subsequent to that, I stumbled upon the work of Elliott Jaques and Stephen Clement (1997) on stratified systems theory, which complemented Wilber's work very well. Finally, I had found in these three individuals a theoretical framework which fit my experience. For the first time, I started to understand why the complexity was overwhelming many of the executives and management. They were simply out of their depth. Some did not have the cognitive power to deal with such complexity.

Future search methodologies are action-oriented and rely on experiential learning. As a result of that, I became a devotee of experiential learning. The more I facilitated future search workshops, the more I learnt about experiential learning—experientially. To this day I am impressed by how simple and yet how hard it is, by its simplicity and its complexity. I also became more and more impressed with Kaplan and Norton's (1996) Balanced Scorecard. It is a tool, and a discipline, which takes strategy from formulation to implementation, and enables one to better manage some of the complexities involved with large-scale change interventions. A big learning curve for me during this time was the power of dialogue and narrative.

As people dialogued and told their stories we were able to extract some phenomenal learning. Soon I was using dialogue and experiential learning as the basis for all these searches, especially during the history sessions. I adapted Table 1 from the work of Danar Zohar (1997) for use in facilitation, and it has served me well ever since.

Another big learning curve at the time was that many of the conflicts we thought were interpersonal were not. To our surprise, we found that executives could actually get on with each other outside the work environment—while at work "all hell broke loose". As we explored this, through dialogue and action learning, we soon discovered that the conflicts resulted from the way organizations are designed. Conflict is built into the system. Because we design organizations in terms of functions instead of processes, the system produces certain behaviours. We keep thinking it's the person, so we get rid of that person and replace them with someone else. Sooner or later the new person reacts in a similar manner. The system creates

Table 1. Dialogue versus debate.

Dialogue	Debate
Finding out	Knowing
Questions	Answers
Equal	Winning/losing
Respect/reverence	Proving a point
New possibilities	Defending a position
Inquiring into assumptions	Justifying/defending assumptions
Learning through inquiry and disclosure	Persuading, selling & telling
Creating shared meaning among many	Choosing one meaning among many
Seeing connections and relationships	Seeing distinctions and differences
Seeing the whole that encompasses the parts	Breaking problems into parts

Source: Adapted from Zohar (1997:139).

its own behaviours. Here I found the work of Barry Oshry (1999) on seeing and leading systems invaluable. In the end, the system is more powerful than the individual. This was the hardest lesson of all. Despite (or perhaps because of) all we had achieved, the company became the target of a hostile takeover in February 1998. I was approached by the Managing Director of the acquiring company to stay on and head up the merger of the two life companies.

It was in this environment that I was asked to assist the executives and senior managers to co-create their strategies, define and design the appropriate processes and structures, and develop a new culture. Over the next six months my colleagues and I flew all over the country facilitating 20 of these workshops. In between, I sat in on all the executive and senior management meetings. Once again I found myself in the position of coaching the executives and senior management, either as teams or on a one-on-one basis. Based on my previous experience, I was starting to be convinced that executive coaching could be a viable profession. When I was not facilitating workshops, I was coaching executives and managers. During the following three years, I experienced a really powerful lesson in how business is run: not on rational principles, but by organizational politics.

Even worse, the executives were battling to cope with the merger, especially with the new levels of complexity, which had increased exponentially. I was eventually asked to relocate to Johannesburg, something I was not prepared to do. Furthermore, I had become convinced that executive management was starting to make decisions which would eventually lead to the company's demise. By the end of July 2000, executive management decided to restructure the group. Given these new circumstances, and my interest in executive coaching, I opted to start negotiating for a retrenchment package. As Executive Manager CRM and E-Commerce, I officially ended my career at the company in February 2001 to open an executive coaching practice. In June 2001 the company's biggest institutional shareholder, which was not happy with developments, stepped in and took it over.

Given my extensive experience in coaching executives, and with all that I had learnt over the years, I founded my own company specializing in executive coaching, strategy formulation, change management and organizational design. However, having established an executive coaching practice in South Africa, I felt the need to become better qualified as a coach. My MBA degree gave me the theoretical business background, and my business experience gave me a solid experiential base. Also, my qualification as a personal fitness trainer gave me a good basis for performance coaching, but I felt I needed more, and so I investigated all the available coaching programmes. Most courses seemed over-simplified; none really catered for the complexity that I was used to working with, but taught a single coaching model on which learners were evaluated. When the Middlesex Doctorate in Professional Studies became available in South Africa I jumped at the opportunity. What appealed to me was that I was expected to develop my own coaching model, and that the programme was based on work-based learning and accredited by an international academic institution.

As a result of my working experience, and as part of the requirements for this doctoral programme, I developed a theoretical integrated coaching model. It must be emphasized, however, that at the time the model existed only in embryonic form, as a broad conceptual construct in the form of a PowerPoint® presentation. The model still had to be written-up and fully developed. I named this model the Integrated Experiential Coaching Model. It is integrated in that it embodies for E.F. Schumacher's (1978) four fields of knowledge, and Ken Wilber's (1996) Integral Model which explores personal development through various levels of consciousness, especially at the personal and transpersonal levels. It is experiential in that it uses David Kolb's (1984) Experiential Learning Model as the injunction and Sheila Harri-Augstein and Laurie Thomas's (1991) concept of Learning Conversations as the primary learning tool.

One of the first clients I acquired after I started my own business was an information technology (IT) company specializing in large outsourcing contracts. I became involved with the company when their relationship with their biggest client was at an all-time low. I was contracted to facilitate experiential learning workshops involving the most senior managers of the company and its client, to try and uncover what had gone wrong, and to develop a way forward. We discovered that both companies were structured incorrectly— their organizational structures did not support their critical business processes, but in fact worked against them. As a result of these findings, the company went through a major restructuring. Until then the entire executive team resided in Johannesburg. In response to the needs of their biggest client, they decided to split the country into two regions, North and South, with the North based in Johannesburg and the South based in Cape Town.

Shortly after arriving in Cape Town, the new General Manager for the South contracted me to do some process improvement work for him in one of his divisions. While doing this work we often used to talk about executive coaching as a possible intervention within the company. This culminated in him asking me to do a formal presentation to him on coaching and the benefits it could have for his business.

Given that I been involved in the process that led to the company's restructuring, and was facilitating some process work for the company, it was only natural to integrate that into the coaching model to show how coaching could support managers with business process design and implementation and how that supported the company's Balanced Scorecard. By its very nature, any change in the company's critical business processes would have an impact on its organizational structure; management's experience with their biggest client had proven that to them. I therefore had to address the issue of organizational design in the coaching model. The Balanced Scorecard, business process design and organizational design were all critical issues that the company was wrestling with at the time, and I had to show how coaching could be used to support these activities.

Having defined the tools that could be used in the coaching model, I turned my attention to what competencies managers would need to effectively implement and manage the Balanced Scorecard, business process design and organizational design. Over the years I had seen leadership models come and go, and I was old enough to have a healthy scepticism of all such fads. One model with which I could, however, increasingly identify was Elliot Jaques and Stephen Clements' (1997) approach to leadership competencies. I especially liked their concept of cognitive power, which is the potential strength of cognitive processes in individuals. Their research seemed to indicate that if an individual's cognitive power did not match the level of complexity required for the task, the complexity would eventually overwhelm the individual.

In my experience I had seen this happen in practice a number of times. Furthermore, I knew that this concept would go down very well within the company as it tested an individual's cognitive power as part of selection processes. The other aspect of Jaques and Clement's (1997) model that strongly appealed to me was their idea that any attempt to define leadership qualities and traits was misguided. Over the years I have seen the damage that has been done to individuals by trying to force them into certain moulds. The leaders I had come to admire and respect over time never seemed to fit into any neat description or model. These individuals all seemed to have a unique set of strengths and weaknesses. So intuitively there was something within me that identified with what Jaques and Clements were saying.

What I did not know at the time was that Jaques and Clement's (1997) leadership competencies were actually implied on Level 3 of the generic key competencies of the company. Level 3 and below are senior executives and board members within the organization. Jaques and Clement's leadership competencies were therefore in complete alignment with that of the organization. This coincidence greatly aided my attempts to sell the coaching model to the General Manager and the rest of the organization.

Early in 2003 I presented the Integrated Experiential Coaching Model to the General Manager of Human Resources, who decided to include 17 people in a six-month pilot coaching project within South Africa. At the same time, I suggested that the pilot project be used as part of my doctoral research. The advantage for the company was that the entire project would necessarily be of a high enough standard to withstand the rigour of academic standards and procedures.

The timing was perfect, as the company was interested in exploring executive coaching to help management and leadership better handle the complexities involved in running a large IT outsourcing company. It was hoped that coaching could help to integrate these issues within the minds of the company's leaders and managers.

Conclusion

This chapter gave a very brief overview of my personal journey towards becoming a coach. It was important to tell some of the story in order to set a context of how and why the Integrated Experiential Coaching model was developed. In fact, the whole Model arose out of my own concrete experience and my reflection on that experience. I hope that telling this story facilitated a process within you, the sudden remembering of an event, theory, connection, or a person that influenced you as a coach. I hope you took note of that, and that it started a process of reflection on your own experience. Chapters two, three and four will deal with the theory of the Model—in other words, with the abstract conceptualization of experiential learning.

CHAPTER TWO

The meta-philosophical framework

Introduction

In this chapter I explore three meta-theories that have influenced, and led to the development of, the Integrated Experiential Coaching Model. The first is the Integral Theory of Ken Wilber. From the outset I want to make it clear that I believe Wilber's theory is **a** theory and not **the** theory. I have found it to be a very useful conceptual framework in which to think and do my work. The second meta-theory that is explored very briefly in this chapter is the Diamond Approach developed by A.H. Almaas. I do little justice to the depth and excellence of his work. But in the context of this book, it was necessary to only briefly make the reader aware of his work, which I would highly recommend to any person exploring a more integrative approach to life. The last meta-theory explored in this chapter is the Experiential Learning Theory of David Kolb. The more I work with his theory, the more respect I gain for its depth. I do believe that, sadly, many people use Kolb's work very superficially.

Robert K. Greenleaf (1977:13–14) once defined the test of true leadership as follows:

The best test, and difficult to administer, is: Do those served grow as persons? Do they, while being served, become healthier, wiser, freer, more autonomous, more likely themselves to become servants? And, what is the effect on the least privileged in society; will they benefit, or, at least not be further deprived?

I believe this is the test that should be applied to any executive coaching model. In the chapters that follow I will present a coaching model and research findings that I believe can meet, and do meet, the test described by Greenleaf.

In 1924 General Jan Smuts wrote a book called *Holism and Evolution*. He proposed that life evolved and continues to evolve into higher levels of complexity and wholeness. Life evolved out of matter, mind evolved out of life, and spirit evolved out of mind. More importantly, this evolution forms an integrated whole; that is to say, there is a continuous progression towards integration and unity. This is not, in itself, a new idea. Schumacher (1978), an economist, pointed out that the four great Levels of Being have been around for thousands of years, and that this teaching can be found in all the great wisdom traditions of the world. The higher levels of evolution comprise all the lower levels. Hence all four levels exist in the human being. Schumacher (1978:15–25) used the following formula to describe this evolutionary process:

$$Mineral = m$$
$$Plants = m + x$$
$$Animals = m + x + y$$
$$Man = m + x + y + z$$

where $m + x + y + z$ = mineral + life + consciousness + self-awareness. He refined this formula even further, where:

$$The\ body = m + x$$
$$The\ soul = y$$
$$And\ Spirit = z$$

Smuts (1973) used the terms matter, life and spirit.

Not only is man considered to be the highest-evolved being, both Smuts (1973) and Schumacher (1978) pointed out that man has an "inner" and "outer" world. There is the external world that can be seen and observed via behaviour and the inner world of thoughts and feelings. Empirical science has had no problem recognizing the former. Within the scientific paradigm, if it can be seen and measured, then it is real. Empirical science continues, however, to have a problem acknowledging the inner world. The problem is compounded even further as one progresses up the levels of evolutionary development.

Traditionally, physics and chemistry are seen to be the more "mature" sciences, yet they deal with the most basic element in evolution, namely matter. As one advances up the evolutionary chain, things become vaguer. Biology is the science of the study of life, but what is this thing called "life"? To get around this vague question, in order to stay "scientific" biology restricts itself to purely material or physical elements. As one moves into the domains of consciousness and self-awareness the vagueness increases exponentially. It is here that empirical science starts to reach its limitations. It cannot study the inner domain of man, which is a higher development in the evolutionary process than the external body. Schumacher (1978:32–33) pointed out that a higher level of development always implies "more inner", while a lower level implies more "external and more outer".

For this reason, Smuts (1973) believed that the world needed a new discipline to study the pinnacle of evolution. He called this discipline "Personology", as in his view personality is the supreme whole of evolution (Smuts, 1973:261). It is a structure that has built on the previous structures of matter, life and mind. Although Smuts (1973) saw the mind as the "most important and conspicuous constituent" of this evolutionary process, the body is an integral part that gives "the intimate flavour of humanity to Personality" (Smuts, 1973:261). However, the whole is more important than the parts:

> The fact is that all these theories have an element of truth; the real explanation being that Mind and Body are elements in the whole of personality; and that this whole is an inner creative, recreative and transformative activity, which accounts for all that happens in the Personality as between its component elements. No explanation will hold water which ignores the

most important factor of all in the situation, and that is the holistic Personality itself. Holism is the real creative agent, and not the entities suggested by the above philosophers (Smuts, 1973:261–262).

There is therefore a "creative Holism in Personality". Even though my body and mental structure can have some resemblance to my parents and ancestors, my personality is indisputably mine. The personality is not inherited; it is a creative novelty in every human being that makes every person a unique individual. The discipline of "Personology" would therefore have to take into account this creative Holism and incorporate all levels of evolutionary development, as well as the inner and outer aspects of the personality. It would incorporate the findings of empirical science, but go beyond it.

Smuts (1973:262) argued that psychology does not "materially assist" in the study of personality, since psychology deals with the average or generalized individual; and in so doing, it ignores the individual uniqueness of the personality. At the same time, psychology limits itself even further by only dealing with the mental point of view, which is only one aspect of personality. His proposed way of studying and developing this discipline was very interesting. He suggested that "Personology" should be studied by analyzing the biographies of personalities as a whole. This study should be done synthetically, and not analytically as in the case of psychology. This would enable the researcher to discover the materials that can help formulate the laws of personal evolution. Smuts (1973:262) called this the science of "Biography", and he believed that it would form the basis of a "new Ethic and Metaphysic" which would have a truer spiritual outlook on personality.

The selection of lives to study would be critical. Interestingly enough, Smuts (1973) mentioned a class of people who would be unsuitable for this kind of scientific study, those who do not have an inner self at all. These are people whose activities and interests are all of an external character. They have no inner life. Smuts (1973) pointed out that this is a common feature among public figures, administrators and businesspeople. Their whole lives seem to be absorbed by the practical interest of their work. They might even be exceptional at what they do, but their inner lives have died as a result of the pressure of external affairs and duties. They might even have great gifts of leadership and have striking and impressive personalities. Yet they lack inwardness, an inner spiritual life, which according to Smuts (1973:287) is the most favourable medium for the study of Personality: "The fact is that the real indefinable quality of true Personality is inward and is not reflected in the life of unrelieved externality which such people live". These are wise words from a very successful public figure, the only man who was a signatory to the founding of both the League of Nations and the United Nations; in fact, he wrote the draft constitutions for both these institutions. His vision was that we would be able to find and study the lives of people who lived strong inner and outer lives, namely, integrated personalities. Sadly, businesspeople do not often fit this profile.

Schumacher (1978) expressed the same concern. We need to study the "inner experience" as well as the "outer appearance". He took the notion even further, and included the context in which the individual finds him or herself. Hence he spoke about the four fields of knowledge. He referred to "I" the individual, and "The World" the communal, both of which have an inner and outer aspect. There is the "I – inner", "The World – Inner", "I – outer" and "The World – outer" (Schumacher, 1978:62). For a truly inte-grated study of the human personality we need to have knowl-edge of all four fields. Given the demands of modern business, businesspeople tend to spend the bulk of their lives in the two outer domains and tend to neglect or sacrifice the inner domains. Business training and development programmes have tended to focus on the outer domains, because they are easier to see and to measure. Yet what so many wise people and sages have taught us through the ages is that it is within the inner domains that the next level of evolutionary development is to be unleashed. The aim is not to deny any of the domains or levels of evolution, but rather to integrate them into a more holistic approach.

Modern business and management theory seems to be par-ticularly poor at being able to develop an integrated approach to executive development. What seems to be missing is an overarch-ing meta-model that integrates business theory and practice. In this book, a theoretical meta-integrated model for coaching will be developed. A meta-integrated model can be defined as a model con-taining many other models. It is not new information; it is a synthe-sis of existing theories and models.

Wilber's Integral Model

Wilber is the author of 21 books, and according to Visser (2003) he is the most widely translated American author of academic works. To try and do justice to his work through a brief introduction is virtually impossible. This section is not an attempt to summarize his work; instead, only parts of his writings that are relevant to this section will be explored. In so doing, large sections of his work will not be dealt with.

The genius of Wilber (1995) is his ability to synthesize an enormous amount of information. He is well-known for his work in integrating Western psychology and Eastern spirituality. His four-quadrant Integral Model (Figure 1) is a synthesis of various disciplines, and includes the works of Smuts (1973) and Schumacher (1978).

Wilber's (1995) four quadrants correspond to Schumacher's (1978) four fields of knowledge. According to Wilber (1995), any integrated model or theory has to take cognizance of all four quadrants. The individual is always part of a collective or communal body of people. One of Wilber's central postulates is that everything exists within a context. It is very difficult to work with an individual if

	Interior Individual experience and consciousness	Exterior Body and behaviour
Individual	• Thoughts/ambitions • Feelings • Mood • Sensory input • Images	• Neuro-muscular system • Genetics • Body sensations • Behaviour • Actions
Communal or collective	Group membership • Language • Social world • Rituals/history • Customs • Culture – organization/family	Social system • Natural and human-made systems • Technology • Processes and structures • Physical laws • Objects

Figure 1. Wilber's four-quadrant Integral Model.
Source: Adapted from Wilber (1996:71).

there is absolutely no understanding of the collective consciousness out of which the individual arises, because nothing can be understood independently of that context.

For both the individual and the communal there is an exterior and an interior domain. In Wilber's (1995) model, the upper-right quadrant deals with the individual's exterior domain. It is that aspect of the individual which can be identified with the senses, such as the body and its behaviour. It can be seen and measured, and consists of things like the neuro–muscular system, genetics, behaviour and actions. For example, if an individual is depressed, a trained technician can perform a CAT scan on them and notice that their neural systems are working in a certain way that has been medically identified as a pattern associated with depression. To treat the depression, a psychiatrist can prescribe Prozac® to manage the condition, a legitimate medical solution to the problem.

However, there is no way that modern medicine can identify why the person is depressed by making use of the right-hand quadrants. To identify the "why", the psychiatrist has to move into the upper-left quadrant, and enter into a dialogue with the patient to explore the latter's interior world. This is the world of inner experience and consciousness, much vaguer and fuzzier than the upper-right quadrant. It is the domain of thoughts, ambitions, feelings, moods and images. Yet it is a world that both Smuts (1973) and Schumacher (1978) saw as being critical to the higher advancement of mankind.

The lower-right quadrant is the exterior manifestation of the collective. It is the domain of social systems, and would include things like natural and human-made systems, technology, processes and structures, physical laws and objects. It is the collective systems that can be identified with the human senses. In Wilber's (1995) model this is the domain of systems thinking. Unlike many who believe that systems thinking is holistic and the solution to reductionism, Wilber (1995) suggests that it is not. In fact, he refers to systems thinking as "subtle reductionism", in that the general tendency of systems thinkers is to deny the inner domain of the system (Wilber, 1995:423). Classical systems thinking focuses its attention on that which can be seen or measured. It can tell you how a system behaves or what its behaviour is, but it does not explore why the system behaves as it does.

That is the domain of the lower-left quadrant. It is the domain of group membership, of things such as language, customs, rituals, history and culture. Individuals are very much influenced by this domain, for example by the culture in which they grew up. The influence of this domain is very powerful, more so than most individuals would like to admit. South Africa and the issue of affirmative action is a prime example of the power of this domain. Companies are battling to deal with all the cultural biases that exist within groups and individuals. Executives will readily admit that the most difficult part of their jobs is to change and manage the culture of the organization. The ineffective management of cultural issues has effectively led to the failure of many mergers and acquisitions.

Through applying some thought to the four-quadrant model (Figure 2), it soon becomes apparent that no one discipline or profession can lay claim to having the ultimate truth. Every profession or discipline contains a partial truth. The value of

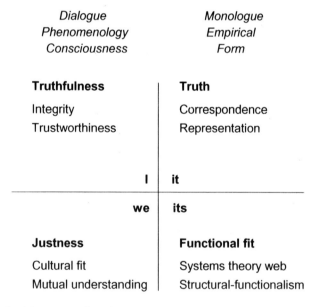

Figure 2. Measures of truth.
Source: Adapted from Wilber (1996:107).

Wilber's (1995) model is that it provides a framework to identify where that partial truth applies. Behavioural psychology, for example, contains partial truths, and it is restricted to the upper-right quadrant. It cannot be used to treat a patient with an existential crisis. That is the domain of Logo therapy, for example, which resides in the upper-left quadrant. In Wilber's model the right-hand quadrants are the world of empirical science. Wilber (1995) refers to this as "flatland", because everything in these quadrants can be identified with the physical senses and can be measured and manipulated. The language that is used to refer to these quadrants is "it", because "it" consists of the behavioural (objective) and the social (interobjective).

The beauty of Wilber's (1995) model is that it gives legitimacy to the world of empirical science, whether that is reductionism or the so-called "new science" of quantum mechanics. Every discipline contains a partial truth, and the measure of "objective truth" is different for every quadrant. In the upper-right quadrant, objective truth is sought through the empirical establishment of perceivable facts. In contrast, the upper-left quadrant is the domain of the inner world of the individual; here the measure is truthfulness, which is the accurate perception by an individual of his or her inner state. What is the objective truth when you are dealing with different cultures? There is no objective truth. Therefore, in the lower-left quadrant the measure of truth is the justness of the mutual understanding among different individuals. The lower-right quadrant is about how the individual fits into the larger system, so the measure is the functional fit.

The left-hand quadrants deal with consciousness, and hence empirical science is of no value; in these quadrants qualitative and phenomenological research is more appropriate and valid. The terms used in these quadrants are "I" and "We" because the focus is the intentional (subjective) and cultural (intersubjective). Wilber (1995) points out that the right-hand quadrants have traditionally been very strong in Western thinking, whereas Eastern thinking has been very strong in the upper-left quadrant.

Wilber's (1995) model is, however, not limited to Schumacher's four fields of knowledge. The model incorporates the evolutionary levels of consciousness, as represented in Figure 3. Like Smuts

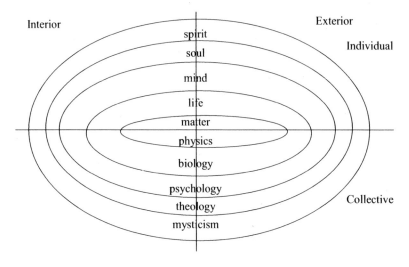

Figure 3. Evolution of consciousness.
Source: Adapted from Wilber (2000:6).

(1973) and Schumacher (1978), he believes that life has evolved from matter to life, from life to mind, from mind to soul and from soul to Spirit.

Wilber's principles

The following principles form the basis of Wilber's Integral Model and his evolutionary/developmental thinking (Wilber, 1995:35–78).

Reality is composed of holons

Reality is composed of holons (whole/parts), and not things or processes. A "holon" is defined as "that which, being a whole in one context, is simultaneously a part of another" (Wilber, 1995:18). By this he means that reality is composed of wholes that are simultaneously parts of other wholes. Even processes exist as holons within other processes. Therefore there are no wholes and there are no parts, they only exist as whole/parts. Because holons exist within holons within holons, there is no ultimate "whole". As a result, everything is open to question, because everything is a context within a context, to infinity.

Capacities of holons

Self-preservation, self-adaptation, self-transcendence and self-dissolution are four fundamental capacities displayed by holons:

- **Self-preservation**. All holons have a capacity to preserve their own wholeness or autonomy. Although all holons exist within a context, it is not the relationship that defines a holon, but its own individual form, structure or pattern. A holon is defined by the relatively coherent and autonomous patterns that it displays.
- **Self-adaptation**. Not only does a holon function as a self-preserving whole; being part of another holon or context, it must adapt to the other holons. Because it is a part, it needs to adapt and fit into its existing environment. As a whole it preserves itself; as a part it must fit in. Hence any holon has a tendency for both agency and communion. Its agency is its ability to express its wholeness to preserve its autonomy; its communion is its ability as a part to be in relationship with something larger.
- **Self-transcendence (self-transformation)**. When different wholes come together to form a new and different whole, transformation has taken place. Transformation results in something new and novel; a new whole emerges. This is achieved through "symmetry breaks" in the evolutionary process. Self-transcendence is the ability of a system to go beyond itself and to introduce something new and novel. Evolution is not only a continuous process; important discontinuities can take place as well.
- **Self-dissolution**. Not only can a holon build up, it can also break down. This is due to the constant tension between a holon's agency and communion: the more a holon preserves its wholeness (agency), the less it serves its communion (being a part). There is thus a conflict between the holon's rights (agency) and its responsibilities (communion). This conflict between agency and communion can introduce pathology into the holon. Vertical tension occurs between self-transcendence (the tendency to build up) and self-dissolution (the tendency to break down). In self-transcendence, for example, particles build up into atoms, atoms build up into molecules, molecules build up into cells, etc. In self-dissolution the process is reversed: cells break down into molecules, molecules break down into atoms, and atoms break down

into particles. Hence every holon is simultaneously a subholon (part of another holon) and a superholon (itself containing other holons).

Holons emerge

Due to the fact that holons have the capacity to self-transcend, new holons emerge. Central to this principle is the idea that the emerging holon is not completely determined by that which went before it, because it contains creativity and novelty. We never know for certain how the holon will emerge or into what it will emerge. The higher we move up the evolutionary scale, the greater the novelty. Physics is a more mature science than psychology, for example, which is not surprising given that humans contain much more novelty than rocks. Humans possess more creativity than rocks, and as a result the human psyche is more vague and more difficult to study than the elements of rocks. Humans are more unpredictable than rocks.

Holons emerge holarchically

Holons emerge holarchically, i.e., they form a developmental hierarchy. Each holon emerges from the previous holon with an increased level of complexity. The higher holon will incorporate everything of the junior holon, and then add its own new complexity or pattern. Holons build on each other, so each holon incorporates and transcends its predecessor. For example, every organism will incorporate cells, but not *vice versa*. Cells will contain molecules, but not *vice versa*.

Unfortunately, "hierarchy" is a word and concept that has been very unpopular in recent years. As Wilber (1995) points out, it has been criticized by social critics, ecofeminists and post-modern poststructuralists, among others, as the major cause of injustice, oppression and domination. These critics of hierarchy called for the end of hierarchies and the instalment of "heterarchy", where governance is established by egalitarianism, i.e., the equality of all parties. Management science bought into this way of thinking during the 1990s. It became the vogue to get rid of hierarchies in organizations and implement self-managed or self-directed teams at all costs.

Hierarchies were seen as the cause of all ills within organizations, and hence the cure to all an organization's problems was to get rid of hierarchies.

This call was especially strong from management theorists like Wheatley, Zohar (1997) and Lewin and Regime (1999), who looked to the so-called "new sciences" to justify the death of hierarchies. According to them, mechanistic science was about hierarchies, while quantum physics was about relationships and self-organized teams. The "new sciences" were the justification for this theory.

According to Wilber (1995), however, the paradox is that while these exponents of the "web of life" and "new science" paradigm deny hierarchies in any form, the actual science on which they base their theories insists on the necessity of hierarchy. Referring to the work of theorists such as von Bertalanffy (the founder of General Systems Theory), Sheldrake (Morphogenetic fields in biology), Birch and Cobb (ecology), Sperry (brain research) and Habermas (social critical theory), Wilber (1995) argues that hierarchy is the "basic organizing principle of wholeness". Normal hierarchy represents an increase in wholeness and integrative capacity. Therefore it is simply a ranking of orders according to their holistic capacity. What is a whole at one stage becomes a part of a larger whole at the next stage, but it does not work in reverse. An acorn can become an oak tree, but an oak tree cannot become an acorn. Hence hierarchy is asymmetrical. There are therefore developmental stages through which holons emerge, with more holistic patterns appearing later in development as they have to wait for the emergence of the parts that they will integrate. The other important feature to remember is that within a hierarchal pattern the elements within that level operate by what Wilber (1995) calls "heterarchy". Here no element is more important or dominant; they all contribute more or less equally to the health of the whole level. Thus, it is possible to see where the idea of self-managed teams comes from. They are heterarchies.

The drive to try to get rid of hierarchies is therefore misguided. The problem is not with hierarchies *per se*, but with the possibility that pathologies can develop within a hierarchy. Pathological hierarchies have led to the condemnation of hierarchies in general. In a pathological hierarchy, one holon assumes dominance to the detriment of all. The problem is that the holon assumes that it is the whole, and no longer sees itself as simultaneously being a whole and a part. On the other hand, in a pathological heterarchy, the holon assumes it is a part—period. It no longer assumes it is a whole. Hence, the cure to the problem is not to substitute heterarchy for hierarchy. Unfortunately, that has, in effect, been the call by management theorists advocating the substitution of self-managed teams in place of hierarchies. A more effective approach is to address the pathology within the hierarchy, to arrest and to integrate the pathological holon. The cure is to root out the holons that have usurped power within the overall system by abusing their capacity for upward or downward causation. The cure is not to substitute hierarchy with heterarchy or *vice versa*, but to address the pathology in both. Wilber (1995) issues a plea to be aware of theorists who push solely for hierarchy or heterarchy. Instead he calls for "holarchy", which maintains the balance between normal hierarchy and normal heterarchy.

Cognitive power and task complexity

Jaques and Clement (1997) have come to the same conclusion through their research and work with organizations and stratified systems theory. They make it clear that the problem is not with hierarchies *per se*, but with dysfunctional hierarchies. A hierarchy becomes dysfunctional in an organizational context when the leadership roles within the structure are occupied by individuals who do not have the cognitive complexity to cope with the level of task complexity associated with that level of work. Cognitive complexity is determined by the individual's cognitive power, where "Cognitive power is the potential strength of cognitive processes in a person and is therefore the maximum level of task complexity that someone can handle at any given point in his or her development" (Jaques and Clement, 1997:49).

From this definition it is clear that cognitive power develops and matures over time. Through their research, Jaques and Clement (1997) found that the greater the individual's cognitive power, the greater was their capability to cope with a mass of information. Therefore the greater the individual's cognitive power the longer was the individual's time horizon, their ability to work into the future.

As a result there is a direct correlation between time horizon and cognitive complexity. In so doing Jaques and Clement (1997:93–97) discovered seven strata or levels of increasing task complexity, namely:

- **Category B–1 task complexity (stratum – I): Direct action in immediate situation**. The time span would be between one day and three months. This is the kind of task that would be found on the shop and office floor. People mostly follow the defined rules.
- **Category B–2 task complexity (stratum – II): Diagnostic accumulation**. The time span would be between three months and one year. This is the type of task complexity encountered by first-line managerial levels. It is the ability to anticipate problems and to develop appropriate solutions and actions.
- **Category B–3 task complexity (stratum – III): Alternative serial plans**. The time span would be between one and two years. Due to more complexity, alternative plans are required to be constructed before action is taken. It calls for the ability to choose one of the plans and implement it serially. Corrective action needs to be taken if it is called for.
- **Category B–4 task complexity (stratum – IV): Mutually interactive programmes**. The time span would be between two and five years. Complexity increases because a number of programmes are interacting with each other. These have to be planned for, managed, and resources moved around where required. It requires the ability to make tradeoffs between resources in order to progress and achieve goals.
- **Category C–1 task complexity (stratum – V): Situational response**. The time span would be between five and ten years. This is the first level of strategic work, and is the world of individuals who manage strategic business units in large corporations. It calls for the ability to start working comfortably with paradoxes and the ambiguity inherent in the complexity of the business world. It calls for on-the-spot judgements while at the same time envisaging the second- and third-order consequences of those decisions. What-if analysis is a continuous requirement.
- **Category C–2 task complexity (stratum – VI): Diagnostic accumulation**. The time span would be between ten and 20 years. Within the context of significant conceptual information and corporate

capital expenditure policies, the individual has to decide when and where to make significant changes in major business units. At this level, the individual applies pressure to influence the external environment, i.e., negotiating with governments.

- **Category C–3 task complexity (stratum – VII): Alternative Strategies**. The time span would be between 20 and 50 years. This is the complexity level of corporate CEOs working on strategic alternatives for global companies. Here the individual starts to operate on a global perspective. Not only do they have to deal with the national economy, but with global economies that affect their business. They have to deal with the complexity of divergent cultures and values and international trade.

According to Jaques and Clement (1997), pathology enters the hierarchy and makes it dysfunctional when an individual occupies a role in which he or she does not possess the required cognitive complexity to match the required task complexity of that stratum of complexity. The problem is not the organizational hierarchy *per se* but the person occupying the managerial role. The solution is not to condemn the hierarchy but to get rid of or develop the pathological holon within that hierarchy. A call for heterarchy (self-managed teams) will not solve the problem. Jaques and Clement (1997) discovered that cognitive power develops and matures over time. Each level incorporates and builds on the previous level and then transcends it. It is therefore not surprising that Jaques and Cason (1994) believe that managerial hierarchies have been around for 3 000 years, and that they are unlikely to ever go away.

Holons include but transcend their predecessors

Each emergent holon transcends but includes its predecessor(s). Each emerging new holon includes the preceding holons and then adds its own defining patterns to it. In each case it preserves the previous holons, but it negates their partiality. It preserves all the basic structures and functions, and drops all the exclusive structure and functions which are replaced by a "deeper agency that reaches a wider communion". In other words, all of the lower is taken up into the higher. At the same time, however, not all of the higher is in the lower. The holon includes but transcends its predecessor.

Wilber (1995) therefore believes that the transition from one stage of human development to the next involves differentiation and integration. Differentiation is when the self becomes aware that its own identity is distinct from the identity it attached to a certain stage of development. Having achieved that, the self can proceed to the next stage, where it can add to the previous stages to create a new whole. This latter development Wilber (1995) refers to as "integration".

The lower sets the possibilities of the higher; the higher sets the probabilities of the lower. Even though a holon transcends its predecessors, it does not violate the laws of the patterns of the lower levels. It is not determined by the lower holon, because it cannot be reduced to the lower level. It cannot, however, ignore the lower level. For example, my body is constrained by the laws of gravity and time and space, but my mind is not. My mind can explore different times and places; it is not limited to the body. If I fall over the edge of a cliff, however, my mind goes with my body.

Depth and span

The number of levels which a hierarchy comprises determines whether it is "shallow" or "deep"; and the number of any given level is called its "span". Very simply, this means that the more levels a holon contains, the greater its depth, and the more holons that exist on that level, the greater its span. Hence man has greater depth than plants and rocks. Rocks, however, have more span than humans and plants.

Each successive level of evolution produces greater depth and less span. The higher a holon is up the evolutionary level, the more precarious its existence. This is because its existence depends on a whole series of other holons that it incorporates. Because the lower holons are components of the higher, the higher-level holons cannot be greater in number than the components. It simply means that more depth equals less span. In addition, greater depth means a greater degree of consciousness. Here Wilber is in complete agreement with Schumacher (1978), who pointed out that a higher level of development always implies "more inner", while a lower level implies more "external and more outer". There are therefore two dimensions at play, a vertical dimension (deep versus shallow) and a horizontal dimension (wide versus narrow). Changes on the horizontal dimension Wilber (1995) refers to as translation, while changes to the vertical dimension are referred to as transformation.

This is best explained by referring back to the seven strata of task complexity defined by Jaques and Clement (1997). If, for example, an individual at Category B–1 task complexity (stratum – I), learns new rules to apply to the work they do, that would be translation. Their world could have expanded exponentially, but they are still stuck at stratum I. They have grown, but the growth has been due to translation. Transformation would happen if that individual, over time, eventually grows and develops into Category C–1 task complexity (stratum – V). The individual would have grown and developed into a whole new world and existence. The reality that a stratum – I individual experiences is totally different to the reality that an individual in stratum – VII would experience. They have totally different worldviews, which in turn lead to different realities. They could be in the same company and the same industry, but they "live in different worlds". This happens as a result of transformation, where new worlds of translation disclose themselves. They are not necessarily new worlds physically located somewhere, but exist as deeper perceptions of the world. There are therefore different worldviews associated with different levels of transformation. Jaques and Clement (1997) believe that the objective world is infinite and unknowable. What the individual knows is limited to what they can make sense of in any given moment, which in turn is dependent on a vast array of data available and their ability to make sense thereof. In a sense, the world the individual inhabits is determined by the data that the individual has managed to transform into meaningful information. The more developed the holon, the more data it can turn into meaningful information.

Evolution and transformation

Wilber (1995) points out that evolution is first and foremost a series of transformations, each producing more depth and less span than its predecessors:

- Destroy any type of holon, and you will destroy all the holons above it, but not the holons below it. There are a number of critics who deny the existence of a higher or lower order of reality; to them this is making judgements. But as Wilber (1995) points out, it is possible to determine the evolutionary sequence of things. The following question will locate the level of the sequence: "What other type of holons would be destroyed if we destroy this type of holon?" (Wilber, 1995:61).

So, for example, if all the molecules in the universe were destroyed, then all living cells would be destroyed. Atoms, however, would still exist. Only the higher-order holons would be destroyed, not the lower-order holons, the reason being that the higher-order holons depend upon the lower holons as constituent parts. So if all plants were destroyed, life as we know it would cease to exist, but matter would still exist. From this, Wilber (1995) deducts the following. The less depth a holon has, the more fundamental it is, because it is a component of so many other holons. The greater the depth of a holon, the less fundamental it is, because fewer other holons depend on it for their existence.

• Holarchies co-evolve. No holon is isolated, so all holons evolve together. Every thing is a system within a system, a field within a field.

• The micro-holon is in relational exchange with the macro-holon at all levels of the depth. For Wilber (1995) this is a very important principle. It means that each layer of depth continues to exist in a network of relationship with other holons on the same level. This is best explained by making use of three levels of existence (matter, life and mind). In the physiosphere (matter), the physical body exists in relation with other physical bodies. It is dependent for its survival on gravitation, light, water and weather. So, for example, the human race reproduces itself physically by maintaining the body through food production and consumption. In the biosphere (life), humanity reproduces itself biologically through emotional sexual relations. This is usually in families within a social environment. And at the same time, the survival of the social environment depends on the ecosystem. In the noosphere (mind), humans reproduce themselves mentally through "exchanges with cultural and symbolic environments". Societies reproduce themselves culturally through exchanging symbols that are embedded in various traditions and norms of that society.

• There is a direction to evolution. The direction is towards increased differentiation, organization, variety and complexity.

The evolutionary process develops from less complex to more complex systems, and from lower to higher levels of organization. This means that there are increasing levels of autonomy within the context of larger systems. The autonomy is relative, because there are no wholes, only whole/parts (holons). Autonomy refers to the holon's enduring patterns, its self-preservation within a given context. To illustrate the importance of this point it is necessary to quote Wilber (1995:72–73) at some length:

> But even the entire integrated and autonomous person of psychoanalysis is not really autonomous, because that individual is actually set in contexts of linguistic structures that autonomously determine meaning without the individual even knowing about it (the critique launched by structuralism, archaeology). But linguistic structures aren't that autonomous, because they exist only in the context of pre-articulated worldviews that use language without language ever registering that fact (the critique by Heidegger, Gebser). But further, worldviews themselves are merely a small component of massive networks and contexts of social practices (in various ways, Marx, Habermas, the later Foucault). And further yet, theorists from Kierkegaard to Schelling to Hegel would insist that these social practices only exist in, and because of, the larger context Spirit. In every one of these cases, the theorist (Freud, Marx, Heidegger, Foucault, Schelling, etc.) tells us something important about the meaning of our existence by situating our existence in a larger context—since meaning and context are in important ways synonymous ... Likewise, each discovery of a new and deeper context and meaning is a discovery of a new therapia, a new therapy, namely: we must shift our perspectives, deepen our perception, often against a great deal of resistance, to embrace the deeper and wider context.

Stratified systems theory and complexity of information

The concept of evolutionary transformation from less complex to more complex systems is fundamental to Jaques and Clement's (1997) stratified systems theory as it is applied to managerial leadership. Even though people live in the same objective world, or in the same organization, they can actually be living in totally different worlds. Given their level of development, and their ability to manage higher levels of complexity, they actually live in different realities. Jaques and Clement believe that the objective world is "infinite and unknowable". Their argument is that what anyone can actually know is limited by what they can make sense of at that moment in time. This depends on the vast array of data available to the individual and how they make sense thereof. Jaques and Clement believe that the world anyone occupies is made up of data which that individual has managed to transform into information that works for them. Every individual therefore determines the size of the world they live in, through the amount of data which they can turn into meaningful information.

As a result, Jaques and Clement have identified four orders of complexity of information. And like all holons they build on the first order of complexity, integrate it and then transcend it to a higher order of complexity. The four orders of complexity are (Jaques and Clement, 1997:54–57):

- **First-order complexity: Concrete things (Concrete Order)**: It is the world of things that can be pointed to: there is a tree, there is a person, that is a car, she has blue eyes, etc. The variables are not tangled together, they are clear and unambiguous. People operating at this level can only deal with a small number of variables. It is usually the world of children and young adults—the juniors in organizations.
- **Second-order complexity (Symbolic Order)**: First level of abstraction, involving verbal variables. This is where verbal information is used in concepts. We no longer have to point to things; we can use the concepts in normal discourse. Here the variables can be broken down into numerous concrete things and actions, while at the same time being interwoven to form complex patterns. It allows individuals to discuss their work, follow rules, discuss orders with customers, etc.
- **Third-order complexity (Abstract Conceptual Order)**: Second level of abstraction, involving concepts. Here more complex concepts can be used to operate in the conceptual world of the organization. It is the world of the CEO. Here the variables are large in number, interwoven in complex systems, and continually

changing. It is difficult in this world to go directly from concepts to concrete reality. Here the individual must be able to translate and pull together a concept like the balance sheet, with all its accounting assumptions, into concrete items like assets, liabilities, expenditure and revenue.

• **Fourth-order complexity (Universal Order):** Third level of abstraction involving universals. This is a world where the level of complexity transcends those that are normally associated with corporate life. Here the concepts develop into universal ideas that address ideologies and philosophy. This level works with the problems of whole societies. It is the world of Einstein, Socrates and Plato, etc. From this it is very apparent that even though a second-order person lived right next door to Einstein, they would actually be living in two different worlds. In terms of Wilber's (1995) thinking, Einstein and his second-order neighbour would inhabit the same physiosphere (matter) and biosphere (life). But in terms of the noosphere (mind), they might as well inhabit different planets. Life would have different meanings for each of them.

Readers familiar with the work of the German philosopher Hegel (1770–1831) and his process of dialectics, i.e., thesis, antithesis and synthesis, will realize that Wilber (1995) is continuing in this tradition. His model is based on dialectical development.

Wilber's developmental process in the individual

Jaques and Clement's (1997) stratified systems theory unfortunately stops development at the upper levels of the noosphere. The tendency in the West has been to stop at the ultimate levels of mind. Wilber (1995), like Smuts (1973) and Schumacher (1978) before him, extends this thinking into the theosphere (divine domain), as can be seen in Figure 3. Wilber (1995) therefore sees evolution as a series of developmental stages from matter, to life, to mind, to soul, and ultimately Spirit. Visser (2003) points out that Wilber identified 17 stages of human development that can be subdivided into three main phases: the prepersonal, the personal and transpersonal, as set out in Table 2.

It is important at this point to mention that, unlike many psychologists, Wilber believes in the existence of a "self" in

Table 2. Wilber's 17 stages of individual development.

Phase of development	Stage of development	Domain of development
	17. Ultimate	
	16. High – causal	
	15. Low – causal	**Spirit**
	14. High – subtle	
Transpersonal	13. Low – subtle	**Soul**
	12. Centaur	
	11. Biosocial	
	10. Mature ego	
	9. Late ego	
	8. Middle ego	
Personal	7. Early ego	**Mind**
	6. Membership	
	5. Image body	
	4. Pranic body	
	3. Axial body	
	2. Oeroborous	
Prepersonal	1. Pleroma	**Body**

Source: Adapted from Visser (2003:82).

the individual which is critical in the developmental process. The argument that there is no self, because the self cannot be seen or perceived, does not hold ground for Wilber. It is the self that integrates, coordinates and organizes the "stream of consciousness", and in so doing forms the basis of the individual's sense of identity. It is the self which climbs the "ladder of development". The ladder of development is a metaphor to illustrate the difference between what Wilber calls the basic structures of consciousness and the transitional or replacement stages of development. Visser (2003), using the metaphor of a ladder, identifies the self with the climber, and the rungs of the ladder with the basic structures of consciousness: a higher view from each new rung with the transitional or replacement stages. So with every basic structure of consciousness is associated a certain worldview. As the self develops, the basic structures of consciousness remain in place and present, while the transitional stages will disappear. So the body (basic structure of consciousness) remains present throughout individual development, but the typhon (where the self is identified and limited to the body) is a transitional stage that is eventually replaced.

Wilber identified more stages than most scientific development models. In his later work he reduced these levels to ten basic structures of consciousness, and specified the ages at which these structures tend to emerge. These are listed in Table 3.

Table 3. The basic structures of consciousness and the ages at which they emerge during development.

Structure of consciousness	Nature of consciousness	Age at emergence
10. Causal	Experience of emptiness	Approximately 35 years
9. Subtle	Experience of archetypes	Approximately 28 years
8. Vision-logic	Visionary thought	Approximately 21 years
7. Formal-reflexive	Abstract thought	11–15 years
6. Rule/role-thinking	Concrete thought	6–8 years
5. Rep-thinking	Thinking in symbols and concepts	15 months–2 years
4. Phantasmic	Thinking in simple images	6–12 months
3. Emotional-sexual	Life force	1–6 months
2. Sensoriperceptual	Sensation and perception	0–3 months
1. Physical	The physical organism	prenatal

Source: Visser (2003:123).

Needless to say, he based his developmental model on Western developmental psychology and the esoteric traditions of

Christianity, Judaism, Islam and Eastern Spirituality. Visser (2003:81) sees Wilber as justifying his choice of the developmental approach as follows:

> Look at any major system of meditation: the Buddha's detailed stages of dhyana/prajna; Patanjali's eight-step Yoga Sutras; Lao Tzu's hierarchic Taoistic contemplation; the encompassing Zen meditation system depicted by the ox-herding stages; the Victorins' multilevel course of contemplation; the specific and detailed stages taught by St Teresa and St John of the Cross; the entire tradition of Kundalini/tantra yoga, both Hindu and Varajanic. What they all have in common is a view of meditation, not as a relaxation response to sensory derivation or a self-regulation strategy, but as a hierarchical unfolding of successively higher structures of consciousness. To be precise, they see it as a developmental process, composed of specific stages, such that each stage embodies a distinct structure of consciousness ... From the Buddha's stages of dhyana to Kundalini's chakric stages of sublimation, the whole point was that of stages of development. Truly, these traditionalists were not only the first structuralists; they were the first *bona fide* developmental psychologists. My point is that in our rush to bridge Eastern and Western psychology, we have looked absolutely everywhere except to developmental/structural psychology. Yet, since the essence of the Eastern traditions is a phenomenological-developmental-structural view of the superconscious realms, and since Western psychology has a rather detailed phenomenological-developmental-structural view of the sub- and self-conscious realms, the most immediate and painless bridge would be simply to add them together, just as they are. Such, anyway, was the approach I took in the Atman Project.

Given the nature of the complexity and wide scope of Wilber's developmental work (19 books), it is outside the scope of this study to go into the developmental stages in great depth. All that is required for this study is a general overview of the developmental processes. Hence the referral to Visser's (2003) summary of Wilber's work.

The prepersonal

According to Visser (2003), Wilber sees the first stages of development as being dominated by the emotions and the body. Here consciousness is merged with physical-emotional reality. Consciousness
is asleep. There is no sense of time, self, space or the environment. It
is prepersonal because the personality has not developed yet. Unlike
many transpersonal theorists, Wilber does not see this as a state of
transpersonal bliss. Washburn (1995), for example, is of the opinion
that this is a blissful state that is lost as the person develops an ego,
and then the self returns to the pre-ego state in the transpersonal
stages. In this view, the ego is seen as something bad, it is the enemy
of the "spiritual".

In his earlier work Wilber agreed with this view. In his later work
he stressed that it was an error in thinking and referred to it as the
Pre/Trans Fallacy. Because Wilber's (1995) model is a hierarchical
developmental model, his argument is that an infant cannot be more
spiritual than an adult. In reality the infant is less spiritual than the
adult because it is merged with concrete reality, in that infants are
totally ignorant of the mental world and the realms beyond that.
Therefore Wilber (1995) does not see the transition from infant to
adult as a fall from paradise, but rather as a difficult emergence from
a state of unconsciousness. It is a developmental way forward, not a
return to a previous state. In Wilber's (1995) thinking the ego is not
an enemy of the spiritual, but a stepping stone to the spiritual. The
implications of this are enormous. How often does one hear consultants, coaches and psychologists speak about the fact that the real
problems in organizations are people whose egos are too big? The
solution, according to them, is to "get rid" of those people's egos, in
effect asking those individuals to repress their egos and their development. In Wilber's (1995) thinking, the problem is not that people's
egos are too big, but that they are in fact too small. The solution is
not to "get rid" of the egos but to grow them as big and as fast as
possible. It is only when a healthy, developed ego reaches its limitations that it can transcend to the next stage of development.

Starting with the body, the child goes on to develop an ego/
personality, and once those are well-established it moves on to the
transpersonal realms of consciousness. As the child develops, it
increasingly identifies with its body as the boundary between the

self and the outside world. The concept of the self is defined by the boundaries of the body. So the self is very much a body-bound self.

At some point in its development the child will enter the "membership self" stage. Here the child becomes aware that it is part of a larger social system or environment. It is this stage that the child starts to talk and communicate with important others in its environment, and at this point that the culture into which the child has been born starts to exert an influence. The child cannot think logically. Aided by language, the child now starts to develop concepts of time and can refer to past, present and future. The child also begins to be able to control bodily impulses. As the child starts to explore the world of language it emerges out of the physiosphere and starts to become a personality.

The personal

The transition from the prepersonal to the personal stage is one of moving from a physical way of functioning to a more mental way of functioning. The child now has an image of itself and is capable of reflecting on that self-image. Whereas the child previously identified itself with the body, identification is now with a mental self. It is at this stage that the id, the ego, and the superego come into existence. An important development here is the ability of the mental self to transcend the physical, while at the same time possessing the ability to suppress the physical. Visser (2003) points out that in Wilber's opinion, this phenomenon is at the core of an important imbalance in the psyche of the modern Western individual. As a mental self (ego), the modern Western individual has virtually lost all contact with the body and its functions, hence the Western ideal to dominate the body and nature.

Towards the end of the mental stages the ego matures and develops the ability to differentiate itself from the ego. For the first time the self can separate itself from the body and the ego. It is now in a position to integrate the body and the ego. Wilber (1995) refers to this as the Centaur Stage, the mythological figure that is half man and half animal. The body and the ego are integrated to form a higher union, and this stage is characterized by the emergence of the existential crisis. Here the individual becomes concerned with meaning, self-realization and self-autonomy. The phenomenological concept of intention becomes very important in that it prompts the individual to ascribe meaning to their lives in the context of a personal vision. Life does not necessarily have meaning, but the individual can ascribe various meanings to it. The individual starts to realize that he or she is not a victim of circumstances, but has the freedom to choose a response to various stimuli, which brings with it a sense of personal freedom. Although Wilber places the existential phase with the personal, it is the gateway to the transpersonal. In Western psychology it is generally believed that this is the pinnacle of human development; the integrated, autonomous and rational individual is the end-point of human development. Even Jaques and Clement's (1997) stratified systems theory is limited to this band of human development. Their four orders of complexity of information clearly limit the concept of the self to Wilber's personal levels of development.

The transpersonal

Drawing on the works of a number of mystics, Wilber (1995) believes that the self continues to develop into the spiritual realms. In the first stages of the subtle level the self begins to transcend the personal, it goes beyond the identity of language, thoughts and the ego. The self realizes that it is more than just the body and the mind. Eventually the self will enter the higher stages where God and the self are one. It is at these levels of development that the self experiences the dissolution of the subject-object duality. All religious traditions speak of this phenomenological experience. At the ultimate stage of development there is no subject-object duality, all that is left is consciousness.

In the East this concept is certainly not strange. In the West this kind of thinking has become more tolerated due to globalization. It is viewed as an Eastern and in particular a Buddhist way of seeing the world. Yet even in the West, and in South Africa where we have very strong Islamic, Judaic, Hindu and Christian religious influences, this kind of thinking is not strange or unique. In Islam one has only to refer to the works of Rumi; in Judaism to Martin Buber; in Hinduism to Sri Aurobindo; in Christianity to St Teresa of Ávila, St John of the Cross, Meister Eckhart, and Fathers Thomas Keating, Bede Griffith,

Thomas Merton, Anthony De Mello, and Evelyn Underhill, to realize that this is the everyday experience of ordinary human beings. It is the pinnacle of human development. Roberts (1993) gives a detailed phenomenological account of her experience of arriving at a state of no-self in her book *The Experience of No-Self*. In the conclusion she writes that the journey to the state of no-self can take on two views. The first is that it is a supernatural event that constitutes a relentless journey into God. The second is that it is the final process of our natural lifespan, where self-consciousness is finally relinquished and we become mature human beings. Either way, the individual is prepared for a new existence.

If that is true, then it is the author's contention that current executive development models have neglected the transpersonal realms of human development. And it is precisely these realms that Smuts (1973) and Schumacher (1978) believed were essential for leadership development. It is only in the transpersonal realms that an executive can truly start to appreciate and experience Greenleaf's (1977) concept of servant leadership and its implications for organizations and societies. Over the years a number of management theorists have tried to expound the virtues of servant leadership. What people forget, however, is that Greenleaf (1977) was a dedicated Quaker, a man who devoted his life to developing the transpersonal realms of human existence. As a Quaker, meditation was an integral part of his life. Moreover, he wrote his essays on servant leadership at a very mature stage in life.

If Wilber's (1995) model is to be taken seriously, then it is the author's further contention that servant leadership is a natural development within the transpersonal levels of development. It is the leadership worldview associated with the transpersonal stages of development. Something as powerful as servant leadership does not make sense to an individual whose identity is still on the lower personal levels of development. The same can be said for the leadership work of Koestenbaum (1991). That kind of leadership thinking and acting comes into existence only in the transpersonal levels of development. Yet executive development programmes have tended to avoid or simply deny these higher levels of development. One of the reasons could be the populist war against hierarchies. Instead of addressing the problem of pathological hierarchies, the tendency has been to deny hierarchies, including developmental hierarchies (**qualitatively ranked levels**) altogether. The call has been for heterarchy (**mutually linked dimensions**), instead of honouring and working with developmental hierarchies. It is therefore not surprising that theorists who support developmental hierarchies are not very popular, and that includes Wilber (1995) and Jaques and Clement (1997). Wilber (1995), however, emphasizes the need for both hierarchy and heterarchy; holarchy is a combination of the two. It is not a question of one at the expense of the other, both are needed.

This simplified developmental process is beautifully illustrated in Figure 4. Starting from the top, everything to the left of the diagonal vertical line is seen as the self, and everything to right is seen as nonself. It is a developmental process in which the identity of the self continually expands until it ends in Unity Consciousness. At each level of development, however, different pathologies can develop. On the left-hand side of Figure 4, Wilber (2001) has listed the various therapies or spiritual interventions that are appropriate for that particular level of development.

So, for example, in the early stages of development the self is identified with the persona, and the shadow is seen as not being part of

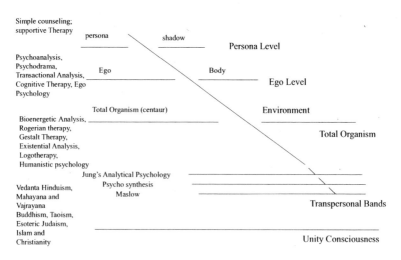

Figure 4. Spectrum of consciousness.
Source: Wilber (2001:14).

the self. This is the first level of integration, and supportive therapy or simple counselling can be used to deal with it. If integration is successful, the identify of the self is expanded to the ego. The self is now identified with the ego, but the body is not seen as part of the self. At this level Psychoanalysis, Transactional Analysis or Ego Psychology, for example, can be effective to deal with the integration struggle or any pathology that arises at that level of development. The centaur comes into being when the ego and the body have successfully been integrated. The self as identity ends with the person's skin; the skin is the boundary of the self. Everything beyond that is again seen as nonself or not part of the self. If this integration process continues and is successful, the individual will eventually reach a state of Unity Consciousness. It is the state of existence that the mystics speak about, the final realization that everything is one. Here the object-subject duality falls away permanently. Mental suffering ceases to exist.

Visser (2003) believes that Wilber's genius has been his ability to map out these developmental levels, to identify the pathologies that can be encountered at the various levels, and the various psychological and spiritual therapies that can treat the pathologies

Table 4. The spectrum of stages, pathologies, and methods of treatment.

Stage	Pathology	Therapy
10. Ultimate	Ultimate pathology	Nondual mysticism
9. Causal	Causal pathology	Formless mysticism
8. Subtle	Subtle pathology	Theist mysticism
7. Psychic	Psychic pathology	Nature mysticism
6. Vision-logic	Existential crises	Existential therapy
5. Formal-reflexive	Identity crises	Introspection
4. Rule/role thinking	Script-pathology	Script-analysis
3. Rep-thinking	Neuroses	Insight therapy
2. Phantasmic	Narcissism/borderline	Structuring therapy
1. Sensory	Psychosis	Relaxing therapy

Source: Visser (2003:144).

(see summary in Table 4). He has shown how Western and Eastern psychological approaches can complement and build on each other. As a result, Wilber (2001) argues that all psychological and spiritual therapies are relevant—one is not better than the other; they each have their place. The question is not which school of therapy is the best, but rather which therapy is relevant for that specific level of development or level of pathology. Hence it is no good trying to treat a patient with an existential crisis using cognitive behavioural therapy; in this case, Logo therapy would be more appropriate. In the same way, traditional Western psychology is irrelevant at the spiritual levels. Wilber's (2001) argument is supported very elo-quently by Roberts (1993:180):

> In keeping with this admission of a gentle man who said he was terrified at the thought of losing the self. What he had obviously failed to realize was that the terror and dread he felt is self, and that without the self there can be no such feelings. In fact, a sure sign self is gone is the absence of these affec-tive symptoms ... But this is why the histories of those who have truly gone beyond self will never be found in psychiatric literature. With no problems in the affective domain, few peo-ple would be in need of a psychiatrist or analyst; indeed, with-out an affective system, or without a self, this whole school of thought would be out of business.

Visser (2003) points out that Wilber's plea is for the conventional psychological schools to learn from the contemplative schools, especially with regard to the higher levels of development. But at the same time he pleads for the contemplative schools to drop their apparent self-sufficiency and open themselves up to vital and important lessons that can be learned from psychology and psy-chiatry. These schools are more effective and efficient at dealing with the pathologies associated with the lower levels of develop-ment. The beauty of Wilber's model is that it gives legitimacy to all the schools, psychological and spiritual, East and West. Every school contains a partial truth. No one school of thought contains the whole truth. Once that is recognized, it is easy to integrate all of the various schools, recognizing the value each adds to the devel-opmental process.

Development is not a simple linear progression

According to Wilber (2000a), the human being is a very complex organism. Rather than seeing development as a simple linear progression where one level builds on another (e.g., the individual first has to be well-developed cognitively before they can develop spiritually), development should be seen as taking place in relatively independent lines or streams. This is illustrated in Figure 5.

The point is that these lines are "relatively independent" in that they can develop independently of each other. They can develop on different time scales, at different rates, and with a different dynamic. So it is very possible for an individual to be highly developed in some lines, and medium or low in others. Wilber's (2000a) argument is that the overall development, what he calls the sum total of all the different lines, does not show any linear or sequential development whatsoever. However, he points out that research continues to find that the "independent" developmental lines do tend to unfold in a sequential, holarchical fashion. The higher stages of each developmental line tend to build on and incorporate the earlier stages. Furthermore, no stage can be skipped because

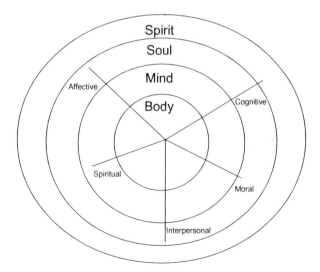

Figure 5. The Integral Psychograph as a holarchy.
Source: Wilber (2000a:31).

one builds on the other. In addition, he argues that these stages emerge in an order that cannot be altered by social reinforcement or conditioning.

Wilber (2000a:29) points out that this conclusion is not based on theoretical speculation, but is based on "massive experimental data". According to Wilber (2000a) there is general consensus that no matter how different the developmental lines are, they tend to unfold holarchically. They develop through a physical/preconvention (prepersonal) stage, a conventional (prepersonal) stage and a more abstract postconventional (personal) stage, and finally into higher post-postconventional (transpersonal) stages, as shown in Figure 5. It is a complex web of development, and there are no guarantees—pathology can enter into and at any stage of these developmental lines. Hence Wilber often talks of "regression in the service of transcendence": sometimes we have to regress to address or heal lower-order pathologies in order to move forward. The point is to not return permanently to the level where the pathology has occurred, but rather to address the pathology and get back to the higher level of development. If such pathologies are not addressed, they can halt the developmental process and/or hinder the integration processes.

The point is that Wilber's model is not a simple linear developmental model. It is a complex web of developmental lines or streams that are relatively independent. A very good example of this can be found in the Christian tradition. One of the literary classics within Christianity is a book called *The Practice of the Presence of God* by Brother Lawrence, written over 300 years ago. By all accounts Brother Lawrence was a very simple man. His application to join a monastery was continually refused on the grounds that he did not have the necessary intellectual capacity. Due to his sheer persistence he was eventually allowed into the monastery, although he was never allowed to join the order. His job in the monastery was to wash the pots in the kitchen, as that was all he was considered intellectually capable of. Yet Brother Lawrence had a very highly-developed "spirituality". In his simplicity, he developed a method to practise the presence of God, which led to him being a very spiritual man. So much so, that in his later years he became a spiritual director to many priests, monks and bishops. These men, no doubt, were intellectually far superior to Brother Lawrence, yet in things spiritual he was far more advanced than they were.

Individual and cultural progress

Not only does the individual develop through various stages, cultures as a whole evolve through similar developmental processes. Visser (2003) points out that Wilber's earlier thinking was very influenced by the work of Jean Gebser, and later by Jurgen Habermas. Wilber found that his stages of individual development corresponded with the stages of cultural development outlined by Gebser. Gebser and Wilber were of the opinion that society as a whole has evolved through four stages: the archaic, magical, mythical and mental. The first stage Wilber called the archaic-uroboric stage/phase. This was the day of primeval man. In this phase man existed in a state of consciousness that was more animal than human, being concerned with pure survival and the search for food.

The second phase, the magical-typhonic, was characterized by a physical-emotional level of consciousness. It was in this phase of development that individuals started to become aware of their mortality. In an attempt to ward off death, magic rituals were devised. In addition, the concept of time started to expand beyond the immediate present, but not much more than that. The most highly-developed individuals at this time were the shamans who possessed authentic paranormal powers. We know about this culture because they left traces of tools, settlements and cave paintings.

During the mythical membership phase, about 100 000 years ago, humanity again advanced. Certain social organizations were called for to cope with increased populations. Visser (2003) points out that according to Wilber, the development of agriculture during this phase was of great importance to the development of human consciousness. At this point humanity became aware of the cyclical nature of time, because of their dependence on the rhythm of the seasons. Hence, individuals had to learn to relate to time in a different way; they had to learn to wait and manage their crops. It was also at this time that language and writing emerged, in order to record the crops. People began to live together in groups, and so the ability to communicate via language developed and cultures flourished. To perpetuate their culture they told stories (hence the term "mythical"). With this development came an awareness of politics or kingship and its shadow side, wars.

The fourth phase, the mental-egoic phase, comes into being around the second millennium BCE. It is at this point in the evolution of humanity that ego develops within both individuals and their culture. By transcending the world of magic and myth, mental development starts to excel. As a result, time now has a past, present and future. Man now has a sense of history, and modern man has arrived.

In his book *Sex, Ecology, Spirituality* Wilber (1995) developed his thinking on this further, incorporating the work of Habermas. Both believe there is a parallel between the development of the individual and the evolution of humanity as a whole, and both incorporate the ideas of Piaget. Wilber, like Habermas, now divides human history into three main periods, as summarized in Table 5.

Visser (2003) points out that according to Wilber, in the first stage culture is magical. Individual identity is associated primarily with the body, thinking is based on images (pre-operational), and the basic orientation is biocentric or egocentric. In the second stage culture is mythical. Self-identity is associated with the group to which it belongs (the role fulfilled in society), thinking is based on concrete concepts (concrete-operational), and the basic orientation is socio- and ethnocentric.

The final stage is the current level of cultural development. Culture is rational. Here the individual becomes an autonomous individual and ego. Thinking at this stage of development is based on abstract concepts (formal-operational), and the orientation is world-centric. Here Wilber's thinking corresponds to that of Jaques and Clement (1997), where his upper level corresponds to the latter's

Table 5. The three stages of individual and cultural development.

Nature of the culture (Gebser)	Level of identity (Habermas)	Types of thinking (Piaget)	Stages of the self (Wilber)
3. Rational	Ego	Formop	Worldcentric
2. Mythic	Group	Conop	Socio/ethnocentric
1. Magic	Body	Preop	Bio/egocentric

Source: Visser (2003:187).

THE META-PHILOSOPHICAL FRAMEWORK   51

Fourth-Order Complexity, which is the third level of abstraction involving universals, and task complexity is stratum VII. This is a world where the level of complexity transcends those levels normally associated with corporate life. Here concepts develop into universal ideas which address ideologies and philosophy. The individual works with the problems of whole societies, and the time span would be between 20 and 50 years. It is the world of Einstein, Socrates and Plato. This is the complexity level of corporate CEOs working on strategic alternatives for global companies. Here the individual starts to operate from a global perspective. Not only do executives have to deal with the national economy, but with global economics which affect their business. They have to deal with the complexity of divergent cultures and values, and international trade.

The rational level is the upper level of our current cultural development. It is the level of development attained by the average person in the population. Wilber is, however, of the opinion that there are levels beyond the rational. Visser (2003) points out that the absence of scientific evidence of transpersonal stages in culture is due to the relative rarity of these stages in our culture. Yet Wilber (1995) points to the mystics who describe the transpersonal levels; these are people who were not just ahead of their own times, but also ahead of our time. These are people who have evolved the highest levels of consciousness, levels of consciousness to which society as a whole still needs to evolve. These transpersonal bands he divides into nature mysticism, theistic mysticism, monistic mysticism and nondualistic mysticism.

It is not within the scope of this study to go into detail on these stages. The point is that our history shows that there have always been individuals, for example Buddha and Christ, who have been more highly developed than the general population. They reach these stages of development long before society as a whole. The tendency has always been for society to try and silence them or to pull them "back" towards the average or median. Just because the median of the population does not experience these levels of development, does not mean that these levels do not exist.

In the corporate world a similar dynamic is at work. It is not uncommon to find individuals whose development or thinking is way ahead of the average level of development within the company. These individuals are usually under enormous pressure to fit in, conform or to leave. Sadly, they often have no choice but to leave the company, because it does not support their growth and development. This dilemma seems to be universal. Another example of where this happens is within monastic orders and the church, the very institutions that should be fostering growth and development in people. Referring to the work of Thomas Merton, Pennington (1996) points out that initially the restrictions of communal service and obedience in the church do liberate the individual from attachments and the self-will. But in trying to channel the energies of the spirit, the church can frustrate and stifle human growth and development beyond the median level. In so doing it tolerates "safe", moderate growth, and blesses the lack of growth and development. The church therefore tolerates those who do not grow.

This thinking is not unique. Beck and Cowan (2000) expressed similar views and stages of development in their book, *Spiral Dynamics: Mastering Values, Leadership and Change*. In his book *Integral Psychology*, Wilber (2000a) shows how their thinking can be integrated with his, for the purposes of a more integrated and holistic view of development. However, Wilber presents a better framework. Like Jaques and Clement (1997), Beck and Cowan (2000) do a brilliant job of mapping personal levels for the individual and culture. It is in the transpersonal realm where they are found wanting, and where Wilber stands out in the clarity of his thinking. Hence Wilber's model appears more robust and more integrative.

A more integrative approach

Wilber's (1995) model gives us an integrated model of human and cultural development that is open-ended. He points out that human growth and development is a never-ending process with limitless potential. At the same time, however, there are no guarantees that every individual will experience healthy growth. At any stage of the developmental process, individual or cultural, pathologies can develop. These pathologies can be treated and overcome, or they can halt or destroy development completely. The beauty of Wilber's model is that unlike so many New Age fads, he does not call for the destruction of old sciences or the establishment of new sciences. Instead, he shows that every discipline contains a partial truth, and no science or discipline contains the ultimate truth. Empirical science and phenomenological science are both valid, and we need to honour both. As Wilber (2003) expresses it in his Foreword to Visser's (2003) book, "integral" means to be more inclusive and embracing; it is an attempt to include as many perspectives, methodologies and styles as possible. Integral approaches are meta-models in that they try to draw together a number of existing, disconnected paradigms into a more enriching perspective.

Critique of Wilber

Rothberg and Kelly (1998) point out that Ken Wilber, Stanislav Grof and Michael Washburn are among the few contemporary theorists who have proposed a comprehensive transpersonal paradigm. It is important to note that Wilber's structural-hierarchical model is only one of the major transpersonal paradigms in circulation. Another alternative to Wilber's transpersonal paradigm is the dynamic-dialectical paradigm of Michael Washburn (1995), Professor of Philosophy at Indiana University and one of Wilber's biggest critics. Both models divide human development along triphasic lines (pre-egoic, egoic and transegoic), and both see development as a dialectical movement (thesis, antithesis and synthesis). But Washburn (1995) argues that that is where the similarities end. The dynamic-dialectical paradigm is based on a bipolar conception of the psyche, with human development being interplay between these two

Table 6. The bipolar structure of the psyche.

Nonegoic or physicodynamic pole	Egoic or mental-egoic pole
Dynamic ground: dynamism, libido, energy, spirit	Ego as organizing and controlling centre of consciousness
Somantic, sensual experience	Reflective self-awareness
Instinctuality	Impulsive control
Imaginal, autosymbolic cognition	Self control, deliberative will
Collective memories, complexes, archetypes	Operational cognition
	Personal, biographical experience

Source: Washburn (1995:10).

psychic poles. At one pole is the ego, and at the other pole is what Washburn (1995:10) refers to as the "Dynamic Ground" which is the source of dynamic life (energy, power, spirit). The two poles are represented in Table 6.

The egoic pole is also known as the mental-egoic pole, whereas the nonegoic pole is known as the physicodynamic pole. This bipolar structure is very similar to the division between Jung's ego and collective unconscious. The egoic pole corresponds to the Jungian ego and the physicodynamic pole corresponds to the Jungian collective unconscious. According to Washburn (1995:5–32), triphasic development happens in five stages as a result of a dialectical interplay between the two poles of the bipolar structure.

1. **Original Embedment**: The ego is blissfully immersed in the nonegoic or physicodynamic potentials as a result of minimal differentiation. Throughout the pre-egoic stage of development the infant continues to be drawn into original embedment.
2. **Pre-egoic Stage**: The ego slowly starts to differentiate itself from the nonegoic pole. However, as this is weak differentiation, it is easily swayed by the physicodynamic potentials. As a result the ego frequently returns to original embedment.
3. **Egoic Stage**: Through primal repression the ego achieves independence from the nonegoic pole. As a result the nonegoic pole is submerged and becomes the deep unconscious. The ego becomes the purely mental or Cartesian ego.
4. **Regression in the service of transcendence and regeneration in spirit**: The ego is regeneratively transformed by the physicodynamic potentials as primal repression gives way. The ego starts to return to the dynamic ground on its way to a higher synthesis within the ground.
5. **Transegoic Stage**: The ego is now rooted in, and an instrument of, the dynamic ground. The psyche is an integrated bipolar system, and fully developed.

Washburn (1995:36–45) mentions five points of disagreement with Wilber:

1. **The central role of conflict in the pre-egoic stage**. Washburn (1995) sees conflict as a primary theme of the pre-egoic stage.

This conflict is brought about as a result of the desire for independence in relation to the dynamic ground, as well as the tension between desires for distance and intimacy in relation to the primary caregiver. The oedipal period and conflict is central, as the child begins to see the father as a rival for intimacy with the mother and a model of egoic independence. Washburn's criticism is that Wilber does not place conflict at the centre of the development stage. In his view Wilber places the emphasis on cognitive development which unfolds without serious "countervailing" challenges. As a result there is no interpolar tension, which is central to Washburn's (1995) paradigm.

2. **Are pre-egoic potentials lost or retained in the transition to the egoic stage?** The dynamic-dialectical paradigm holds that the ego resolves the early childhood conflict through primal repression which submerges the nonegoic potentials into unconsciousness. For the child to continue developing, it must disconnect itself from the original source of its being. To assert its independence, the child has a choice between repression and regression, and in making this choice there is a forfeiture of the physicodynamic potentials of the psyche. Washburn (1995) points out that although Wilber does see a forsaking of some pre-egoic structures, these are transitional structures and not basic structures. As a result, the transition to the egoic stage involves a higher reorganization of the pre-egoic psychic resources, but it does not forfeit them. Washburn (1995) believes that the repression and forfeiture of psychic resources is a normal and necessary part of the developmental process. Wilber does not.

3. **Does the mental ego alienate itself from its source in the egoic stage?** Washburn (1995) is of the opinion that repression of the nonegoic pole of the psyche during the transition of the egoic stage puts it out of touch with the Ground. This is done through repression. However, once development of the ego is complete, it no longer needs to repress the physicodynamic potentials. It is then that it is ready to reopen itself to the nonegoic pole of the psyche. The structural-hierarchical model, on the other hand, sees the mental ego as remaining in touch with its foundations. "As Wilber puts it, the mental ego's existential difficulties at midlife do not express alienation from a pre-egoic Eden but rather reflect the fact that the mental ego has not yet reached

transegoic heaven. The mental ego's sense of alienation arises in relation to future possibilities not yet realized rather than past actualities that have been repressed and submerged" (Washburn, 1995:41).

4. **Is it a spiral movement or straight ascent through the stage?** The dynamic-dialectical paradigm sees development as a spiral loop. It is a going back in order to move beyond. There is a regression back into the pregoic in order to ascend into the transegoic. Wilber sees it as a straightforward ascending movement to higher levels. However, Wilber does point out that rather than seeing development as a simple linear progression where one level builds on another, i.e., the individual first has to be well-developed cognitively before they can develop spiritually, development should be seen as taking place in relatively independent lines or streams (refer to Figure 5). Washburn (1995), on the other hand, sees this spiral as a regression process in which the ego is disempowered and brought into direct contact with resurging nonegoic life. In so doing the ego is transformed by the power of the Ground. So, as Washburn (1995) points out, none of Wilber's stages require a redeeming of resources that have been forsaken or lost. There is no spiral movement.

5. **Are there two selves or none?** Washburn (1995:43) believes that there is "small-s self", which is one pole on the biopole that needs to be reunited with or transformed by the other pole, the "large-S self". He is of the opinion that with Wilber the self is seen as an illusion that needs to dissolve. It is merely a transitional structure. That might have been true of Wilber's earlier work, which is the work to which Washburn actually refers. In his later work, Wilber believes in the existence of a "self" in the individual which is critical in the developmental process. The argument that there is no self, because the self cannot be seen or perceived, does not hold ground for Wilber. It is the self that integrates, coordinates and organizes the "stream of consciousness", and in so doing forms the basis of the individual's sense of identity. It is the self which climbs the "ladder of development". The ladder of development is a metaphor to illustrate the difference between what Wilber calls the basic structures of consciousness and the transitional or replacement stages of development (Visser, 2003:122).

Stanislav Grof (1998:89–94) believes that Wilber has a blind spot in terms of the significance of prenatal and perinatal experiences for the theory and practice of psychotherapy, psychiatry and psychology. Grof feels that Wilber does not understand that the perinatal domain is completely different as a logical type to all the subsequent developmental stages. He is also of the opinion that Wilber trivializes the importance of life-threatening situations like birth and death. As a result, his theory cannot make sense of essential features of psychopathology such as the linkage between sexuality and aggression. Grof is of the opinion that Wilber's pre/trans fallacy is too simplex, and believes it is a complex process in which the personal and transpersonal coexist in a state of interpenetration. So Grof's criticism of Wilber is very similar or close to that of Washburn.

Washburn (1995) has some very compelling arguments, and I think his work adds richly to the field. Both Wilber and Washburn are very well-grounded in psychological theory, and both provide an understandable framework for transpersonal experience. I believe that Washburn's (1995) model is a very powerful and useful model to use if you are a psychotherapist or psychologist—especially if you have been trained in and understand the conflicts brought about by pre- and perinatal experiences. I, however, have never been trained in psychology, and as a result I do not practice therapy on my clients. In doing so I would be acting unprofessionally and crossing professional boundaries. The criticisms that Washburn and Grof level against Wilber involve issues with which I as an executive coach never work. If I pick up any indication of a need for therapy, I immediately refer my clients to the relevant professionals. It is simply outside my scope of work; I do not work with pathology.

I believe that the criticisms of Washburn and Grof are valid. However, I have chosen to work with the structural-hierarchical paradigm because Wilber not only provides us with a well-developed theory of human development, but he also gives the executive an integrated framework in which to think. The problem in many organizations is that people do not tend to see how different interventions support each other. Instead, all interventions are seen as the latest management fad that will come and go. What is missing is to see how the various interventions can actually support or build on each other. Once the organization is seen from this point of view, it immediately becomes apparent that any intervention is relevant but partial. No intervention or leadership model or methodology is a "silver bullet" containing the ultimate truth; they all contain a partial truth which they contribute to the ultimate truth. Figure 6 sets out some of the more well-known interventions that have been implemented in organizations, showing where they could fit into Wilber's Integral Model. The important thing to remember is that all four quadrants are necessary for an integral theory of consciousness. The problem in business is that reality is often reduced to the two right-hand quadrants, the so-called "hard stuff". The left-hand quadrants are often ignored, or at the very least tolerated as the "soft stuff". Yet everybody knows that this is the most difficult domain in which to work. Wilber's call is for the executive to work within all four quadrants.

Visser (2003) believes that one of the main advantages of the four-quadrant model is that it enables the identification of all kinds of precise correlations within the various quadrants. As an example, when an individual is capable of abstract thought (upper-left quadrant) due to the fact that the neocortex has developed in the

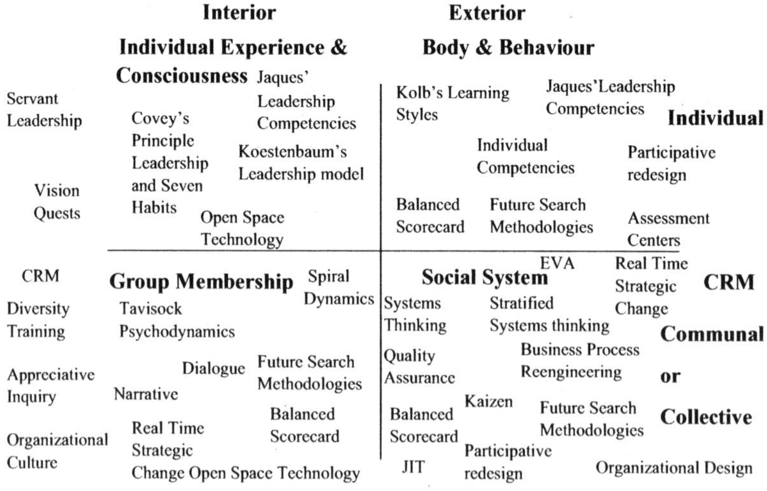

Figure 6. Organizational interventions in Wilber's model.
Source: Adapted from Wilber (1996:71).

brain (upper-right quadrant) and is a prerequisite for thought, the individual can create a culture (lower-left quadrant) that is rational. And that rational culture can in turn develop industrialized economies (lower-right quadrant)

In the same way, it is going to be very difficult for servant leaders to evolve within a company if the individuals and the company as a whole are not at that level of consciousness. At the same time, a company will find it very difficult to come up with a strategy addressing strategic issues which can span ten to 20 years, when the most highly-developed individuals in the organization can only work four years into the future. These are highly complex problems that have to be addressed in an integrated way. Wilber's (1995) Integrative Model therefore provides the framework for integrated growth and development.

Given that Wilber has tried to come up with a theory of everything, it is understandable that there will be gaps in his theory. As we know, reality is actually way beyond the conceptual ability of any individual. Wilber (1995) cautions us to remember that any theory is just that—a mere theory. The point is not to know the theory intellectually, but to live the reality and to experience it. Not only is Wilber a gifted theorist, he actually lives what he preaches. But this is precisely the point Grof uses to criticize Wilber's theory, and I tend to agree with Grof:

> However, for a theory of such importance, it is not sufficient to integrate material from many different ancient and modern sources into a system that shows inner logical cohesion. While logical consistency certainly is a valuable prerequisite, a viable theory has to have an additional property that is equally, if not more, important. It is generally accepted among scientists that a system of propositions is an acceptable theory if, and only if, its conclusions are in agreement with observable facts (Frank, 1957). Since speculations concerning consciousness, the human psyche, and spiritual experiences represent the cornerstone of Ken's conceptual framework, it is essential to test their theoretical adequacy and practical relevance against clinical data. Ken himself does not have any clinical experience, and the primary sources of his data have been his extensive reading and the experiences from his personal spiritual practice. For this

reason, evaluating his ideas in the light of actual experiences and observations from transpersonal therapy and from modern consciousness research seems particularly important and necessary (Grof, 1998:88–89).

I believe one of the reasons Wilber's work has not been researched is that he actually does not have an integrated methodology for development. There is no integrated injunction, i.e., the how-to-do-it. Research into the model can only happen once an integrated methodology for it is developed or found. In Chapter three I will show that a research methodology does actually exist that can be used to research aspects of Wilber's model.

Integrative growth and development

Having an integrated theoretical framework for growth and development is all very well; the question is, of course, how does one facilitate this growth and development within individuals, or in the culture within which the individual lives and operates? Interestingly enough, Wilber does not offer an integrated developmental methodology. Part of the reason could be that he refers to himself as a Pandit as opposed to a guru. Wilber (2000b) believes that a Pandit does not accept devotees, whereas a guru does. Pandits are usually scholars of a tradition, and spend their time researching, writing and teaching. They do not engage in spiritual or therapeutic work with individuals; that is the domain of gurus and therapists. To the latter we can also add the profession of coaching. The point is that anybody looking to find an integrated developmental methodology in Wilber's work will be disappointed; they will not find one. Wilber's view is "work it out for yourself". Wilber (2000b) does, however, suggest that any individual who wants to grow in an integral way, should practice a number of disciplines at the same time—and these disciplines should cover all four quadrants.

According to Wilber (2000b), the general idea is to take a practice from each of the levels of being (body, mind, soul and spirit) and exercise all of them to the best of your ability. The aim is to practice them individually and collectively, and to find those disciplines that suit the individual and that are practically possible. In his view, the more categories that are engaged, the more effective they become. The problem is that people tend to concentrate on only one discipline, which leads to individuals not growing in an integrated way. Furthermore, it seems to be a very impractical suggestion for executives. In a world that is constantly demanding "more with less", executives are already having a difficult enough time trying to manage their lives and their time effectively. Multiple practices demand a tremendous amount of time and discipline.

An alternative integrated model

Given the time constraints, resource constraints, and the pressures under which most executives live in modern corporations, it is highly unlikely that Wilber's approach is practicable for these individuals. The question has to be asked whether there is not a more pragmatic approach which can be used to help individuals develop in an integrated way. One possibility is the Diamond Approach developed by A.H. Almaas (2002). Like Wilber, Almaas has been working on an integrated approach to human development which incorporates both Western psychology and spiritual wisdom. In his book *The Eye of the Spirit*, Wilber (1998a) gives a 13-page critique of Almaas's work. His main criticism is that Almaas falls into the romantic notion of the prepersonal being the same as the transpersonal; in doing so he is supporting the Pre/Trans fallacy. However, Almaas has been able to develop an integrated praxis, which Wilber has not. And it is because of this, that Wilber (1998a) holds Almaas's work in such high esteem, despite the criticism that he levels against parts of his theory:

> Here I will simply say that, in my opinion, the Diamond Approach is a superb combination of some of the best Western psychology with ancient (spiritual) wisdom. It is one type of a more integral approach, uniting Ascending and Descending, spiritual and psychological, into a coherent and effective form of inner work (Wilber, 1998a:267).

> This, nonetheless, is an extraordinary achievement, and certainly ranks it as one of the premier transformative technologies now available on any sort of widespread scale (Wilber, 1998a:372).

On one level Almaas's (2002) methodology is very simple, yet at another level it is very complex and involved. It is simple because all that is required of any individual is an open-ended exploration into the immediacy of their own experience. It is about continuously inquiring into one's own personal experience. The beauty of it is that it is a developmental and spiritual technique that uses the inherent natural capacity of the human consciousness. Human beings are curious by nature, and it is just a matter of using that curiosity to inquire into our own experience. All that is required is a certain amount of discipline and desire to want to do it. It is actually so simple that an individual can do it on their own through journaling or silent contemplation, or via engaging in a dialogue with another human being. The inquiry into the experience is then analyzed and explored even further by continuously asking open-ended questions. It is about inquiring into personal thoughts, behaviours, feelings and sensations. Like most things in life, it is a discipline that needs to be learnt.

What makes it complex is the language and terminology that Almaas (1998) uses. To really come to terms with this approach, the individual is required to do a tremendous amount of reading, or to attend group training sessions to learn the terminology used in this approach. And the terminology is very important, because Almaas (1998) is very precise with the terms that he uses; the words have very specific meanings. The problem, however, is not in the words or the description, but that people who read the words often don't really understand them due to a lack of experience. Almaas (1998) points out that the usual contention in spiritual literature, that ultimate reality cannot be described, is not accurate. Ultimate reality or "essence", as he refers to it, can be described. The problem, however, is that in describing essence it does not guarantee that someone who has not experienced essence will actually understand it. A person who has had first-hand experience of essence will, however, easily understand what the description is referring to. Almaas (1998a:77) describes the dilemma as follows:

> If somebody has never seen or eaten a persimmon, he will not be able to understand a description of a persimmon; but on hearing a description, he will likely envision something else, familiar from his past experience. The same holds true

for descriptions of essence. The difficulty is not in describing it in words but in making sense to someone who does not have the experience. The person will be able to understand the words but will be incapable of connecting the description to his experience. He will construct something in his mind that will correspond to the description. This construction will be false because he lacks the actual experience ... So when I say 'existence', a person who has had the experience of existence will understand. The person who has not will either see that he does not understand or will take something else in his experience to mean existence.

As a result of this, Almaas goes to great lengths to describe what he means. For the novice this can be overwhelming. He does, however, make the point that this dilemma applies to anything and all levels of existence, not just essence. A simple example of this dilemma in the organizational context is the word "strategy". Executives use the word freely, believing that when they use it everybody sees the same reality to which they are referring. That reality, however, is often very different. Enough of the concept "strategy" is conveyed for people to have a general or vague idea of what strategy is. The question, however, is whether people are seeing the same picture. Almaas will say no, because it depends on the person's level of development and their actual experience.

One can return to the work of Jaques and Clement (1997) to see a similar point of view. A person operating at Category B–1 task complexity (stratum – I) will have a totally different view and experience of strategy to a person operating at Category C–3 task complexity (stratum – VII). Hence people at different levels of development often use the same word, but the experience and the worldviews associated with the word are literally worlds apart. To overcome this problem, Almaas has to go to great lengths to develop an appropriate terminology, which can often be confusing and overwhelming for the novice. This is what makes his methodology complex and involved.

On closer inspection, however, it becomes apparent that Almaas (1998a) is actually referring to the Prehension Dimension in David Kolb's (1984) Experiential Learning Model. His description of the actual experience corresponds to Kolb's (1984) concrete experience and the grasping of knowledge through direct apprehension. When Almaas (1998a) refers to description, he is talking about Kolb's (1984) abstract conceptualization and the ability to grasp knowledge via comprehension. The beauty of this is that Almaas clearly points out the weakness of working only with the prehension dimension as a source of true knowledge. Some things are simply impossible to pass on via comprehension, because it will be distorted and governed by the receiver's actual experience. Hence it is easy to understand why the Christian Church, for example, has often executed or banished its more highly-developed saints: although they spoke the same language, they experienced totally different realities. Be that as it may, the point is that Almaas (1998) is referring to Kolb's (1984) Prehension Dimension.

Fortunately, Almaas (1998a) does not stop with the Prehension Dimension. He goes on to say that to be a genuine human being is to be essence. But to be essence is not only an inner experience, it is the inner and outer. Essence is the inner experience in the privacy of your heart and it is the shared outer experiences with others. With a bit of reflection it becomes clear that Almaas (1998a) is referring to what Kolb (1984) would call the transformation dimension of his Experiential Learning Model. In Kolb's model this is the growth dimension. When Almaas (1998a:82) refers to the "inner and privacy of our hearts" he is talking about Kolb's (1984) concept of transformation via intension. It is the journey inwards and the activity of reflective observation. Reflective observation takes the individual inwards. The danger, of course, is to get trapped in this inner world where it becomes mere escapism. Hence Almaas's (1998a:82) call that reflective observation must be completed or complemented with the "outer and shared experience with others". He is talking about Kolb's (1984) transformation via extension, the going outwards and being engaged with active experimentation. Interestingly enough, the test of true mysticism has always been that the journey inwards is the journey outwards. Both dimensions of the journey have to be present.

It can therefore be argued that at the most elementary level, Almaas's (2002) integral methodology uses inquiry as a developmental tool by making use of Kolb's (1984) Experiential Learning Model. This is not an attempt to simplify a very complex methodology; it is rather an attempt to arrive at a methodology that a novice can use to get started in order to mature into more complex and complicated levels of inquiry. I would therefore argue that Kolb's (1984) Experiential Learning Model can be used as an appropriate starting methodology, which can at a later stage lead to more complex levels of inquiry.

Kolb's Experiential Learning Model

Kolb (1984) developed his Experiential Learning Model by drawing on the work of Dewey, Lewin and Piaget's cognitive development tradition. In effect, his model is a synthesis of their work, and is a four-stage learning cycle that involves four adaptive learning modes. The four adaptive learning modes are (Kolb, 1984:68–69):

- **concrete experience** (the ability to involve oneself fully and openly and without bias in new experiences);
- **reflective observation** (the ability to reflect and to observe the experience from many perspectives);
- **abstract conceptualization** (the ability to create concepts and to build logically sound theories from the observations); and
- **active experimentation** (the ability to use the constructed theories to make decisions and experiment with new behaviours and thoughts).

Within this model there are two distinct dimensions, representing two dialectically opposed adaptive orientations:

- concrete experience versus abstract conceptualization; and
- active experimentation versus reflective observation.

The important thing to remember is that these dimensions are independent but mutually enhancing, and each makes a contribution to the learning process.

Learning requires the resolution of conflicts between these conflicting dialectical orientations. Hence, by its very nature, learning is a conflictual and tension-filled process. The first dialectical orientation Kolb (1984:43–51) refers to as the prehension dimension, as it represents two different and opposing ways of experiencing the world:

- the reliance on symbolic representations or by making use of concepts, which he calls "comprehension"; and
- another which is more tangible and makes uses of the directly-felt experience, which he calls "apprehension".

There are therefore two distinct modes of grasping experience. When I walk outside on a very cold morning, for example, I will feel the cold directly. That is, I will have experienced the cold via direct apprehension. This direct apprehension I cannot pass on directly to my family or colleagues; the best I can do is to describe to them that it is cold. To do that, I need to pass on the concept that it is cold. They, in turn, can grasp the reality via comprehension. I have passed on my experience via a concept. I can never, however, pass on the actual experience. As pointed out by Almaas (2002), the problem with grasping via comprehension is that it is very much governed by my past experience and the level of my development. My concept of coldness as a South African will be very different to an Alaskan's concept of coldness. Concepts can only pass on so much of experience; it will always be limited. That is why it is preferable to have both apprehension and comprehension. Herein lies the dialectical tension: there is a difference, for example, between a consultant who knows all the theory on how to run organizations (grasping via comprehension), and managers who actually have the hands-on experience (grasping via apprehension). In Kolb's (1984) view you need both. In this regard he is supported in his thinking by both Almaas and Wilber.

The active/reflective dialectic, Kolb (1984) calls the transformation dimension. It represents two opposed ways of transforming experience, either by reflecting on it, which is called "intension", or through "active external manipulation of the external world", which is called "extension". It is this dimension that is responsible for the creation of meaning and the awareness of consciousness. Quoting Yeats, Kolb (1984:52) writes:

> The human soul is always moving outward into the external world and inward into itself, and this movement is double

because the human soul would not be conscious were it not suspended between two contraries. The greater the contrast, the more intense the consciousness.

In addressing the transformation dimension, Kolb is honouring the call by many to integrate the inner and outer domains of human existence. Interestingly, Kolb (1984) believes that traditionally the Eastern traditions have been stronger on transformation by intension, while the West with its pragmatism has placed more emphasis on transformation via extension. The real power in Kolb's (1984) model is that he recognizes and honours this dialectical tension, and reminds us that both are required for learning and growth to take place within the individual. Intension on its own is mere escapism or fantasy, while extension on its own can be very dangerous and meaningless. As mentioned above in connection with Almaas's (2002) Diamond Approach, the test of true mysticism has always been that the journey inward is always the journey outward. Mother Teresa of Calcutta expressed the transformation dimension very eloquently when she said, "The fruit of silence is prayer. The fruit of prayer is faith. The fruit of faith is love. The fruit of love is service. The fruit of service is peace" (Vardey, 1995:39). The transformation dimension is an integrated whole.

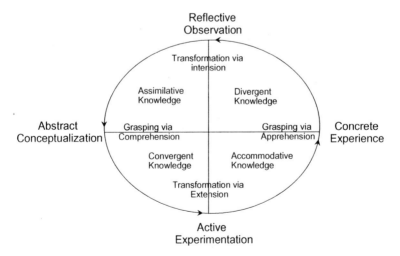

Figure 7. Kolb's experiential learning model.
Source: Adapted from Kolb (1984:42).

According to Kolb (1984), learning happens as a result of the transaction between these four adaptive modes and the way in which the dialectical tension gets resolved. As a result there are four forms of knowledge, as presented in Figure 7. (Those familiar with Kolb's model will realize that the order of the four forms has been altered. Instead of moving clockwise around the cycle, the order has been reversed to anti-clockwise. The reason for this adaptation will be made clear later.) The four forms of knowledge are defined as follows (Kolb, 1984:42):

- **Divergent knowledge** is the result of grasping experience via apprehension and transforming it via intension.
- Experience grasped via comprehension and transformed via intension results in **assimilative knowledge**.
- **Convergent knowledge** is a result of experience being grasped via comprehension and transformed through extension.
- When experience is grasped via apprehension and transformed via extension the result is **accommodative knowledge**.

Kolb's (1984) point is that grasping knowledge is not sufficient for learning. For learning to take place it has to be acted on; in other words, the grasping has to be transformed either via intension or extension. At the same time, transformation on its own is also meaningless. There has to be something, an experience or concept, which is to be transformed. Kolb (1984) points out that all adults are capable of using all four modes. The learning processes is not, however, identical for all human beings. As a result, individuals tend to emphasize some adaptive orientations over others. In other words, individuals tend to use some orientations more than others. It is not that they cannot use all four; they just prefer certain orientations more than others. This can lead to people getting stuck in those orientations. Kolb's (1984) Learning Style Inventory (LSI) was developed to identify an individual's preferred learning style.

The Learning Styles Inventory (LSI)

The LSI is a self-description questionnaire that measures an individual's relative emphasis on each of the four modes. On the prehension dimension it measures the extent to which an individual emphasizes abstraction over being concrete (AC–CE). The transformation dimension measures the extent to which an individual emphasizes action over reflection (AE–RO). The four basic learning modes are (Kolb, 1984:68–69):

- **An orientation towards concrete experience focuses on immediate experience.** The individual tends to get personally involved, and uses feelings more than thinking. There is a concern for the complexity involved with reality, as opposed to working with theories and generalizations. The approach to problem resolution is more intuitive and "artistic", as opposed to scientific and systematic. These are usually people-oriented individuals who relate well to other people. They tend to have an open-minded approach to life, and as a result they generally function well in unstructured situations.
- **An orientation towards reflective observation focuses on the understanding and meaning of ideas.** The individual tends to try and understand the meaning of ideas by observing and impartially commenting on them. The emphasis is on understanding how things happen, as opposed to what works. These people tend to be good at seeing the implications of ideas and at looking at things from many different perspectives. They tend to value impartiality and patience, and are the kind of people who drive action-oriented business executives mad.
- **An orientation towards abstract conceptualization focuses on concepts and ideas.** Here the emphasis is on thinking as opposed to feeling. This is a more logical, scientific orientation concerned with building general theories. It is the opposite of the artistic, intuitive approach. These people tend to be good at quantitative analysis, systematic planning, and the manipulation of abstract symbols. They tend to be disciplined when it comes to analyzing ideas.
- **An active experimentation orientation focuses on changing situations and influencing people.** Here the emphasis is on practical application and a pragmatic concern for what works. Action is valued above observation, and these people enjoy getting things done. Because they love to see results, they are willing to take risks and to try and influence the environment in which they find themselves.

Based on research and clinical observation of the LSI scores, Kolb (1984) developed descriptions of the characteristics of the four learning styles. The four descriptions are (Kolb, 1984:77–78):

• **The convergent learning style**. Here an individual prefers to employ abstract conceptualization and active experimentation. This approach is strong at decision-making, the practical application of ideas, and problem-solving. This learning style solves problems through hypothetical-deductive reasoning. People who prefer this style of learning prefer to deal with technical tasks and problems. Social and interpersonal issues tend to be avoided.
• **The divergent learning style**. Here the individual prefers to utilize concrete experience and reflective observation. These people tend to like working with people and are more feeling-oriented and tend to be imaginative. They love to look at things from many perspectives and tend towards observation rather than action. They are good at brainstorming because of their ability to generate alternative ideas and to think of the implications of these.
• **The assimilation learning style**. This style draws on abstract conceptualization and reflective observation. Individuals who prefer this style tend to have an ability to create theoretical models, synthesizing disparate observations into meaningful explanations using inductive reasoning. The focus is more on ideas and abstract concepts than on people. Theories are valued more for their precision and logic than for their practical value.
• **The accommodative learning style**. Here concrete experience and active experimentation are employed as the preferred learning abilities. It is action-oriented and excels at getting things done, completing tasks, and getting involved with new experiences. This style is accommodative, because it is best suited for those situations where an individual must adapt to the changing circumstances. These individuals will tend to discard plans or theories when they do not suit the facts. Problems are solved in an intuitive, trial-and-error manner. These people tend to rely more on other people for information than on their own analytical ability. Although they are comfortable with people, they can be seen as pushy and impatient.

Again, it must be emphasized that these are preferred learning styles. The ideal is for an individual to move through all four learning styles to optimize learning and growth. The problem, as was mentioned previously, is that individuals tend to get stuck in or concentrate on only one of the four learning abilities, and in so doing limit their own learning and development. Kolb (1984:78–95) found that the following factors can affect or shape individuals' preferred learning styles, which could lead to them concentrating on a preferred learning style:

- **Personality Type.** Quoting research done by Margerson and Lewis on 220 MBA students, Kolb (1984) argued that there is a strong relationship between learning styles and the Jungian personality types. The accommodating learning style is associated with the sensing type, the assimilative learning style with the intuitive type, the divergent learning style with the feeling personality type, and the convergent learning style with the thinking personality types.
- **Educational specialization.** Given that we are taught how to learn, it can be expected that early educational experiences shape learning styles. The longer an individual spends in the educational system, the more specialized the learning becomes. So, for example, postgraduate studies are more specialized than graduate studies, which in turn are more specialized than high school. Hence Kolb (1984) found that some of the differences in the learning orientations of managers can be explained by their early educational specializations in university.

  Evidence seems to suggest that undergraduate training is a major factor in the development of learning styles. The open question is whether the field shapes the learning style or whether individuals choose fields that suit their learning style. Kolb (1984) is of the opinion that both factors are at play. Those individuals choose a field based on their preferred learning style, which is then reinforced by the field or the discipline.
- **Professional career.** The choice of a professional career not only exposes an individual to a specialized learning environment, it also involves adopting a common set of values and beliefs about professional behaviour shared by peers with a certain professional mentality. A learning style is shaped through habits

acquired in professional training and normative pressure. Kolb (1984) found that certain learning style orientations characterized certain professions. Social workers, for example, tended towards the divergent learning style, while the converger learning style was associated with accountants, engineers and medical doctors. Professional managers tended to fall between the converger and assimilator learning styles.

- **Current job role.** A person's adaptive orientation tends to be shaped by current job demands and pressure. An accommodative learning style is required by executives who have to make decisions in uncertain circumstances, while at the same time having a strong orientation towards task delivery. Jobs which involve working with people, where personal relationships are critical, demand a divergent learning style. Assimilative learning is called for where the work is centred on data gathering, analysis and conceptual modelling. Technical jobs like engineering and production require a convergent learning style.
- **Adaptive competencies.** According to Kolb (1984), the specific task or the problem that an individual is currently working on is the most specific force that shapes learning styles. Each task or job requires a specific set of skills. The effective matching of task demands and personal skills is what Kolb (1984) calls "adaptive competence". Hence the need to test for competencies, as opposed to aptitudes that are too generalized to relate to specific tasks for a given job. The aim is to identify adaptive competencies that lead to congruence between personal skills and task demands. Kolb (1984) found that adaptive competencies did relate to learning styles:

  - The divergent learning style is associated with "valuing" skills like being sensitive to people's feelings, imagining implications of ambiguous situations, gathering information, listening with an open mind, and being sensitive to values.
  - "Acting" skills like committing yourself to objectives, seeking and exploiting opportunities, being personally involved, dealing with people, and influencing and leading others, are associated with the accommodator learning style.
  - The assimilator learning style is related to thinking skills which include organizing information, analyzing quantitative

data, testing theories and ideas, building conceptual models, and designing experiments.

- Decision skills such as creating new ways of thinking and doing, making decisions, setting goals, experimenting with new ideas, and choosing the best solutions, are related to the converger learning style.

Hence it can be concluded that tasks requiring certain skills will influence the preferred learning style.

Experiential learning and development

Unlike the classical Piagetians who believe that learning is a subordinate process that is not actively involved in human development, Kolb (1984:133) believes that learning is the process through which development occurs:

> Without denying the reality of biological maturation and developmental achievements (that is, enduring cognitive structures that organize thought and action), the experiential learning theory of development focuses on the transaction between internal characteristics and external circumstances, between personal knowledge and social knowledge. It is the process of learning from experience that shapes and actualizes developmental potentialities. This learning is a social process; and thus, the course of individual development is shaped by the cultural system of social knowledge ... Through experiences of imitation and communication with others and interaction with the physical environment, internal development potentialities are enacted and practised until they are internalized as an independent development achievement. Thus, learning becomes the vehicle of human development via interactions between individuals with their biological potentialities and the society with its symbols, tools, and other cultural artefacts.

The first thing that becomes very apparent is that Kolb's (1984) language and concepts are very similar to those of Wilber. Kolb talks about the inner and outer world, personal knowledge and social knowledge. In so doing he is describing Wilber's (1995) four-quadrant model. The last sentence of the quote (Kolb, 1984:133) contains all four quadrants:

> Thus, learning becomes the vehicle of human development via interactions between individuals [upper-left quadrant] with their biological potentialities [upper-right quadrant] and the society with its symbols [lower-left quadrant], tools, and other cultural artefacts [lower-right quadrant].

The similarities between Kolb (1984) and Wilber (1995) do not end there. They share a very similar view of human development. Kolb's (1984) development model can be summarized in Figure 8.

Like Wilber (1995), Kolb (1984) sees development as a dialectical process, which requires a confrontation and resolution of dialectical conflicts, and it is marked by increased differentiation and integration. In this regard, his hierarchical integration is the same as Wilber's (1995) fifth principal, that an emergent holon

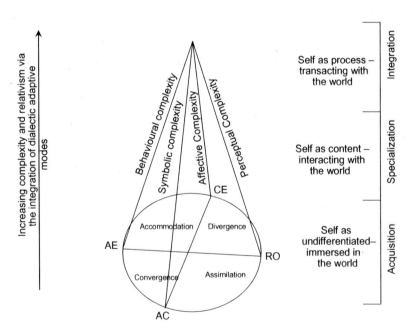

Figure 8. The Experiential Learning theory of growth and development. *Source:* Kolb (1984:141).

transcends but includes its predecessor(s). Each emerging new holon includes the preceding holons and then adds its own defining patterns to it. In each case it preserves the previous holons but it negates their partiality. Kolb (1984) says exactly the same thing, in that each developmental stage is characterized by the acquisition of a higher level of consciousness then the stage before it. Yet at the same time the previous or earlier levels of consciousness remain intact. So in Kolb's (1984) model, an adult can display all three levels of consciousness, namely registrative, interpretative and integrative. Both therefore believe in a developmental hierarchy which evolves towards higher and higher levels of complexity. Furthermore, they both believe that each successive stage of development builds on its predecessor, by adding something new, while at the same time preserving the previous stage. Although Kolb (1984) does not say it, from his work it is clear that he would not support the popular idea of trying to do away with hierarchies. Development hierarchies are inherent in Kolb's (1984) Experiential Learning Theory.

Experiential Learning Theory believes that there are four interrelated developmental dimensions: perceptual complexity, affective complexity, behavioural complexity and symbolic complexity, as represented in Figure 8. The important thing is that although these dimensions are interrelated, they can develop separately/independently of each other or at various rates/speeds. Hence Kolb (1984) differs from Piaget in that he sees individuality not only being manifested in the stage of development, but also in the personal learning style that the person adopts. This is very similar to Wilber's idea of separate and independent development lines, as represented in Figure 8. Hence both Wilber (1995) and Kolb (1984) break away from the pure linearity of the Piagetian approach, in that they see development as being multilinear. Yet both agree that the more integrated the individual becomes, the more the various lines of development become integrated or converge.

Kolb's developmental stages

Kolb (1984) believed that the human development process can be divided into three broad developmental stages: acquisition, specialization and integration. Acquisition extends from birth to adolescence, and it is the stage where the basic learning abilities and cognitive structures are acquired. At the beginning the self is experienced as undifferentiated and immersed in the environment. As the child develops through the acquisition phase, there is a gradual development of an internalized structure that allows the self to distinguish and separate itself from the surrounding environment. It is at this stage that the discrimination between internal and external stimuli are developed which matures into the **delineation of the boundaries of selfhood**.

The specialization phase extends through formal education and/ or career training into early adulthood. Given their culture, education and socialization, the individual becomes more specialized to adapt and master their careers. It is at this stage that the individual will work very intensely with the transformative dimension for the first time, the dynamic tension between internal personal dynamic and external social forces and expectations. Kolb (1984) points out that during this phase there is a closer and closer match between self characteristics and environmental demands. And there are two ways in which this happens: social pressure forces the person to fit in, and people tend to select environments that are consistent with their characteristics. At this stage the self is defined in terms of "content"—professional skills, achievements and past experiences, both good and bad. The sense of self is based on the rewards and recognition received for doing well in a chosen life task. The primary mode of interacting with the world is through interaction. The individual acts on the world, and the world acts on him or her in return through the rewards it gives. Kolb (1984) does point out that although this interaction is bi-directional, neither is fundamentally changed by the other. This stage brings about social security and achievement.

The integration phase is ushered in with the existential crisis, the conflict between personal fulfilment and meaning versus social demands and expectations. The individual strives more to influence than to be influenced by the environment. There is an exploration of aspects of the personality that was suppressed during the specialization phase. Hence, the concept of the self moves from self as "content", to self as "process". Sadly, this is where Kolb (1984) stops with the stages of development, at the same level as Jaques and

Clement (1994). Both stop their thinking on human development at the highest level of rational development, the existential level.

Integrating the models of Wilber and Kolb

In Wilber's (1995) model, the highest level of rational development is referred to as Vision-Logic, and is seen as the transition point into the transpersonal bands. As can be seen from Table 7, Wilber (1995) and Kolb (1984) are in complete agreement on the symbolic complexity via comprehension for the personal bands of development. In short, they are saying the same thing. If any criticism can be levelled at Kolb, it could be that he has done himself an injustice by stopping at the integrative level. This could be due to the fact that he was writing for a mainly "pragmatic" Western audience that was less open to the notion of transpersonal levels of development. Be that as it may, it is clear that in terms of human development and how it happens, Wilber (1995) and Kolb (1984) seem to be in agreement. The only difference is that Wilber's (1995) model is more integral than Kolb's (1984) model, in that Wilber does not stop at personal levels of development but allows for transpersonal levels of human development. However, in my personal correspondence with David Kolb he has made me aware of the fact that although he does not directly address the transpersonal realm, he does allude to it in Chapter eight of his book.

Given that Wilber's (1995) integrative model caters for more developmental stages, and that his theory as a whole is covered in more depth than Kolb's (1984), it can be argued that Wilber's model provides a more comprehensive framework for integrated growth and development. It is more holistic than Kolb's (1984) model, and hence should be used as the meta-theory for human growth and development within an integrated coaching model. However, Wilber's (1995) Integral Model is weak in terms of the praxis of human development, and it is here that Kolb's (1984) Experiential Learning Model is far superior. Kolb's (1984) model provides a practical, experiential way to learn and grow in an integrated way. In order to develop an Integral Experiential Coaching Model, it is suggested that the two models be integrated to form a higher synthesis, as represented in Figure 9. By comparing Figure 7 on page 67 with

Table 7. Wilber's stages of development in relation to Kolb's stages.

Wilber's stages	Wilber's symbolic complexity via comprehension	Kolb's stages	Kolb's symbolic complexity via comprehension
10. Causal	Experience of Emptiness		
9. Subtle	Experience of Archetypes		
8. Vision-logic	Visionary thought	Integration	Attaching concrete meanings to symbol systems and finding and solving meaningful problems
7. Formal - reflexive	Abstract thought	Specialization	Formal hypothetic-deductive reasoning
6. Rule/ role-thinking	Concrete thought	Specialization	Concrete symbolic operations
5. Rep-thinking	Thinking in symbols and concepts	Acquisition	Object constancy; "ikonic" thought
4. Phantasmic	Thinking in simple images	Acquisition	Recognizing enactive thought
3. Emotional -sexual	Life force	Acquisition	Recognizing enactive thought
2. Sensori perceptual	Sensation and perception	Acquisition	Recognizing enactive thought
1. Physical	The physical organism	Acquisition	

Source: Adapted from Visser (2003:123); Kolb (1984:152).

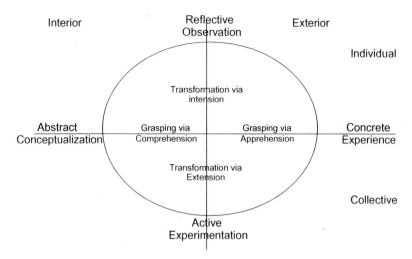

Figure 9. Integrated Experiential Coaching Model.
Source: Adapted from Wilber (1996:71); Kolb (1984:42).

Figure 1 on page 20, it will be clear how Figure 9 superimposes the four forms of Kolb's model on the four quadrants of Wilber's Integral model.

Wilber's (1995) model provides the meta-framework for integrated growth and development; while Kolb's (1984) model provides a practical, experiential way to learn and grow in an integrated way. Figure 9 is an oversimplified presentation of two very complex models, yet it provides a simple framework to explain the synthesis of the two models. An individual will generally experience something concrete in the context of the collective, unless the individual lives in complete isolation. To make sense of that experience the individual needs to make use of the intension dimension, move inwards, and reflect on the experience. Having reflected on it, the individual starts to develop some theory or concept about the experience. Abstract conceptualization, however, is not something that belongs purely to the individual; it is influenced by the culture or system in which the individual finds him or herself. Kolb (1984) conceptualizes experiential learning as a developmental process that is the product of both personal and social knowledge. The individual's state of development flows from the transaction of the individual's personal experience and the particular system of social knowledge with which they interact. Here Kolb (1984) disagrees with Piaget, who sees it purely as an individual issue.

Having developed a theory, the individual then needs to engage the extension dimension and actively experiment within the collective environment. The beauty of Kolb's (1984) model is that it is context- and content-independent. The same methodology can be used to facilitate the learning of meditation, personal fitness training, the design of organizational processes and structures, or learning how to manage people. Done correctly and in a disciplined way, experiential learning will automatically move the individual through all four quadrants, and develop all four learning capabilities that are a prerequisite for human growth and development. And the more developed the person becomes, the more integrative the experiential learning experience becomes (as illustrated in Figure 9), thereby facilitating personal growth, development and the transformation of consciousness.

Thus the Integrated Experiential Coaching Model proposes that coaching is about facilitating integrated experiential learning in individuals in order to enhance personal growth and development. It is integrated in that it caters for Schumacher's four fields of knowledge and Wilber's Integral Model which caters for personal development through various levels of consciousness, especially in the personal and transpersonal levels. It is experiential in that it uses Kolb's Experiential Learning Model as the developmental tool.

Summary

This chapter explored three meta-theories that influenced the development of the Integrated Experiential Coaching Model: the Integral theory of Ken Wilber; the integral theory of A.H. Almaas; and the Experiential Learning Theory of David Kolb. Finally, the chapter showed how these three meta-theories were integrated or synthesized to develop the Integrated Experiential Coaching Model.

CHAPTER THREE

The methodological framework

Introduction

Having a philosophy and theory on coaching is all good and well. A theory without a practical methodology, on the other hand, is of no practical use whatsoever. This chapter deals with the further enhancement of the Integrated Experiential Coaching Model by integrating it with the transcendental phenomenology of Moustakas (1994) and Harri-Augstein and Thomas's (1991) Learning Conversations. The Integrated Experiential Coaching Model proposes that coaching is about facilitating integrated experiential learning in individuals, in order to enhance personal growth and development. It is **integrated** in that it caters for Schumacher's four fields of knowledge, and for Wilber's Integral Model which analyzes personal development through various levels of consciousness, especially in the personal and transpersonal levels. It is **experiential** in that it uses Kolb's Experiential Learning Model as the methodology and Harri-Augstein and Thomas's concept of Learning Conversations as the primary learning tool.

Phenomenology

A further interesting aspect of Kolb's (1984) Experiential Learning Model is how well it integrates with phenomenology. Ernesto Spinelli (1998) points out that Edmund Husserl (1859–1938) is credited with developing an investigative approach known as the phenomenological method. Husserl wanted to develop the science of phenomena, a science that could clarify how objects are experienced and presented to consciousness. The task was to explore the subjective experience of individuals. The aim, as Spinelli (1998:2) points out, was **"to expose how our consciousness imposes itself upon, and obscures, 'pure' reality"**. In so doing, the individual becomes more aware and is able to bracket (or set aside) conscious experience so that a more adequate approximation of reality can arise. Central to phenomenology is the idea of imposing meaning on the world. Phenomenology argues that things exist in the way that they exist because of the meaning that each individual assigns to them:

> Simply stated, this conclusion argues that true reality is, and will forever remain, both unknown and unknowable to us. Instead, that which we term reality, that is, that which is experienced by us as being reality, is inextricably linked to our mental processes in general, and in particular, to our in-built, innate capacity to construct meaning (Spinelli, 1998:2).

Consequently, our reality is a phenomenological reality that is open to a multiplicity of interpretations. What many people take to be objective reality, based on objective laws or truths, actually consists of judgements that are influenced by a consensus viewpoint. This consensus viewpoint is one agreed upon by a whole culture or a group of individuals or professionals; it is an interpretation. It is an interpretation which works and has meaning for the group that has constructed the meaning. Kolb (1984) refers to this consensus viewpoint as the "selectivist paradigm", and it is this higher level of integrated learning which uses the act of purpose (meaning) to integrate the psychological world (feeling, thought, desire) with the physical world (the individual and world as physical/chemical substances). Quoting Von Glasersfeld regarding the selectivist paradigm, Kolb (1984) makes the point that theories and constructs survive for as long as "they serve the purposes to which we put them". The theory, knowledge or construct is viable because it works for us, not because it is any sense a replica or picture of reality. This, however, does not imply that validity is unique, because there could be a host of other constructs as viable as the one constructed. Phenomenology holds that whatever the meaning is, it cannot be concluded to be a true or correct reflection of reality. This is a view that is held by Jaques and Clement (1997) as well.

Subjective versus objective reality

Does this mean that reality is a purely subjective process—nothing more than mere mental constructs? Not at all. Kolb (1984) speaks about the act of purpose integrating both the psychological (subjective) and physical (objective) worlds. The problem, as phenomenologists point out, is that we never only perceive the objective world or mental phenomena; we experience the interaction of the two. All agree that there is a physical reality, which we have labelled objective reality, that remains free of our consciousness. It is our interpretation of that objective reality that can be questioned. Christian de Quincey (2005) states it very simply, that the world consists of things and our experience of things. Where things are made up of energy and consciousness is what feels and knows those things. Consciousness is our concrete experience within that context of things. Moustakas (1994:85) sums up the dilemma as follows:

> The phenomenological Epoche does not eliminate everything, does not deny the reality of everything, does not doubt everything—only the natural attitude, the biases of everyday knowledge, as a basis for truth and reality. What is doubted are the scientific 'facts', the knowing of things in advance, from an external base rather than from internal reflection and meaning.

These interpretations or facts, as mentioned previously, are influenced by a whole culture or a group of individuals or professionals; they constitute a paradigm which has been created and in which we operate. These interpretations and this paradigm are therefore open to change, and from history we know that they do change over time.

Phenomenology's fundamental issues

Spinelli (1998) mentions that Husserl focused on two issues in an attempt to examine how we construct our reality. The first is the notion of intentionality as the basis of mental experiences, and the second is the noematic and noetic foci of intentionality which are the shapers of experience.

Intentionality is the basis of all meaning-based constructs of the world:

> As it is employed by phenomenologists, intentionality is the term used to describe the fundamental action of the mind reaching out to the stimuli which make up the real world in order to translate them into the realm of meaningful experience. In other words, intentionality refers to the first, most basic interpretative mental act—that of 'translating' the unknown raw stimuli of the real world, which our senses have responded to, into an object-based (or 'thing'-based) reality. Franz Brenato first coined the term 'intentionality' in order to clarify his assertion that a real physical world exists outside our consciousness and that, as such, all consciousness is always directed towards the real world in order to interpret it in a meaningful manner (Spinelli, 1998:11).

Human consciousness is therefore always aware of some thing; the mind is directed towards some entity, whether the entity exists or not. The object can be real or imaginary; it can be a tree or I can be worried. In the case of the latter, I am still worried about some entity. According to phenomenologists, it would appear that human beings are programmed to interpret an object-based or thing-based world. Thus Moustakas (1994) asserts that intentionality refers to the internal experience of being conscious of something; the act of consciousness and the object of consciousness are intentionally related. The senses respond to unknown stimuli from the physical world, which undergo a translation or interpretation that leads the individual to respond to the stimuli as if they are objects or things. The meaning that the individual ascribes to the object or thing is, however, determined by various socio-cultural influences that have informed the individual's mental framework.

Hence, the knowledge the individual has of the external world is not as a result of his or her direct access to external reality. That knowledge has undergone a number of complex interpretations that have been influenced by past experience, socio-cultural influences and the level or stage of the individual's development. For this reason it is possible for two individuals to have exactly the same experience, but to experience and interpret it differently. Spinelli (1998) argues that because of the act of intentionality, "ultimate reality" can never be known. As a result, our interpretations of the world and the meaning we ascribe to it are not unique or fixed. Through the act of intentionality we constantly interpret and assign meaning to our world.

In effect, therefore, the phenomenological concept of intentionality is the same or very similar to Kolb's (1984) transformational dimension of experiential learning. Meaning is created through the synergetic role of the dual transformation processes of intension and extension:

> What I propose here is that the transformation processes of intension and extension can be applied to our concrete apprehensions of the world as well as to our symbolic comprehensions. We learn the meaning of our concrete immediate experience by internally reflecting on their presymbolic impact on our feelings, and/or by acting on our apprehended experience and thus extending it … Learning, the creation of knowledge and meaning, occurs through the active extension and grounding of ideas and experiences in the external world and through internal reflection about the attributes of these experiences and ideas (Kolb, 1984:52).

Every act of intentionality does, however, have a noematic and noetic focus which are the shapers of experience. The thing that is being experienced is the noema or noematic correlate, and is the object (the "what") towards which we direct our focus. The mode of the experience is the noesis or noetic correlate; it is the "how" we experience an object. As an example, assume two individuals from two different race groups are listening to a diversity lecture. At the end of the lecture one individual agrees completely with what has been said, while the other is furious. In Kolb's (1984) terms, both have grasped the lecture via direct apprehension; they had the same experience.

The noematic focus is made up of the content of whatever is being focused on or being experienced, in this case the content and arguments presented in the lecture. The noematic focus is the same as Kolb's (1984) concept of grasping via direct apprehension. Yet, although they experienced the same lecture, each individual's experience of the lecture was different. This is due to the noetic focus, which contains the referential elements of the individual and deals with the various cognitive and affective biases that add more elements of meaning to the experience.

The noetic focus corresponds to Kolb's (1984) concept of grasping via comprehension. Kolb (1984) sees this as a secondary and arbitrary way of knowing. Comprehension is the way in which we introduce order into an "unpredictable flow of apprehended sensations". Yet by doing that, as Kolb (1984) points out, we distort and forever change the flow. In theory it would appear that we can distinguish between the noetic and noematic foci; in practice, however, the two are not distinct from each other. When it comes to experience we evoke both foci, the events contained in the experience (noema) and the way we experienced it (noesis). Hence we see that the noema and noesis foci of phenomenology are the same as Kolb's (1984) prehension dimension, while the concept of intentionality is the same as Kolb's (1984) transformation dimension.

The phenomenological method

Spinelli (1998) points out that the concept of intentionality, and its noematic and noetic foci, enabled Husserl to develop the phenomenological methodology to help clarify the interpretational factors contained in each experience. The aim of the phenomenological method is to raise an awareness of how consciousness imposes itself and obscures "pure" reality. It is therefore concerned with wholeness, in that it examines experience from many sides, angles and perspectives until an integrated vision of the essence of the phenomenon is achieved. In this methodology, subject and object are integrated:

> Phenomenology is rooted in questions that give a direction and focus to meaning, and in themes that sustain inquiry, awaken further interest and concern, and account for our

passionate involvement with whatever is being experienced. In a phenomenological investigation the researcher has a personal interest in whatever she or he seeks to know; the researcher is intimately connected with the phenomenon. The puzzlement is autographical, making memory and history essential dimensions of discovery, in the present and extensions into the future (Moustakas, 1994:59).

In Wilber's (1995) terms, the methodology deals with the inner (noesis) and external (noema) quadrants, as well as dealing with the individual within the context of the communal, covering both the inner and outer quadrants.

In this methodology, as Moustakas (1994) points out, phenomenology tries to seek meaning and the essence of an experience by reflecting on it. This in turn leads to ideas, concepts, understanding and judgements. This methodology therefore uses personal experience, subjective thinking, intuition, reflection and judgement as primary evidence for scientific investigation. The phenomenological methodology therefore contains all the elements of the experiential learning processes: concrete experience, reflective observation, abstract conceptualization, and active experimentation. In addition to facilitating learning and growth, experiential learning at a more mature level turns out to be a powerful methodology for scientific investigation as well.

The important thing to remember, however, is that it is always individual experiential learning within a communal or collective context. It is an intersubjective experience, since the world is a community of persons. Moustakas (1994) points out that it is through conversations and dialogues with other people that the individual continuously corrects their interpretation of reality. Other people help us to validate our experiences through the interchange of perceptions, judgements, feelings and ideas. Schumacher (1978) emphasizes the same point when he refers to the four fields of knowledge: I-inner, the world (you)-inner, I-outer, and the world (you)-outer. He suggests that any individual has direct access only to the I-inner and the world (you)-outer fields of knowledge. An individual can feel what he or she is feeling, and can directly see what the other looks like. But what it feels like to be the other, and what the individual looks like in the eyes of the other, cannot be known directly. To gain access to those fields of knowledge, the individual needs intersubjective dialogue and conversations to help validate their reality.

Moustakas's (1994) phenomenological research method is known as transcendental phenomenology; it is called

> ... 'phenomenology' because it utilizes only the data that is available for consciousness—the appearance of objects. It is considered 'transcendental' because it adheres to what can be discovered through reflection on subjective acts and their objective correlates (Moustakas, 1994:45).

It is transcendental because it helps to uncover the ego for which everything has meaning. It is phenomenological because it transforms the world into mere phenomena. The methodology process consists of four steps: Epoche, phenomenological reduction, imaginative variation, and synthesis (Moustakas, 1994:84–101).

The Epoche process

Epoche is a Greek word which means to abstain, stay away from or to refrain from judgement. In our day-to-day lives we tend to hold knowledge judgementally, that is we are biased due to our expectations and assumptions. The Epoche requires that we bracket as far as possible our biases, understandings, knowing and assumptions, and look at things in a new and fresh way. As Moustakas (1994:33) says, we need to revisit our experiences "... from the vantage point of a pure or transcendental ego". This does, of course, assume that the individual has developed a healthy and mature ego that can be transcended. An underdeveloped ego will not be able to do this. The Epoche does, therefore, assume and call for a certain level of ego maturity. In so doing, the individual is able to bracket their ordinary thought processes and look at experience from a fresh perspective.

The Epoche urges the individual to impose an openness on to their immediate experience. In so doing, subsequent conclusions drawn about the experience (whatever it may be) would be based more on the immediate experience than upon prior expectations and assumptions. The aim is to see and experience the "experience" in a completely open manner. It is a way of seeing and experiencing before any form of reflection, judgements or reaching conclusions happens. Of critical importance is that in the Epoche no position is taken; everything is of equal value. Nothing is determined in advance. Everything is experienced and valued for what it is; it is a fresh way of perceiving and experiencing. This is not an easy state to achieve, and as was mentioned previously it assumes and calls for a certain level of ego maturity. As Moustakas (1994:88) points out:

> The challenge is to silence the directing voices and sounds, internally and externally, to remove from myself the manipulating or predisposing influences and to become completely and solely attuned to just what appears, to encounter the phenomena, as such, with a pure state of mind.

The Epoche process therefore requires sustained attention, presence, discipline and concentration. Moustakas (1994) refers to the process as a form of reflective-meditation. In this process the individual allows prejudices, preconceptions and prejudgements to arise in consciousness and leave freely. The aim is to be as receptive to these phenomena as to the unbiased actions of looking and seeing. Those familiar with the work of De Mello (1990) will immediately recognize that it is all about "awareness", i.e., just learning to be aware of the phenomena and then to let them go. Eventually the essence of the experience is seen for what it is. It is impossible to completely bracket everything, but the aim is to become more aware and disciplined in the process in order to experience life and phenomena in a less biased way. With practice the individual will learn to become more open to their own experience, and be more aware of how their biases predetermine and influence their reality.

The Epoche process corresponds very well with Kolb's (1984) concept of concrete experience. For a person to learn from concrete experience they must be able to involve themselves fully, openly, and without bias in new experiences. The aim, like the Epoche process, is to be open to experience and to move beyond or to transcend personal and social biases. The way of experiencing via the Epoche process is the same as Kolb's (1984) grasping via apprehension. Like the phenomenologists, Kolb (1984) is very aware of how using words to put the experience into a concept can take something away from the direct experience:

> What you see, hear, and feel around you are those sensations, colours, textures, and sounds, that are so basic and reliable that we call them reality. The continuous feel of your chair as it firmly supports your body, the smooth texture of the book and its pages, the muted mixture of sounds surrounding you—all these things and many others you know instantaneously without need for rational inquiry or analytical confirmation. They are simply there, grasped through a mode of knowing called apprehension. Yet to describe these perceptions faithfully in words, as I have attempted here, is somewhat difficult. It is almost as though the words are vessels dipped in the sea of sensations we experience as reality, vessels that hold and give form to those sensations contained, while sensations left behind fade from awareness. The concept 'chair', for example, probably describes where you are sitting ... It is a convenient way to summarize a whole series of sensations you are having right now, although it tends to actively discourage attention to parts of that experience other than those associated with 'chairness' (Kolb, 1984:43).

Both concrete experience and the Epoche process therefore encourage the individual to continuously open themselves in a fresh, non-biased way to their own experience, free of preconceptions and prejudgements.

Phenomenological reduction

Phenomenological reduction is a process of prereflection, reflection and reduction with the aim of explicating the phenomenon's essential nature. The task is to derive a textural description of what the individual experiences in terms of the external object and the internal act of consciousness, describing the relationship between the phenomenon and the self. The rule is to describe and not to explain. The problem with explaining is that it tries to make sense of the experience in terms of a hypothesis or theory. Spinelli (1998) gives the example of a hypochondriac who has failed to apply the rule of description. Instead of describing the somatic experience in concrete terms, the individual jumps to abstract, disease-model explanations. In so doing the individual provokes levels of anxiety that reinforce the debilitating situation. Descriptions are derived from the immediate sensory-based experience. Explanations try to make sense of experience within the boundaries of a hypothesis or theory. The aim is to reflect, reflect again, and then to describe the experience in terms of textural qualities, varying intensities, special qualities and time references. The experiencing person therefore turns inward in reflection and describes whatever shines forth in consciousness. Whatever stands out and is meaningful for the individual is explored and reflected on. Individual memories, judgements, perceptions and reflections are reflected on and described, as they are integral to the process. The process allows the individual to return to the self, in that the world is experienced from the vantage point of self-reflection, self-awareness and self-knowledge. The more the individual reflects, the more exact the phenomenon becomes.

Phenomenological reduction is about observing and describing. In this regard we can see that phenomenological reduction is the same as Kolb's (1984) reflective observation:

> An orientation towards reflective observation focuses on understanding the meaning of ideas and situations by carefully observing and impartially describing them. It emphasizes understanding as opposed to practical application; a concern with what is true or how things happen as opposed to what will work; an emphasis on reflection as opposed to action ... They are good at looking at things from different perspectives and appreciating different points of view. They like to rely on their own thoughts and feelings to form opinions (Kolb, 1984:68).

He goes on to discuss how we learn the meaning of immediate concrete experience by reflecting on their "presymbolic impact" on feelings. The issue is that both methodologies call for inner reflection that tries to describe the experience rather than explaining it.

More importantly, reflection is never-ending. Although the individual might reach a point where they consciously stop the reflective process, the possibility for reflection and discovery is unlimited. In phenomenological reduction this is known as horizontalization.

No matter how many times the individual reconsiders or reflects on the experience, the experience can never be exhausted because horizons are unlimited. Even the final textural description, although completed in a point of time, remains open to further reflection. Another requirement of horizontalization is that all statements are treated as equal, and that the applying of hierarchies of significance should be avoided. By avoiding hierarchical assumptions, the individual is in a better position to examine the experience with less prejudice.

Imaginative variation

Through the utilization of imagination, varying the frames of reference, different perspectives and points of views, the individual tries to derive a structural description of the experience and the underlying factors that account for what is being experienced. The aim is to understand the "how" that brought about the "what" of the experience. The question that needs to be explored is how did the experience come to be what it is? By using the textural descriptions, the aim is to derive structural essences of the experience and how it came about. It creates a picture of the conditions that give rise to the experience and connect with it. According to Moustakas (1994:99), imaginative variation consists of the following four steps:

- continuously looking for varying and different structural meanings that underlie the textural meanings;
- becoming aware of and recognizing the underlying themes that have brought about the phenomena;
- becoming aware of the universal structures that give impetus to the thoughts and feelings with reference to the phenomena. Considering things like time, space, causality, relation to self and others and bodily concerns;
- "searching for exemplifications that vividly illustrate the invariant structural themes that facilitate the development of a structural description of the phenomenon".

In essence, it can be said that imaginative variation is an attempt to develop an understanding or "theory" about how the experience came about. Thus it is very similar to, if not the same as,

Kolb's (1984) abstract conceptualization, where the individual is able to create concepts that integrate their observations into logically sound theories.

Synthesis of meaning and essences

The final step in the methodology is the integration and synthesis of the textural and structural descriptions into a unified statement of the experience as a whole. The important thing to remember is that the textural-structural synthesis represents the essence of the experience from the point of view of an individual researcher at a definite point in time and place, and as such it is open to further exploration. The essence of any experience is never totally exhausted. Hence this research methodology is often used for hypothesis-generating research as opposed to hypothesis-testing research. For this reason it can be seen as a form of active experimentation. The findings have to be taken further and researched further. It generates a hypothesis that needs to be researched and tested empirically. The hypothesis has to be applied and tested; it is an ongoing experiment.

Integrating transcendental phenomenology with the Integrated Experiential Coaching Model

Based on the above logic it can be argued that Kolb's (1984) Experiential Learning Model integrates very well with Moustakas's (1994) transcendental phenomenological research methodology. It can be argued further that the latter is just a higher or more mature form of learning than the former. In other words, experiential learning matures into transcendental phenomenology. Both can therefore be used as integral developmental methodologies. Transcendental phenomenology is therefore easily integrated with the Integrated Experiential Coaching Model, as represented in Figure 10.

In the Integrated Experiential Coaching Model it is suggested that Kolb's (1984) Experiential Learning Model initially be used as an integrative developmental methodology for coaching and learning. As the individual becomes more skilled in using the experiential learning process, they will eventually mature and develop into using transcendental phenomenology for their own personal growth and development. Done in a disciplined way, these methodologies

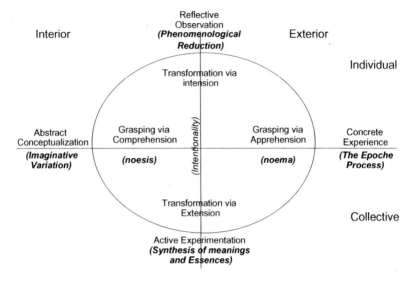

Figure 10. Integrated Experiential Coaching Model expanded.
Source: Adapted from Wilber (1996:71); Kolb (1984:42).

could facilitate growth and development right up to the highest
rational level, which is Wilber's (1994) Vision-logic stage and Kolb's
(1984) Integration stage. Eventually, if this development continues,
transcendental phenomenology will mature into Almaas's (2002)
Inquiry method. It is Almaas's (2002) Inquiry method that will facilitate growth into and in the transpersonal bands of development.
The method requires that the individual continuously inquires into
their own direct experience. The need to inquire into personal experience is defined as follows by Almaas (2002:5):

> To experience the richness of our Being, the potential of our
> soul, we must allow our experience to become more and more
> open, and increasingly question who we assume we are. Usu-
> ally we identify with a very limited part of our potential, what
> we call the ego or personality. Some call it the small self. But the
> identity is actually a distortion of what we really are, which is a
> completely open flow of the mystery of Being. A human being
> is a universe of experience, multifaceted and multidimensional.
> Each of us is a soul, a dynamic consciousness, a magical organ

of experience in action. And each of us is in a constant state of transformation—of one experience opening to another, one action leading to another, one perception multiplying into many others; of perception growing into knowledge, knowledge leading to action, and action creating more experience. This unfolding is constant, dynamic, and full of energy. This is the nature of what we call life.

It is through constantly inquiring into these dynamic experiences that we arrive at our true Essence. It is therefore argued in the Integrated Experiential Coaching Model that experiential learning matures and develops with the individual from experiential learning to transcendental phenomenology to Almaas's inquiry method. This process is represented in Figure 11.

The strength of the Integrated Experiential Coaching Model is that it allows for continuous growth and development in the personal and transpersonal levels, and it provides a practical methodology to facilitate this continuous growth and development.

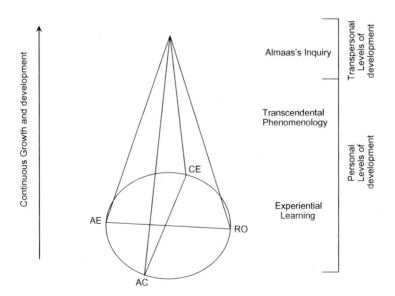

Figure 11. The maturity phases of the Integrated Experiential Coaching Model.
Source: Adapted from Kolb (1984:141).

Most Western methodologies tend to stop at the upper levels of rational development; some of them do not recognize the transpersonal levels. The Integrated Experiential Coaching model honours body, mind, soul and Spirit, and provides a practical methodology to help facilitate their integration.

Mastery

In one sense the Integrated Experiential Coaching Model is quite simple. All that it requires is for the individual to continuously go through the experiential learning process. There is nothing new about that. So the question to be asked is why have we not seen more people applying the methodology to their own lives in order to facilitate growth and development? There could be two possible answers. One reason could be that not many individuals actually understand the power of experiential learning. As a result, due to ignorance, it is not being used as powerfully as it could be. A more likely reason could be what Leonard (1992) calls a lack of mastery. Leonard (1992) has dedicated his life to learning, education and the study of human potential. The question that continuously fascinated him was why some people master something while others do not. He soon realized that everything in life starts and ends with the individual's ability to learn, what they learn, and how they learn. For Leonard (1992) the road to mastery is through learning certain skills, whatever those skills might be. The important thing to remember, however, is that all significant learning happens not in a straight line, but rather in stages. There are brief spurts of progress separated by periods when nothing seems to be happening. Yet it is in these times that we can learn another important skill—how to learn. In Leonard's understanding, mastery is not reserved for the super-talented or those born with exceptional talents. The journey of mastery starts when any individual decides to learn a new skill. In the Integrated Experiential Coaching Model, the individual is challenged to learn the skill of experiential learning: learning how to learn, and to practice the skill of lifelong learning.

According to Leonard (1992), learning any new skill involves relatively briefs spurts of growth followed by a slight decline and a plateau which is somewhat higher than that which preceded it.

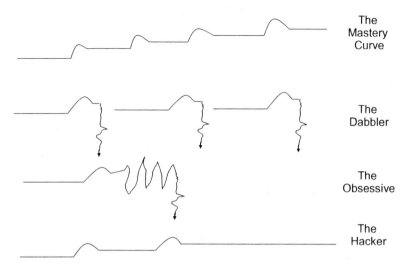

Figure 12. The Mastery Curve and its enemies.
Source: Adapted from Leonard (1992:15–23).

This is referred to as the Mastery Curve as represented by the top curve in Figure 12.

To take the master's journey the individual has to practice diligently, striving at all times to hone the new skill and to try and attain new levels of competence. The individual has to be willing to spend most of their time on the plateau, to keep on practising the skill even when they do not seem to be getting anywhere. The reason being that as soon as the individual learns a new skill they have to think about it and actively try to replace old patterns of thinking, sensing and moving with new ones. People who have mastered a skill have learnt to love the plateaus, and they practise their skill primarily for the sake of the practice itself. Masters have learnt that learning is ongoing, and is not limited to the brief spurts of noticeable progress.

The Dabbler, Obsessive and Hacker

Sadly, as Leonard (1992) points out, most people go through life choosing not to take the master's journey. Instead they opt to go through life as Dabblers, Obsessives or Hackers. Dabblers love the rituals involved in getting started. They love everything that is new. These individuals love all the latest management fads. When a new fad comes along they embrace it wholeheartedly, but when the plateau strikes, as it always does, they find it unacceptable if not incomprehensible. As a result they give up and look for the next fad.

Obsessives are bottom-line people; they do not believe in settling for second best. In their lives it is results that count, no matter how they get them. Somehow the business world has excelled at breeding these kinds of people, or conversely these kinds of individuals are drawn to the business world where this kind of mentality is highly prized and rewarded. When these individuals hit the plateaus they cannot accept it, and try harder and do more of the same. The end result of this kind of behaviour is what Senge *et al.* (1994) call the "fixes that backfire" archetype in systems thinking. The thinking and behaviour that underlies this archetype is the belief that one needs to try the same solution just a little more, and then just a little more. Eventually the individuals concerned resist the idea of trying anything else:

> The central theme of this archetype is that almost any decision carries long-term and short-term consequences, and the two are often diametrically opposed ... A solution is quickly implemented (the fix) which alleviates the symptom (the balancing loop). But the unintended consequences of the fix (the vicious cycle of the reinforcing loop) actually worsen the performance of the condition which we attempt to correct (Senge *et al.*, 1994:126).

Companies face this problem all the time. The Obsessive individual does not understand the necessity for periods of development on the plateau. They are too impatient to see results, and as a result they create deep systemic problems through their behaviour and actions of doing more of the same or just trying harder. They eventually burn out.

The Hacker, on the other hand, is prepared to stay on the plateau indefinitely. They do not mind skipping stages essential to the development of mastery and themselves. They do just enough to get by. These are the qualified professionals who do not invest in continuous learning and professional development.

Organizations are filled with these people who believe that they have arrived due to the fact that they have degrees and professional qualifications.

In reality, most individuals probably have some of the Dabbler, Obsessive and Hacker within them, and these characteristics prevent them from getting on the path to mastery and lifelong learning. What is required for the individual to start on the path of mastery is a willingness to want to learn, the discipline to keep on practising, an openness to their own experience, and an emptiness that allows new things to come into being. The latter is an emptiness that makes them humble enough to realize that they do not know everything, and that there is always something to learn. It is the kind of emptiness, according to Leonard (1992), that Jigro Kano, the founder of Judo, showed when he was lying on his death bed. He called his students together and requested that they bury him in his white belt. The highest-ranking judoist in the world was humble enough to realize that he was actually just a beginner. Leonard's (1992) plea is therefore that individuals start the journey of mastery by committing themselves to the discipline of lifelong learning. It is only through disciplined long-term practice that change and development come about. After a lifetime of studying and exploring human potential and learning, Leonard and Murphy (1995:8) have the following to say:

> In a culture intoxicated with promises of the quick fix, instant enlightenment, and easy learning, it was hard to accept one of the most important lessons … Any significant long-term change requires long-term practice, whether that change has to do with learning to play the violin or learning to be a more open, loving person. We all know people who say they have been changed by experiences of a moment or a day or a weekend. But when you check it out you'll generally discover that those who ended up permanently changed had spent considerable time preparing for their life-changing experience or had continued diligently practising the new behaviour afterward.

Similarly the Integrated Experiential Coaching Model calls for disciplined long-term practice and application. It is not enough to know the theory of experiential learning for growth and development to take place; the individual needs to practice the skill of experiential learning over a lifetime. It is a never-ending discipline and journey.

Valid knowledge

Long-term practice and discipline of the Integrated Experiential Coaching methodology is what moves the individual onto the road to mastery. If the Integrated Experiential Coaching Methodology is to become a valid form of empirical and phenomenological research it will, however, have to meet what Wilber (1998) calls the "three aspects of scientific inquiry" or the "three strands of all valid knowing". Long-term practice is not enough. The methodology has to be validated empirically and phenomenologically. The three aspects of scientific inquiry, according to Wilber (1998b:155–160) are:

- **Instrumental injunction.** This is the actual practice of doing the methodology or inquiry. De Quincey (2005) refers to this as the Procedure. It is an injunction, an experiment, a paradigm, an agreed-upon set of protocols to conduct the inquiry. According to Wilber (1998b) it always takes the form "If you want to know, do this". Here Wilber (1998b) draws on the work of Thomas Kuhn who showed that science advances by means of a paradigm or exemplars. Unfortunately the New Age movement and theorists have tended to misuse the word paradigm, and in their teaching they only emphasize part of what Kuhn meant by paradigm. The New Age view of paradigm has come to mean that if you want to change something, all that is needed is to change the way you think (change your paradigm). By paradigm, Kuhn meant a concept and a way of doing within that concept:

  > A paradigm is not merely a concept, it is an actual practice, an injunction, a technique taken as an exemplar for generating data. And Kuhn's point is that genuine scientific knowledge is grounded in paradigms, exemplars, or injunctions. New injunctions disclose new data (new experiences), and this is why Kuhn maintained both that science is progressive and cumulative, and that it shows certain breaks or discontinuities (new injunctions bring forth new data) (Wilber, 1998b:159).

Kuhn, therefore, emphasizes the injunctive strand of valid knowledge. Thinking differently is not enough, you have to practice the injunction or the methodology. In the Integrated Experiential Coaching methodology the injunction is experiential learning. You need to know the theory and you need to practise the methodology; the one without the other is useless. So on one level, Kolb's (1984) Experiential Learning Model is the injunction, but on another level it is the active experimentation aspect of the Experiential Learning Model.

- **Direct apprehension**. This is the direct experience or the apprehension of data that is brought about by the injunction. In Kolb's (1984) language, this is grasping the data via direct apprehension as a result of active experimentation. Hence de Quincey (2005) names it the Observation phase, in that the investigator observes and records the data of experience. This is the data of direct and immediate experience. It is what Almaas (2002:78) refers to as basic knowledge:

> So our experience is not knowledge in the usual sense of knowledge. It is not what we call ordinary knowledge—the information we have in our minds that we remember about things in the past. It is knowledge now. Basic knowledge is always direct knowledge in the moment—the stuff of our immediate experience. We usually don't call it knowledge; we call it experience, and if we are a little more sophisticated we call it perception. Perception carries more of the sense of being aware of our immediate experience, which is a palpable sense of knowingness that is basic knowledge.

As Wilber (1998b) points out, it is this data on which science anchors all its concrete assertions. Hence Wilber is in total agreement with empiricism, which demands that all knowledge be grounded in experiential evidence. The only difference is that he recognizes sensory, mental and spiritual experience. That is why Wilber argues that scientific inquiry can be applied to empirical, phenomenological and spiritual research. All are valid fields of scientific inquiry. Experiential learning can be used for empirical learning, such as how to improve business processes or to explore a spiritual practice like meditation. Both levels will generate experiential data via direct apprehension that can be validated or invalidated. Wilber (1998b) goes on to argue that knowledge that is brought forth by valid injunctions is genuine knowledge due to the fact that bad data can be rejected. His argument is that paradigms disclose data, they do not invent them.

• **Communal confirmation (or rejection)**. De Quincey (2005) simply refers to it as Reporting. This is where the data or experiences are checked by a community of people who have completed the injunction and the apprehensive strands. In a sense this is a combination of reflective observation and abstract conceptualization. Having had the experience and collected the data, an individual will reflect on it, and via comprehension share it with a community who will either validate or invalidate the data. Here Wilber (1998b:159) draws on the work of Sir Karl Popper:

> Sir Karl Popper's approach emphasizes the importance of falsifiability: genuine knowledge must be open to disproof, or else it is simply dogma in disguise. Popper, in other words, is highlighting the importance of the confirmation/rejection strand in all valid knowledge; and, as we will see, this falsifiability principle is operative in every domain, sensory to mental to spiritual.

Hence it is important that the Integrated Experiential Coaching methodology must take place within the context of a community who can validate or invalidate the data. So for example, if the Integrated Experiential Coaching methodology is used to coach business executives, then there must be a community of executives or managers who can validate or invalidate the data. Likewise, if the methodology is used to teach meditation, there must be a community of meditators who can validate or invalidate the data.

In summary, it is argued that experiential learning be used as the injunction in the Integrated Experiential Coaching methodology in order to facilitate growth and development. The data will then be collected via direct apprehension, and validated in the context of a community that has adequately completed the injunction and the apprehension strands.

Learning conversations

Integrated Experiential Coaching is facilitated via a Learning Conversation. According to Harri-Augstein and Thomas (1991), a Learning Conversation includes three different levels of conversation over time, as represented in Figure 13.

Every Learning Conversation, whether it be level one or level three, will always take place within the context of a bigger life relevance situation (level two conversation). So it is not uncommon for the conversation to move between levels one, two and three. It might start at level one (task-focused), but the individual might start questioning his or her bigger life purpose or the value of doing the particular work that they are doing. In so doing they move the conversation into a level two Learning Conversation. Once that has been dealt with, the conversation might move back to level one. Learning Conversations are therefore very dynamic.

Level one is a task-focused Learning Conversation. For example, a coach is requested to help an individual improve his or her performance or to learn certain managerial leadership skills. Task-focused Learning Conversations are intermittent and they can extend over many cycles of task or topic activity. Experiential learning is the basis of these conversations, and can be implemented by means of an adapted version of Harri-Augstein and Thomas's (1991) Personal Learning Contract (PLC) as represented in Figure 14.

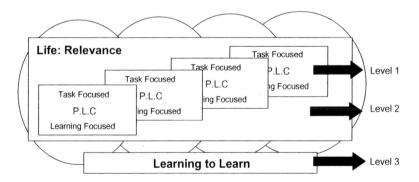

Figure 13. Learning conversations.
Source: Adapted from Harri-Augstein and Thomas (1991:151).

Personal Learning Contract

Name:...

Date:...............................

Purpose	What is my Purpose?		What actually was my purpose?	Describe the essential differences?
Outcome	How shall I judge and measure my success?	Action (go and do)	How well did I do?	Describe the essential differences?
Strategy	What actions shall I take?		What did I actually do?	Describe the essential differences?
What have I learnt from this exercise?				

Figure 14. Personal Learning Contract (PLC).
Source: Adapted from Harri-Augstein and Thomas (1991:151).

The client will usually come into the coaching session with a real problem or difficulty that he or she is facing (their concrete experience). In the Integrated Experiential Coaching Model it is very important that the client always sets the agenda. The coach and client will then reflect on the experience (reflection-on-action) together. The client will be encouraged to make sense of what is going on by developing their own understanding or theory as to what is happening or going on (abstract conceptualization). If needs be, the coach can give some experiential or theoretical input into the conversation. The client will then decide on some course of action that they will experiment with to address the issue (active experimentation).

For learning to happen, it is very important that everything is made very explicit, and this is where the Personal Learning Contract is such a powerful tool. It makes the learning experience very explicit. Once the client has decided what they want to do (active experimentation), they fill in the first column of the contract, i.e., what is my purpose, what is it that I want to achieve? They also specify how they are going to measure themselves to determine whether they have been successful or not. Furthermore, the strategy and the action steps that they will follow are made explicit and writ-ten down. The client then goes away in between coaching sessions and actions what they said they were going to do. This takes care of the active experimentation part of the learning process. Prior to the next coaching session, the client will document what their actual purpose was, how well they actually did and what action they actu-ally took. This teaches them to reflect on their actual concrete expe-rience. They are also required to describe the essential differences between what they said they were going to do and what they actu-ally did, both positive and negative, and explain why those differ-ences exist. In so doing they raise their own levels of awareness and they start to develop their own theories about why the differences exist. This helps to improve their abstract conceptual abilities. The coaching session combined with the Personal Learning Contract ensures that the client goes through the entire experiential learning processes in a structured way. It is an iterative process where the one contract can build on the other.

The main advantage of the Personal Learning Contract is that it makes the learning experience explicit. It thereby facilitates the abil-ity of the client to learn how they learn, which is a level three Learn-ing Conversation. In the long term, learning how to learn is the most important learning that can happen. The more individuals can learn about how they learn, the more independent and autonomous they can become as human beings. The ultimate aim of the Integrated Experiential Coaching Model is to help the client become what Harri-Augstein and Thomas (1991) term a Self-Organized Learner (S-O-L). The essential characteristics of a Self-Organized Learner are (Harri-Augstein and Thomas, 1991:89–90):

- When individuals accept responsibility for managing their own learning, and are no longer dependent on other people's directives and initiatives. The individual gives personal meaning to the events.

- Individuals become aware of how they learn; in other words, they start to reflect on the functional components of the learning processes. They can recognize their need and translate it into a clearly defined purpose. They develop their own strategies to achieve the purpose, and are able to recognize the quality of the outcome they have achieved. More importantly, they can critically review the cycle and implement more effective learning cycles.
- Individuals learn to appreciate the dynamic nature of the personal learning process, while at the same time striving for more self-organized learning.
- To learn how to learn by continually challenging their existing partially-developed skills. The aim being to transform these skills in order to achieve higher standards of personal competence.
- For individuals to recognize the value of S-O-L and to practise it as a way of life regardless of the social context.
- Individuals redefine S-O-L in their own terms in such a way that the S-O-L expertise generates new dimensions of personal innovation and experimentation.
- Individuals constantly strive for quantum improvements in their own ability to learn. The person becomes better at learning on the job, from training courses, from experienced colleagues and from their own and other people's mistakes.

Harri-Augstein and Thomas (1991) point out that self-organized learning cannot be achieved through direct instruction (provider-centred), as this often leads to complete dependency, alienation and negatively-valued learning. On the other hand, to leave the individual to discover how to become a self-organized learner can take too long, hence the need for Learning Conversations and learner-centred learning. People need support and coaching to learn what Beard and Wilson (2002) call "reflect-on-action" so that they eventually develop the independent ability to "reflect-in-action". The important thing about the conversation is that it starts with where the individual is (i.e., the individual's experience and preferred learning style), and allows as much freedom to learn as the individual can cope with. The client sets the agenda, not the coach. It is a gradual process of expanding the quality and scope of the individual's learning capability. Hence, in the Integrated Experiential Coaching Model the coach starts working with and honouring the preferred learning style of the individual and gradually enhancing the individual's ability to move through the complete experiential learning cycle. This means that the coach must make use of appropriate coaching skills, depending on where the client is at that point in time in order to facilitate the experiential learning process more effectively. A schematic presentation of the process is found in Figure 15.

Brooks-Harris and Stock-Ward (1999) came up with the idea of organizing facilitation skills into four quadrants that correspond to the four learning styles. They referred to these facilitation skills as engaging, informing, involving and applying skills. These four skills apply as easily to coaching individuals as they do to facilitating groups:

- **Engaging coaching skills**: These skills are used to fully involve the client in the Learning Conversation. Engaging skills are used to activate the knowledge that the client already has, and it builds bridges between their past experience and the current learning experience. Due to the reflective nature of engaging skills, individuals with Divergent Learning Styles respond well to engaging exercises. Engaging skills include: getting clients to tell their story (narrative); reflecting; paraphrasing; asking for more information clarifying issues; probing; challenging assumptions; brainstorming with the client; and self-disclosure by the coach as and when it is relevant.
- **Informing coaching skills**: Informing involves teaching factual information and allowing the clients to gain new knowledge. Here there can be an element of provider-centred learning, in that the coach brings experience and theoretical knowledge to the table. Clients learn new information and are encouraged to use the concepts to understand their own experience. What is important to remember is that there is an element of provider-centred learning, but it is within the bigger context of learner-centred learning, which is the primary mode of learning. People with a preferred Assimilation Learning Style react well to informing. Informing skills include: clarifying assumptions; giving factual or theoretical information; answering questions; pointing out what was not mentioned and what was inconsistent; identifying

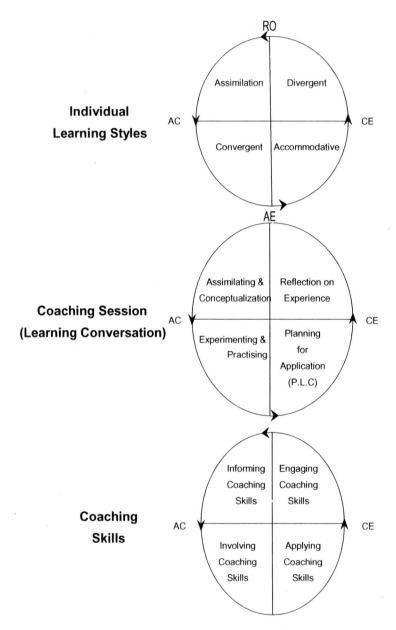

Figure 15. Integrated Experiential Coaching Model skills.
Source: Adapted from Brooks-Harris and Stock-Ward (1999:16).

themes; modelling new behaviour; summarizing; explaining; and self-disclosure by the coach as and when it is relevant to provide information.

- **Involving coaching skills**: This involves active experimentation, in that it allows the client to play with new knowledge and skills. Learning is encouraged through practising with the new knowledge they have gained. This is hands-on experience, where the client experiments with what works for them. Involving activities and skills work well for people with a preferred Convergence Learning Style. Involving skills include: playing with new behaviour in the coaching session; playing with repertory grids; playing with Personal Learning Contracts; connecting various ideas; interpreting and offering ideas about possible explanations for why the individual is feeling, acting, or behaving in a certain way; challenging the client to see and do things differently; helping to make the client's way of learning explicit; concentrating the discussion on the here and now; asking the client what they are feeling to get them in touch with their feelings; and asking for feedback, focusing and getting the conversation back on track.

- **Applying coaching skills**: Here the clients personalize what they have learnt by drawing up an action strategy by means of a Personal Learning Contract, the aim being to apply what they have learnt. Because people with a preferred Accommodative Learning Style are highly action-oriented, they respond well to application activities. Applying skills involve: scenario planning; exploring the future; encouraging new behaviour outside the coaching session; pointing out opportunities for application; encouraging action and goal-setting; developing Personal Learning Contracts; and self-disclosure that helps and encourages application.

The advantage of this approach is that it caters for clients' preferred Learning Styles and then aims to help them move through the complete experiential learning process to help them become Self-Organized Learners. This model encourages the coach to use different coaching skills for different clients and different situations. At times it might be very valuable to use engaging skills, but in a different situation informing skills might be more appropriate. Yes, the client will eventually get there if you keep asking questions, but sometimes the coach and client can be up against time constraints. On the other hand, engaging skills could fail with a very strong Accommodator. The person could see the coach as being too fuzzy. Hence there is a danger that some coaching models opt for "a coaching style" and ignore or deny the value of other styles. The Co-Active Coaching Model of Whitworth, Kimsey-House and Sandal (1998:4), for example, has as one of its four cornerstones an Engaging Style:

> The coach does not have the answers; the coach has questions
> ... This is why we say that the coach's job is to ask questions, not
> to give answers. We have found that clients are more resource-
> ful, more effective, and generally more satisfied when they find
> their own answers. And because they found the answers them-
> selves, they are more likely to follow through with action.

Yet at the same time Whitworth, Kimsey-House and Sandal (1998) believe that coaching is a Learning Conversation, because it is a conversation that wants to deepen learning which in turn leads to action. However, it is not a conversation that informs, explains or rectifies. The objective is action and learning, not specific results. What is very clear is that their coaching model is not an experiential learning conversation. They have limited their coaching model to be an engaging learning conversation, and decided to ignore the other three aspects of experiential learning. Sadly, even coaches who claim to use experiential learning as the basis of their coaching often tend to limit themselves to an Engaging Style.

Harri-Augstein and Thomas (1991) suggest that the coach helps the client to externalize the Learning Conversation (reflection-on-action) in order to improve its quality and to make the conversation as explicit to the client as they learn. As the client's awareness and skill develops, the coach gradually passes control of the Learning Conversation over to the client. If the Learning Conversation has been successful, over time there should be evidence of the client moving from dependence on the coach to more self-autonomy. The individual starts to take responsibility and control of their own learning. Not only do they move beyond their own preferred Learning Style to using the complete experiential learning cycle, they even start to identify and challenge their own learning myths. Based on the cumulative impact of past history, every individual brings certain attitudes and assumptions about learning into the learning situation. These attitudes, assumptions and beliefs are personal constructs or myths that the individual holds in regard to themselves, in terms of their ability to learn and how they learn. As a result of 20 years of action research, Harri-Augstein and Webb (1995) have identified a category system of personal myths about learning that are represented in Table 8.

Table 8. A simple category system of personal learning myths.

A. Myths about "conditions" of learning

Physical

Time of day: Just after sunrise; just after midnight. Place: Small and intimate; airy and well-lit. Span of time: Short; long. Body position: Sitting still; walking; lotus position. Noise levels: Peace and quiet; radio as background.

Social

Solitude: Alone; with others; in a team; in a family setting; with a chosen friend; in a unisex context.

B. Myths about opportunities for learning

Situation

Within a problem-solving environment. In a crisis. When everything is running smoothly. In a lecture. Using a business game. In a laboratory doing project work. In an intensive experiential workshop. With a simulator that logs my action for replay. In a discussion with a consultant/advisor. Quality circles. Using computers. Using videos/books. On the job.

Type of event

A week's intensive course. An outdoor leadership course. A competitive event. A final-year project. Preparing for an exam. Attending a relate session. A well-structured lecture.

Nature of resources

Spreadsheet. A counsellor. Observing an experienced worker. Videos with rich examples. Research journals and specialist books. Work placement. Feasibility exercises.

(Continued)

Table 8. (*Continued*)

C. Myths about processes of learning

Learning by: Doing. Listening. Questioning. Feeling. Making patterns. Repetition and drill. Selecting principles. Making a mental map. Visualizing. Affirmation.

D. Myths about capacities for learning

A memorizing capacity. A mind for figures and relations. Linguistic skills. Brainstorming abilities. A colour sense. A spatial awareness. Manipulative skills. Risk-taking. Long concentration. Sustained commitment.

E. Attitudinal myths: personal characteristics, traits and talents

Practical bent. Sharp eye. Feminine touch. Musical ability. Persistence and doggedness. Mathematical talent. Macho nature.

Source: Harri-Augstein and Webb (1995:20).

Obviously every one of these myths has some truth and relevance about them, that is to say that they might have a physiological base; they do not just exist in the mind as a "myth". Levine (2002) has identified the following eight neurodevelopmental categories or systems involved in learning processes: the attention control system, memory system, languages system, spatial ordering system, sequential ordering system, motor system, higher thinking system, and social thinking system. These systems do not perform as soloists, they all interact to aid the learning process and to form an individual's unique mind profile. Some children, and even adults, have deficiencies in one or more of these systems, which leads to them having some kind of learning problem, or a profile that does not operate optimally within a given context.

The point, however, is that personal learning profiles are a partial truth and not "the absolute truth". Dr Levine (2002:35–36) sums up their significance as follows:

> Every one of our children ambles down the highly judgemental corridors of school each day dragging his mind's profile, a partly hidden spreadsheet of personal strengths and weaknesses. And throughout every moment of the school day that profile gets

put to the test. Some of our children are blessed with profiles that are magnificently matched to expectations, while others are saddled with profiles that fail to mesh with demands—an all too common disparity that can arise at any age. If a child you know has a profile that is not conforming to demands, don't give up and don't allow him to give up either. That profile has a great chance of coming into its own sooner or later. That's because we know a pattern of strengths and weaknesses may operate particularly well at specific ages and in certain contexts but not nearly so optimally in other times and under alternative circumstances.

Individuals therefore need to continuously challenge their personal learning myths, which may have been valid at a certain age or in a certain context, in order to improve their learning abilities. Part of the learning experience is to make these myths explicit so that the individual can distance themselves from their supposed "limitations". Harri-Augstein and Webb (1995) believe that individuals can only distance themselves from their own thoughts, feelings, beliefs and myths through a process of gradual but deepening reflection on personal learning experiences.

Not only is it important for the client's myths to be surfaced and made explicit, the same applies to the coach. The coach might have their own personal learning myths, as well as myths about the learning of others. Hence in the Integrated Experiential Coaching Model, the coach shares his or her preferred Learning Style and any personal learning myths they are aware of. By adopting a Learning Conversation stance, the client and the coach can work together for personal growth. It is a Learning Conversation for both parties; both client and coach can grow and develop as a result of the learning experience. It is an ongoing learning process which should lead to self-organized learning. Harri-Augstein and Webb (1995:46–47) define Self-Organized Learning as follows:

> The conversational construction, reconstruction and exchange of personally significant, relevant and viable meanings, with purposiveness and controlled awareness. The patterns of meaning we construct are the basis for all our actions. By 'significant' we mean how the new meaning is valued in the person's life space.

By 'relevant' we mean how it relates to the person's intentionality and specific purposes. By 'viable' we mean how it works for
the learner in their actions in life. By 'purposiveness' we mean
a deep understanding of how we motivate ourselves—how we
channel our energies in particular directions to meet our needs.
By 'controlled awareness' we mean deep personal conversations which tap inner processes in ways which open up the richness of personal experience.

It is clear that this definition applies to the client as well as to the
coach. If, for example, the coach is bored, and the conversation has
no relevance or viable meaning for them, they could hinder the
learning process of the client. Learning Conversations call for an
openness and natural curiosity from both the client and the coach.
The coach is an expert in facilitating the Learning Conversation, but
like the client, remains open to the learning process as it unfolds, and
is therefore continuously on the journey of Self-Organized Learning. It is a journey that starts with experiential learning, and eventually matures into transcendental phenomenology and ultimately
Almaas's inquiry method.

Thus the definition of the Integrated Experiential Coaching
Model can be enhanced by saying that coaching is about facilitating integrated experiential learning in individuals in order to
enhance personal growth and development. It is "integrated" in
that it embodies Schumacher's four fields of knowledge, as well
as Wilber's Integral Model, which caters for personal development
through various levels of consciousness, especially in the personal
and transpersonal levels. It is "experiential" in that it uses Kolb's
Experiential Learning Model as the paradigm or injunction, and
Harri-Augstein and Thomas's concept of Learning Conversations
as the primary learning tool.

Stages in the coaching relationship

The Integrated Experiential Coaching Model follows an adapted
version of Kilburg's (2000:80–86) coaching stages as represented in
Figure 16. The stages are the same at the macro and micro levels.
At "macro level" we mean the contractual coaching agreement, i.e.,
from the time the contract starts to the time it ends. At "micro level"

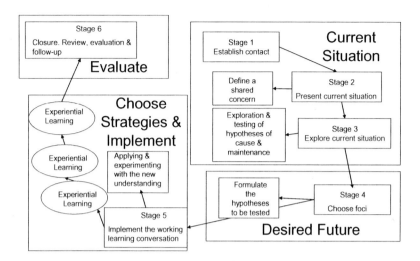

Figure 16. Stages in the coaching relationship.
Source: Adapted from Kilburg (2000:81).

we mean that every coaching session will go through the same or a similar process. What follows is a description of the macro-level process.

Stage 1: Establish contact

Stage 1 involves establishing contact with the client. The client could have contacted the coach directly, or the coach could have been selected by the Human Resources department. In this stage the coach and the client are introduced, and the two parties agree on whether or not they want to work together. In Lane's *Case Formulation Method* (1990), which was initially used in Cognitive-Behavioural Psychology and later adapted to coaching, this stage is about trying to define a shared concern that both parties are interested in exploring. Here the coach and the client discuss and agree on things like the purpose of the coaching, the process that will be followed, who the players are, and other important stakeholders that should be involved. The aim is to arrive at a contracted piece of work based on a shared concern. This last point is a valuable contribution that Lane (1990) has made to the profession of coaching. It is important that both parties define a shared concern; if no shared concern can be defined, it is better for the coach to walk away from the situation. The coach must be interested in the issue at hand; if not, the coaching relationship is doomed to failure before it even starts.

Stage 2: Present current situation

Stage 2 involves presenting the current situation. Here the client is asked to share their life story. Critically important is that it is the client's story, not the story as told or understood by a third party. The client shares his or her subjective story. Egan (2002) is of the opinion that helping the client to tell their story is very important and should not be underestimated. Referring to the work of Pennebaker, he notes that:

> An important ... feature of therapy is that it allows individuals to translate their experiences into words. The disclosure process itself, then, may be as important as any feedback the client receives from the therapist (Egan, 2002:139–140).

According to Egan (2002), self-disclosure through storytelling can help reduce the initial stress, in that it helps the client to get things out in the open which in turn can have a cathartic effect. It is not uncommon to hear clients say to the coach, "you are the only person who knows this about me". Storytelling helps the client to unburden themselves by getting rid of secrets they have carried around for years. It also helps to clarify problem situations and unexploited situations, especially if the story can be told in a nonjudgemental environment. It is important to help the client tell their story in as much detail as possible, i.e., specific experiences, behaviours and emotions. As Egan (2002:140) points out, "Vague stories lead to vague options and actions".

More importantly, storytelling can help facilitate relationship-building building between the coach and the client. To facilitate the relationship-building process, the coach must learn to work with all styles of storytelling. Every individual is unique, and has a different story and way of telling it. Therefore, it is important to start where the client starts. Stories are a valuable aid in identifying the client's deficits, as well as their resourcefulness. The aim in the

Integrated Experiential Coaching Model is to help the client build on their own resourcefulness. This is in full agreement with Egan (2002), who believes that incompetent helpers tend to concentrate on the person's deficits. Skilled professionals, although not blind to the person's deficits, capitalize on the person's resources and resourcefulness. Through storytelling it is possible for the coach and the client to spot and develop unused opportunities.

Stage 3: Explore current situation

In Stage 3 the coach and the client explore the current situation even further. In Egan's (2002) model this stage is about helping the client break through blind spots which may prevent them from seeing their unexplored opportunities, themselves, and their problem situations as they really are. In so doing, it is possible to help the client screen or choose possible problems and/or opportunities on which to work.

Lane (1990) refers to this stage as the exploration and testing of hypotheses of cause and maintenance. Every problem and/or opportunity that is selected is a hypothesis. It is a hypothesis because at the time it is the most obvious leveraged problem and/or opportunity with which to work. The hypothesis might change over time, and it is therefore an open-ended experiment. It is what Bruch and Bond (1998) refer to as "pseudo-experimenting", because it involves interview logic instead of controlled experiments: the clinical context and experimental rigour of controlled experiments are either not possible or not desirable. In this regard, Lane's (1990) and Bruch and Bond's (1998) hypothesis-testing experimentation is similar to that used by reflective practitioners:

> Their hypothesis-testing experiment is a game with the situation. They seek to make the situation conform to their hypothesis but remain open to the possibility that it will not. Thus their hypothesis-testing activity is neither self-fulfilling prophecy, which insures against the apprehension of disconfirming data, nor is it the neutral hypothesis-testing of the method of controlled experiment, which calls for the experimenter to avoid influencing the object of study and to embrace disconfirming data. The practice situation is neither clay to be moulded at will

nor an independent, self-sufficient object of study from which the inquirer keeps his distance. The inquirer's relation to the situation is transactional. He shapes the situation, but in conversation with it, so that his own models and appreciations are also shaped by the situation. The phenomena that he seeks to understand are partially his own making; he is in the situation he seeks to understand. This is another way of saying that the action by which he tests his hypothesis is also a move by which he tries to effect a desired change to the situation, and a probe by which he explores it. He understands the situation by trying to change it, and considers the resulting changes not as a defect of experimental method but as the essence of its success (Schön, 1983:150–151).

In Stage 3 the client and the coach therefore experiment with various options and hypotheses. The first three stages deal with the current reality of the client.

Stage 4: Choose foci

In Stage 4 the emphasis moves on to the desired future. The client is encouraged to spell out possibilities for a better future. According to Egan's (2002) model, this is where the coach helps the client to choose realistic and challenging goals which are real solutions to the problems or unexploited opportunities identified in Stage 4. Lane (1990) refers to this stage as the formulation of the hypothesis to be tested. It involves getting a sense of what the issue is that the client wants to work with. Here the client creates a model with which they can go and experiment in the world. It is here that the client defines ways to change that are desirable, feasible and lead to action.

In the Integrated Experiential Coaching Model this is done by means of a Personal Learning Contract (PLC). The client defines their purpose (i.e., what they want to achieve), how they will know whether they have been successful (measurement criteria), and the strategies that they will implement to achieve their purpose. This is the overarching Personal Learning Contract. It is, however, important to remember that the Integrated Experiential Coaching Model does cater for various levels of consciousness, and that the clarity of goal-setting will depend on what level the client is working on. If, for example, the client wants to lose weight or achieve certain business objectives, then it is very important to set clear and realistic expectations and goals. On the other hand, if the client is exploring the transpersonal levels of consciousness, goal-setting can actually be a major stumbling block to their progress. The Jesuit psychologist De Mello puts it beautifully, "You don't have to do anything to acquire happiness", and quotes the great Meister Eckhart who said "God is not attained by a process of addition to anything in the soul, but by a process of subtraction. You don't do anything to be free, you drop something. Then you're free" (De Mello, 1990:82). However, if you then set yourself a goal or objective to "drop something", you have completely missed the point.

Stage 5: Implement the working Learning Conversation

Step 5 involves implementing and going through a number of Learning Conversations for the specified contractual period. According to Lane (1990), it is the process of applying and experimenting with the new understandings gained in the coaching sessions. In the Integrated Experiential Coaching Model, each Learning Conversation is followed by a two-week break during which the client experiments with and applies what they defined in their PLC. Before the next session they will evaluate what they actually did, compare it to what they said they were going to do, and explain the differences. The sessions can be iterative, in that the PLCs tend to build on each other, or they can fluctuate between the three different types of Learning Conversations. Sessions generally last for two hours.

Stage 6: Closure and review

The final step, Stage 6, is closure and review. Here the coach, client, and if needs be an organizational representative, will review the process and decide on whether to renew the contract or to terminate the coaching relationship. To bring the coaching relationship to closure, each client is asked to write a reflective essay about what they have learnt from the coaching experience. The reason for doing this is twofold; it is a helpful way to bring final closure to the learning experience and the coaching relationship, and it further enhances the ability of the client to reflect on their actions and their own learning.

Case study: How the Integrated Experiential Coaching Model is applied

The first thing that needs to be emphasized is how I use the four-quadrant, multilevel part of the Model. The four-quadrant Model is the perceptual map I, as the coach, use to try and make sense of the reality that is presented to me by the coachee. It is the tool I employ to make sense of, or manage, the complexities involved with working with the person and the situation. So, for example, if the coachee said to me that they needed help in formulating their strategy for their division or department, in my mind I would see that as being in the social system domain that includes the natural and human-made systems like technology, processes and structures. It is an activity that fits into the rational level of the lower-right quadrant, and as such it can be measured. It means we would be working with something relatively easy to measure, and the sessions could be more easily structured using a tool like the Balanced Scorecard.

Alternatively, if the coachee said to me that they needed help with time management, in my mind I would see that as fitting into the rational level of the upper-right quadrant, the individual's exterior domain. Once again, it would be a piece of work that could be reasonably well-structured and measured. For example, we could use a tool like Covey's priority grid to help the coachee logically prioritize all their activities and time. So the measure could be as simple as: prior to coaching I could not manage my time and activities effectively; after six months of coaching, however, a noticeable improvement was visible (or not).

If, on the other hand, the coachee said to me that they needed help with defining a purpose for their lives, I immediately know that the coaching sessions would be less structured and "fuzzy", because we would be dealing with the world of inner experience, the upper-left quadrant. Being an existential issue, it means that we would be working with the upper rational level of consciousness, and starting to touch on the transpersonal levels of consciousness. Here the coaching would involve more exploration and use of dialogue, and the outcomes could be more difficult to measure.

Mentally "mapping" the type and level of work gives me, as coach, a sense of security and ease, which helps me relax and be more present to the client's needs. It helps me to simplify the complexity in my mind. Naturally, as the session progresses, this hypothesis-testing would be going on in my mind all the time, and I would continuously test it with the client.

The coaching sessions themselves involve me as coach facilitating an experiential learning experience for the client; this is best illustrated by means of an actual case, as follows. At the initial meeting, the coachee's immediate manager had raised some concerns that, despite having run a very successful business over the years, he was starting to see some cracks appearing in the business for which the coachee was responsible. The coachee's manager was concerned about the quality and sustainability of the annuity income side of the business (i.e., the problem was manifesting in the lower-right quadrant). In the manager's opinion, the coachee was not as hands-on in the business as he used to be, and the manager wanted to see the coachee take more responsibility for the business and to become more hands-on again. In the manager's mind, the cause of the problem originated in the upper-right quadrant, and that is where he wanted the "problem" to be fixed.

When the coachee and I explored what he would like to achieve from coaching, he mentioned that he needed help in defining his life's purpose (this was clearly an issue related to the upper-left quadrant). He wanted to discover what his real purpose in life was; he felt that somewhere along the way he had lost the meaning of life. He mentioned that he was not so excited about his work any more. A few years back he used to enjoy getting out of bed and coming to work. Now he found it an effort to come to work. He was starting to question whether he was in the right job and whether it was not time for him to make a change. But given that he was a married man with two children, and the implementation of affirmative action in South Africa, he wanted to make sure what his purpose was before he made any radical career changes. He mentioned that since he had completed his MBA, asset management seemed to be an attractive alternative. These were the issues he was wrestling with; this was his concrete experience, the reality that he was living with.

Having discussed this for some time, we moved into reflective observation. I asked him why he thought that things had changed for him. His response was that he honestly did not know. So we started to reflect on his work and life experience, from which it became clear that he was a very bright and successful individual. For example, he completed his Master's thesis in electronic engineering at the same time as his MBA degree. He had an immaculate career track record, having already made a change from the electronic defence industry, where he was involved in designing guidance systems for missiles, to a highly successful career in information technology. He was in his forties, happily married and living in a good house, but he could not work out why he was so discontented. As we explored these issues, he realized that there were some aspects of his current job that he still enjoyed, but also some that he absolutely hated. However, he could not put his finger on his discontent, or on why he was losing interest in his work.

He then asked me what I thought was going on with him. Was he abnormal? I suggested that there was a strong possibility that he was starting to experience what is generally known as an existential crisis, and that it was common for successful people at his age to experience this. I explained to him that it was a normal developmental process, and that he could be starting to make the transition into the transpersonal realms of human development. I also explained a bit of Victor Frankl's Logo Therapy to him, and how discovering our meaning in life gets us through the existential crisis. Immediately he saw how his search for purpose fitted into this theory. In so doing, he realized he was not abnormal, and that he was experiencing an aspect of normal human development. The conversation had moved into the abstract conceptualization aspect of experiential learning. Some theoretical input was interjected into the conversation which helped the coachee to better understand his current predicament.

We then explored some options with which he could experiment, to help facilitate the process of discovering his purpose in life. The option which most appealed to him was keeping a reflective journal in which he would reflect on those parts of his job that he found meaningful and energizing. I encouraged him to especially monitor his feelings and energy levels, which parts of his job excited him and gave him energy, and which parts drained him of energy. Using the Personal Learning Contract, we contracted that he would experiment with this approach for a specified time. This step effectively took him into the active experimentation aspect of experiential learning. We were using an upper-right quadrant activity, writing and journaling, to help him discover and explore an upper-left quadrant dilemma, the search for purpose and meaning in his life.

Summary

This chapter enhanced the Integrated Experiential Coaching Model further by integrating it with Moustakas's (1994) transcendental phenomenology, Schumacher's (1978) four fields of knowledge, and Harri-Augstein and Thomas's (1991) Learning Conversations. The Model proposes that coaching is about facilitating integrated experiential learning in individuals in order to enhance personal growth and development. It is "integrated" in that it caters for Schumacher's four fields of knowledge, and Wilber's Integral Model, which analyzes personal development through various levels of consciousness, especially in the personal and transpersonal levels. It is "experiential" in that it uses Kolb's Experiential Learning Model as the paradigm or injunction, and Harri-Augstein and Thomas's concept of Learning Conversations as the primary learning tool.

CHAPTER FOUR

The business framework

Applying the Integrated Experiential Coaching Model in business

In the previous chapter it was proposed that the Integrated Experiential Coaching Model facilitates integrated experiential learning in individuals in order to enhance personal growth and development. This chapter will attempt to give that meta-theoretical model a business context, in order to arrive at a theoretical executive coaching model. The discussion moves into a more micro level, dealing with tools that can be applied in the various quadrants. I explain that executive coaching is a one-on-one developmental initiative within the context in which the individual coachee operates, as represented in Figure 17.

The Integrated Experiential Coaching Model is about working with the executive or senior manager's behavioural and intentional content within the context of the social (system) and cultural (world space) in which they operate. By emphasizing a more holistic and systemic approach to executive development, the Integrated Experiential Coaching Model is in agreement with O'Neill's (2000) systems approach to executive coaching. However, as was previously pointed out, a systems approach tends to be limited to the lower-right

125

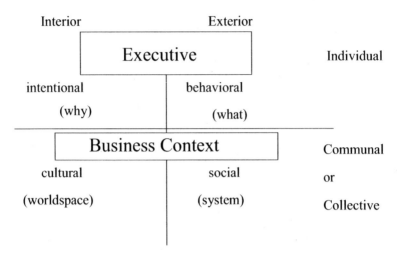

Figure 17. The context of executive coaching.
Source: Adapted from Wilber (1996:71).

quadrant; in contrast, this model is more holistic than a pure systems thinking approach.

Strategy formulation and implementation

Executive work is about strategy formulation and implementation. For years, strategy seemed to be a very fuzzy and vague concept. Executives would design amazing strategies for their organizations, and then create even more amazing explanations as to why they could not implement the desired strategies. Somehow, strategy formulation was limited to the question, "What must we do to outperform the competition?" The "what" was the burning question, and in an attempt to answer the "what question" a whole strategic consulting industry was born. Soon all major corporations were hiring strategy consulting firms to help them define what they needed to do.

Not surprisingly, it was not long before most companies in the same sector had similar strategic objectives. A good case in point is the financial industry in South Africa. Despite all financial sector firms claiming to have a unique strategy, on closer inspection they have very similar strategies; they all want to be the first to successfully implement a workable Customer Relationship Management

(CRM) solution. Yet they all face the same problem: they do not have an integrated view of their clients. Their clients exist as a number of disjointed records in various unintegrated databases. So the true strategic question is therefore not what they need to do, because they know that; they all hired the same consultants to help them define the "what". The more relevant strategic question is why they can't implement what they need to do—what is stopping them from actually implementing these chosen strategies?

Could the problem be that for years, we have created an artificial belief, or assumption, in our minds? An assumption based on a distinction that only exists in our minds and not in reality; i.e., the distinction between strategy formulation and implementation/ operations. Strategy formulation was seen to be the work of the executive team, and implementation was seen to be the work of the rest of the organization. To that must be added the very real problem of communicating the strategy to the entire organization. How many people in organizations actually have a clear understanding of what the executive's strategy is, and what their contributing role is in implementing that strategy? The reality is that in many organizations strategy implementation continues to be an ongoing challenge for the executive team. How do you formulate a strategy, and then align a whole organization with that strategy, in such a way that there is continuous feedback on whether the strategy is actually being implemented and delivering the desired strategic objectives?

The Balanced Scorecard

Thankfully, a methodology and a tool now exist that, in my opinion, enable a more holistic approach to strategy formulation and implementation. That tool and methodology are contained in the Balanced Scorecard model developed by Kaplan and Norton (1996). The Balanced Scorecard is built on four perspectives. The first two perspectives answer the "what" question of the strategy: what is it that the organization must do to outperform its competition? Those two perspectives are (Kaplan and Norton, 1996:25–26):

• **The financial perspective**: The critical question which needs to be answered is, "What must the company do to satisfy its shareholders?"

- **The customer perspective**: Here the question is, "What do customers expect from the company—what must the company do to satisfy its customers?"

The last two perspectives address the "how" question of strategy: how is the company going to deliver on the first two perspectives? It is often the absence of these last two perspectives that explains why many organizations are not able to implement the strategies they have formulated. The last two perspectives are (Kaplan and Norton, 1996:26–29):

- **The internal perspective**: Here the strategic question is, "At what internal processes must the organization excel in order to satisfy its shareholders and customers?"
- **The learning and growth perspective**: "What competencies need to be developed to enable the internal business processes?"

The strength of the Balanced Scorecard is that it forces executive management to test their assumptions via cause-and-effect relationships. Strategy formulation has always depended on making certain assumptions in very complex and uncertain environments, and given the reality of the business environment it will stay that way. Prior to the Balanced Scorecard, however, those assumptions were often not made explicit, tested or challenged. Given that the Balanced Scorecard is built on cause-and-effect relationships, assumptions now have to be made explicit and be tested. (That does not imply that it is possible to reduce the business context into a simple cause-and-effect model; we all know that reality is far too complex for that. It does, however, challenge us to make our assumptions explicit, and to test and challenge those assumptions to the best of our abilities.)

So, for example, the company needs to make x amount of profit. To make that profit it needs profitable customers, which forces it to identify those customers by carefully segmenting the market to understand its various needs. As a result there are two internal processes at which management must excel. One is the ability to segment the market (or at least manage a company that can do the segmentation for them), and the second is product development. In order to carry out these processes, certain competencies are needed within the company. By thinking through the relevant cause-and-effect relationships, all the underlying assumptions are made explicit and can be tested.

Testing and challenging assumptions are not enough. The question is, does the logic work in reality? That is why, in the Balanced Scorecard, all four perspectives need to identify measurable indicators. The old adage, "what is not measured is not managed", still applies, and even more so. The Balanced Scorecard employs both leading and lagging indicators. Financial measurements are lagging indicators. Annual financial statements come out at the end of a financial time period; the damage is done and there is nothing that can be done about it. Employee discontent, on the other hand, is a leading indicator. It does not take a rocket scientist to work out that discontented staff will affect business processes, which will eventually have an impact on client satisfaction, and ultimately on the bottom line.

Built into the Balanced Scorecard is a process of dynamic feedback, via the cause-and-effect relationships. Given that all four perspectives are being measured, the executives are continuously receiving feedback on the state of the organization and their ultimate strategy. In so doing, the Balanced Scorecard facilitates learning within an organization. It integrates very well with experiential learning. In fact, it is a tool that can be used for experiential learning. Strategy is a function of reflecting on concrete experience. Based on their concrete experience of the organization and the industry in which they function, executives continually need to reflect on what they need to do within that environment. Based on their reflection, they should come up with a strategy that they believe is appropriate for their organization, and formulate a Balanced Scorecard (abstract conceptualization). They will then actively experiment with that strategy via implementation of the Balanced Scorecard, continuously adapting the strategy to the needs of the business environment (concrete experience).

The Balanced Scorecard is therefore not a once-off event, but a continuous learning process. It is a dynamic learning experience. In so doing, the Balanced Scorecard methodology facilitates a movement away from traditional strategic planning to what Perry, Scott and Smallwood (1993:3) call "Strategic Improvising". In this approach, strategy is seen as a continuous process of improvising operational strategies in response to the dynamic environment. Improvisation, in turn, is dependent on people's ability to learn from their own experience.

The Balanced Scorecard is a powerful methodology, which integrates strategy and operations by making all assumptions explicit, and testing them through a disciplined process analyzing the cause-and-effect relationships between all four perspectives. Unfortunately, due to a lack of **mastery**, this is often not the way the Balanced Scorecard has been implemented in practice. What it has degenerated into is a measurement tool used to gauge companies' often disassociated strategic thrusts. Various strategic thrusts are identified and then slotted into one of the four perspectives. And if a particular strategic thrust does not fit neatly into one of the four perspectives, a fifth or sixth perspective is created. For example, it is currently not uncommon to see a fifth perspective, Black Economic Empowerment (BEE), in South African Balanced Scorecards. BEE is at present a critically important issue in South Africa, and has to be a strategic thrust because it is a legislative requirement. The problem is that BEE is seen as an independent thrust, with no connection to strategy at all. Yes, it is a legislated requirement, and as such every company in South Africa should see it as a critical business process at which they need to excel. Hence it should be treated like any other critical business process, and form part of the internal perspective of the Balanced Scorecard. Cause-and-effect relationships must be determined to show how BEE affects strategy, and what competencies the company needs in order to excel at BEE. Creating a fifth perspective for BEE completely misses the point of the Balanced Scorecard.

Over the years, many executives have knowingly or unknowingly come to believe that their emphasis should be on the first two Balanced Scorecard perspectives, i.e., the financial and customer perspectives. Kaplan and Norton (1996) point out that this is an incorrect notion or belief. Their methodology clearly shows that the first two perspectives are the result of the last two perspectives. Customer satisfaction and financial rewards are the result of having the correct business processes and competencies in place. Kaplan and Norton (1996) suggest a new way of thinking about what is important, and in so doing shift executive attention to what Goldratt's (1990) Theory of Constraints refers to as Throughput. Both agree that it is a fundamental switch in executive thinking.

Goldratt (1990) believes that it is a fundamental flaw to specify operating expenses as the dominant measure, because it gives the impression that the organization is made up of independent variables. Putting the emphasis on Throughput forces the organization to realize that resources have to work in concert in an interlinked process for a substantial time. By doing this, executives will realize that the organization "operates as an assemblage of dependent variables". It is business processes that are primary, not operating expenses. The work of executives is to structure the architecture of organizations for long-term sustainability. Enron and Arthur Andersen are good examples of companies which went into liquidation because the executives were focusing on manipulating finances instead of designing the organization to continuously deliver to their customers. Somehow, in our day and age we have lost the art or science of structuring and designing organizations for long-term sustainability.

The design problem

The reason why so many organizations cannot deliver or implement their strategies is because their business processes and structures do not align with and support each other. Even worse, the structures often prevent the business processes from functioning correctly, or the information technology architecture does not support the desired business processes. There is no alignment between the financial and customer perspectives, the internal business processes, organizational structure, the required competencies and the reward system. What the Balanced Scorecard provides is a disciplined learning methodology that enables executive management to align all these elements and to design an appropriate organizational architecture. If any of these perspectives are missing or not aligned, strategy and its implementation will remain an ever-elusive goal. Galbraith, Downey and Kates (2002:5) believe that an unaligned organizational design will result in any of the following:

- **Confusion**. If there is no clear or agreed-upon strategy the consequence will be confusion throughout the organization. There will be no common direction, and as a result people will be pulling in different directions. At the same time, there will be no well-defined criteria for decision-making, and as a result everything becomes a strategic thrust. It is then difficult to decide what is and is not important. In a world of unlimited resources and no constraints that is not a problem. The reality, according to Goldratt's (1990) Theory of Constraints, however, is that every organization has some form of constraints. If that was not true, the throughput for any organization would be limitless. Given the Theory of Constraints and resource limitations, the art of strategic leadership, according to Perry *et al.* (1993), involves the ability to say "no". How can anybody say "no" in the absence of well-defined criteria for decision-making?

- **Friction.** If the organizational structure is not aligned to the strategy it will result in friction. There is an inability to mobilize resources which leads to ineffective execution. This in turn leads to lost opportunities for competitive advantage. Jaques and Clement (1997) believe that an organizational structure lies in the pattern of relationships among the various roles that people fulfil within the organization. Roles set the limits and expectations on the behaviour that is required. Hence all social relationships take place within the context of social structures that are defined by specific roles. If all relationships were totally unstructured, people would not know what to do or how to act. Leadership accountability and authority are therefore defined by specified roles, and not by personal characteristics or traits. That is why they believe that leadership is context-dependent and tied to a role. Using Winston Churchill as an example, they ask whether Churchill was a great "leader". The answer seems to be that he was during the Second World War, but not before or after it. Hence they conclude:

> Does this mean he somehow grew a new personality for the war, and then lost it again? That hardly seems possible. What happened was that he got into a role during the war, in which he was able to use his capabilities to the full and to function with extraordinary competence and effectiveness ... Did Churchill thus undergo a great personality change—absolutely not; what we see is the same person with great competence to cope with one role but not another. It is therefore no use asking whether a person is a great "leader". The real question should be whether the person is a great manager, or a great commander, or a great

political representative, or a great wartime president, or a great peacetime prime minister, or is great in any other role that carries leadership accountability (Jaques and Clement, 1997:6–7).

The right way to go about this is first to define the required role, and then to look for a person who has the competencies to fill that role. That is why, in their view, it is so important to get the structure right, because it sets the roles and role relationships that specify the types of people needed to fill those roles, and defines how they should behave towards one another. It is impossible to have effective managerial leadership if there is no clear managerial structure.

Not only do you need a clear managerial structure, it has to function effectively. In an attempt to get structures to function more effectively some management theorists, as was mentioned previously, called for the end of hierarchies and the need for self-organized organizations (**heterarchy**). But, as Wilber (1995) and Jaques and Clement (1997) have pointed out, the problem is not with hierarchies *per se*, but with the pathology within the hierarchy or dysfunctional hierarchies. What Jaques and Clement (1997) found was that hierarchical structures are dysfunctional when the roles are not defined and designed correctly. What they discovered was that the level of work in any role can be objectively measured in terms of the target completion times for the longest assignment (tasks, programmes, projects) in that role. The longer the time to complete the task, the heavier the weight of responsibility and accountability. In other words, the boundaries between successive managerial layers occur at certain specific time-spans:

> Equivalent firm boundaries of real managerial layers were found to exist at time-spans of 3 months, 1 year, 2 years, 5 years, 10 years (and 20 years) ... This regularity, which has so far appeared consistently in over 100 projects, points to the existence of a structure in depth, composed of true managerial layers with boundaries measured in time-span ... (Jaques and Clement, 1997:113).

This discovery has enabled the design of hierarchical structures according to strata, which make it possible to align the nature of task complexity, human nature and capability, as represented in

Time Span	Too Many	Just Right	Stratum
10 years			Str VI
5 years			Str V
2 years			Strl V
1 year			Str III
			Str II
3 months			Str I
1 day			

Figure 18. The underlying structure of organizational layers.
Source: Jaques and Clement (1997:115).

Figure 18. In other words, the true organizational layer at stratum I coincides with the category B–I in task and cognitive complexity. So at stratum I you need individuals who follow orders and do what they are told; they proceed along a prescribed linear pathway to a goal. At stratum III the task and complexity corresponds to category B-3; here you need individuals who can work with alternative serial plans. Stratum VI corresponds to Category C-2 task complexity; here you need individuals who can handle the complexities involved with international trade. In this regard, we can see that Jaques and Clement (1997) and Kolb (1984) are talking a similar language; it is Kolb's concept of "adaptive competencies". According to Kolb (1984), each task or job requires a specific set of skills. The effective matching of task demands and personal skills is what Kolb (1984) calls "adaptive competence". Hierarchies become dysfunctional when individuals are promoted into positions where the level of task complexity exceeds their cognitive ability to manage the task complexity involved.

• **Gridlock.** In the absence of clearly defined business processes the organization experiences gridlock and output constraints.

Lack of collaboration across boundaries and an inability to share information means that the organization cannot leverage best practices. This in turn results in long decision time-frames and long innovation cycle times.

- **Internal competition.** If the metrics and the reward system do not support the goals it will result in internal competition. The end result is low standards, wrong results, frustration, high staff turnover, and diffused energy.

- **Poor performance.** If people do not understand what they are meant to do, or they are not empowered, it will result in poor performance and low employee satisfaction. Rehm (1997) believes that there are six basic human needs that must be present for human beings to be productive; in fact he sees them as the foundation for designing effective organizations. In an unaligned organization, these six criteria will be adversely affected or they will not be optimized, which leads to lower productivity. The six psychological criteria for productive work are (Benedict Bunker and Alban, 1997:139):

  - **Elbow-room for decision-making.** People need to know what their parameters are. They need to feel that they are their own bosses and that, except in exceptional circumstances, they have room to make decisions that they can call their own. On the other hand, they do not need so much elbow-room that they do not know what to do.
  - **Opportunity to learn on the job and keep on learning.** Learning is a basic human need, and is only possible when people are able to set goals that are reasonable, challenging for themselves, and they get feedback on results in time to correct their behaviour. Without feedback no learning can take place.
  - **Variety.** People need to vary their work to avoid extremes of fatigue and boredom. On the other hand, if people have so much variety due to too much work they can become overwhelmed which leads to high levels of stress. This is a common problem in the modern workplace, where the call is for people to continuously do more with less.
  - **Mutual support and respect.** People need to get help and respect from their co-workers.
  - **Meaningfulness.** Meaningfulness includes both the worth and the quality of a product, and having knowledge of the whole

product and process. The more an individual can see the bigger picture or the bigger process, the more meaningful their work becomes.
- **A desirable future**. People need a job that leads them to a desirable future for themselves, not a dead end. This desirable future is not necessarily a promotion, but a career path which continues to allow for personal growth and increase in skills.

Structuring and designing the organization

Having defined the financial and customer objectives, executives have to design the appropriate organization that will enable them to deliver on their strategy. Unlike the approach suggested by Galbraith, Downey and Kates (2002) and Jaques and Clement (1997), which starts with designing the organizational structure first and then designing the appropriate business processes, the Balanced Scorecard approach starts with the critical business processes. So why start by designing the processes first? The business processes have to be designed to enable the chosen strategies to meet shareholder and customer expectations.

If a company has, for example, decided that they can better serve their customers by having a Customer Relationship Management (CRM) programme in place, they will have to design and build relationship management, knowledge management and solution development processes. Or, if their customer strategy is to satisfy their clients by providing the best products in the market, they will have to design and build market research, innovation management and product development processes. The art is to learn to identify the critical processes that will enable the chosen strategy and then to design and build them. Galbraith, Downey and Kates (2002) point out that there are a number of processes that exist in any organization, but there are typically only a few which are critical to the strategy and the organization, and these usually involve multiple functions within the organization to carry them out. These critical processes will in turn be supported by sub-processes. The problem for most organizations is that their current processes have usually evolved over time, and hence need to be reviewed and re-designed on an ongoing basis.

Once the critical processes have been identified, defined, mapped and/or designed, the required competencies can be defined, in terms of the skills, knowledge and behaviours required to make the processes work. Only then can the roles and responsibilities be defined, as represented in Figure 19. This process should take into account the design principles set out by Jaques and Clement (to align the nature of task complexity and human nature and capability), as well as Kolb's adaptive competencies (the effective matching of task demands and personal skills).

Having designed the business processes, and defined the required competencies, roles and responsibilities, it becomes possible to design the appropriate architecture for the organization. The executives are in a position to ask, "What is the appropriate information technology (IT) architecture that is required to support these processes?" However, as Boar (1994) points out, it is not about deciding on a single IT architecture, but the strategic ability to move across IT architectures. He points out that the debate around the demise of the mainframe and elevation of client/server is an incorrect debate. It is a tactical debate and not a strategic one, because the use of any singular architecture is tactical. The strategic move is the ability to move across various architectures, as dictated by the ever-changing environment and needs of the business.

Having decided on the appropriate IT architecture, executives need to design the appropriate organizational structure that will support the strategic business processes. At the same time, executive management must define and build desired leadership style, values and culture that the executive team wants to instil within the organization. Finally, they need to design the reward and

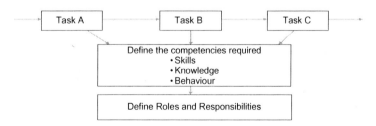

Figure 19. Designing the internal processes of the organization.
Source: Chapman (2006:109).

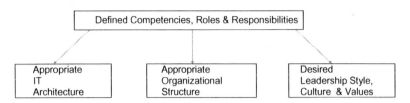

Figure 20. Designing the architecture of the organization.
Source: Chapman (2006:110).

remuneration system which will support the organizational architecture. The process is represented graphically in Figure 20.

In so doing, both the interior quadrant (desired leadership style, culture and values) and the exterior quadrant (business processes, competencies, organizational structure, and IT architecture) of the business context are taken into account.

Managerial complexity

In theory and on paper, the process of structuring and designing the organization is easy to explain. Most executives have no problem grasping the idea or concept of strategy formulation and organizational design. The problem, however, arises with the actual implementation. Why is it that so many companies and executives battle with the implementation or the actual doing of the design? An answer can be found in the work of Jaques and Clement (1997) on stratified systems theory. According to them, the problem has to do with the level of complexity involved. The complexity is not in the formulation of the strategy, but in the implementation thereof. Furthermore, the complexity is compounded by the fact that the strategy has to be formulated and implemented within an ever-changing environment. It has to become real-time strategy, constantly responding to the changing demands of the market. And as Goldratt (1990) points out, even the best solutions, including solutions and designs that worked in the past, can actually become the next source of constraints. The problem is compounded further as many individuals tend to underestimate the level of complexity involved, where complexity can be defined as:

> ... a function of the number of variables operating in a situation, the ambiguity of these variables, the rate at which they are

changing, and the extent to which they are interwoven so that they have to be unravelled in order to be seen (Jaques and Clement, 1997: xvii).

And these variables can be numerous and very elusive, as Kilburg (2000) points out; there can be hundreds if not thousands of variables that contribute to the success or failure of an organization. Given that these variables interact in both observable and non-observable ways, he argues that "true prediction and control are elusive". In short, the reason that executives sometimes find it difficult to implement their designed strategies is because they become overwhelmed by the complexity involved with modern managerial leadership.

Individual competencies

Given the complexity of the business environment, what is it that the individual executive needs to do or have to function effectively within that environment? According to Jaques and Clement (1997:44–82), the following competencies are required to effectively manage the levels of complexity involved:

- (CP): Cognitive power (CP) is the potential strength of cognitive processes in an individual, and it is therefore the maximum level of task complexity that the individual can handle at any given point in his or her development. CP is the maximum number, ambiguity, rate of change, and interweaving of variables that an individual can process in a given period of time. It is therefore the necessary level of cognitive complexity required to manage the level of task complexity of the specific managerial role. Underpinning CP are the cognitive processes by means of which an individual is able to analyze, organize and synthesize information to make it available for doing work. Jaques and Cason (1994:30) found that it was possible to observe an individual's pattern of mental processing:

  In simplest outline, we found that the pattern of people's mental processing could be observed in the manner in which they organized their information, or arguments, in the course of an engrossed discussion or argument in which they were really concerned to set out their point of view and to make themselves perfectly clear to whomever might be listening.

Their research found that there are only four mental patterns or types of mental processes that individuals use. The four patterns are:

- **Declarative processing:** The individual explains their position by using a number of separate reasons. Each reason is seen as separate, and no attempt is made to connect the reasons. They all stand alone and independent of each other. This processing has a declarative quality.
- **Cumulative processing:** The individual explains their position by bringing together a number of ideas. The individual ideas are insufficient to make the case, but taken together, they do. This processing has a pulling-together quality.
- **Serial processing:** Here the individual builds up an argument through a sequence of reasons, each reason building on the other. The ultimate result is a chain of linked reasons.
- **Parallel processing:** Using serial processing, the individual explains their position by examining a number of other possible positions as well. The lines of thought are held in parallel, and can be linked to each other. It involves working with various scenarios at the same time. This kind of processing has a conditional quality. Not only do the various scenarios link with each other, but they can condition each other.

By combining these observable thinking patterns with the observable levels of information complexity (concrete order, symbolic order, abstract conceptual order, and universal order) Jaques and Cason (1994) were able to develop their categories of complexity of mental processing. Using these categories of mental processing they were able to define an individual's current potential capability (CPC) by observing and analyzing the mental processes being used. Based on their research they concluded *inter alia* that the complexity of mental processing can be reliably observed by trained observers. The important thing is that this mental processing could be observed when subjects were engrossed in discussions that were of interest to them. From this they were able to observe the complexity of mental processing being used and make a valid judgement of their current potential. Interestingly enough, these thinking processes were only observable when the subjects were engrossed in discussion of topics of interest to them. The discussions had to be of interest to the subjects; in other words, the study had to take the subjects' concrete experience into account. Having defined the field of interest, the subjects got so involved that the researchers could observe their thinking processes.

Be that as it may, Jaques and Cason (1994) showed that it is possible to identify the amount of complexity any individual could handle at that point of their development by observing and analyzing their thinking processes. They concluded that there are categories of complexity of mental processes, and that these mature over time. Individuals become overwhelmed by complexity when their cognitive power does not match the level of task complexity demanded of them. This could be due to the individual not having matured into the required cognitive complexity, or they simply do not have what it takes. Cognitive power is therefore the most critical requirement to handle organizational complexity, but it is not the only criteria for success. The competencies listed below are just as important.

- (V). A strong sense of values for the required managerial work, and for the leadership of others. Even if an individual has the required cognitive complexity, they must want to do the work at hand; that is, they must value the work they are doing. Their personal values have to be aligned with the work they do so that their mental energy can be focused and unleashed. If people believe in what they are doing, they have much more energy to do the work. The converse is also true; even if the individual is a genius, if the work is no longer meaningful for that individual, mental and physical energy evaporates.
- (K/S). This is the appropriate knowledge, and skills to do the work. Having the appropriate skills and knowledge, however, is not enough. Jaques and Clement (1997) believe that the individual needs experienced practice in both. Furthermore, when it comes to executive-managerial leadership it is important to distinguish between technical, managerial and personal skills as represented in Figure 21.

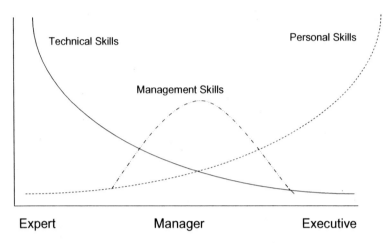

Figure 21. Evolution of managerial skills.
Source: Adapted from Goldsmith, *et al.* (2000:211).

Most individuals start their careers as some form of expert or professional in which they make use of their technical skills. As they
move out of being functional or technical experts they move into
management and have to learn managerial skills. If they happen to
move into an executive position, personal skills become more important than technical or managerial skills. Technical and management
skills are task-based skills, in that they are aimed at addressing a
certain task at hand. These skills are usually learnt by making use of
Kolb's (1984) prehension dimension of experiential learning. There
is a task or a problem that needs to be solved or addressed (concrete
experience); people are then trained in various theories or methods
by means of abstract conceptualization on how to apply the theory
to the concrete problem or task at hand. Traditionally, this kind of
learning has usually been done via what Beard and Wilson (2002)
refer to as **provider-centred** as opposed to **learner-centred** learning.
The differences between the two approaches are set out in Table 9.
Traditionally, provider-centred learning has tended to be aligned
with classroom training and learning.

Personal skills, on the other hand, are more environmentally-
based skills, such as flexibility, adaptability, intuition, and imagination. These types of skills are very difficult to learn in a classroom

Table 9. A dichotomy of power and control in learning.

Learner-centred	Provider-centred
Providers work with the natural curiosity and concerns of the learner	Passive learning is encouraged
There is a learning contract	The provider has a rigid syllabus to get through
Real issues and problems are worked on and used as vehicles of learning	Trainees learn by memorizing, and use artificial case studies
Feedback on self-performance is encouraged	Learning is monitored, examined and assessed by trainer
Learners are considered to have a valuable contribution to make	The trainer is the repository of knowledge
Learners are trusted to learn for themselves	The teacher/trainer knows best
Responsibility for learning is shared with the learners	Trainees wait for the trainer to lead
The learning provider offers resources to learn	Learning is limited to the trainer's knowledge
Learners continually develop the programme	The trainer dictates the flow of the programme
Learners and providers have joint responsibility and power	The trainer has responsibility and power
There is a climate of genuine mutual care, concern and understanding	Trust is low; trainees need constant supervision, and the trainers remain detached
The focus is on fostering continuous learning, asking questions and the process of learning, and learning is at the pace of the learner	Knowledge is dispensed in measured chunks decided by the trainer
Emphasis is on promoting a climate for deeper, more impactful learning that affects life behaviour	Emphasis on here-and-now acquisition of knowledge and skills to do the job
There are no teachers, only learners	The teacher/trainer is, and remains, the expert

Source: Beard and Wilson (2002:166).

environment. In a sense, these are the skills that an individual learns from their own experience, and are highly dependent on Kolb's (1984) transformation dimension of experiential learning, i.e., reflective observation and active experimentation. It is the ability to develop and practice what Schön (1983) calls **reflection-in-action**. It is about reflecting and experimenting in a real-time environment. Schön does, however, distinguish between the Technical Rational model of controlled experimenting and what he calls exploratory experimentation:

> In association with the model of controlled experiment, there is also the requirement for a particular kind of stance to inquiry. The experimenter is expected to adhere to norms of control, objectivity, and distance. By controlling the experimental process, he is to achieve objectivity, seeing to it that other inquirers who employ the same methods will achieve the same results. And to this end, he is expected to preserve his distance from experiential phenomena, keeping his biases and interests from affecting the object of study. Under the conditions of everyday professional practice the norms of controlled experiment are achievable only in a very limited way. The practitioner is usually unable to shield his experiments from the effects of confounding changes in the environment. The practice situation often changes very rapidly, and may change out from under the experiment. Variables are often locked into one another, so that the inquirer cannot separate them. The practice situation is often uncertain, in the sense that one doesn't know what the variables are. And the very act of experimenting is often risky ... In the most generic sense, to experiment is to act in order to see what the action leads to. The most fundamental question is, 'What if?' When action is undertaken only to see what follows, without accompanying predictions and expectations, I shall call exploratory experiment ... Exploratory experiment is the probing, playful activity by which we get a feel for things. It succeeds when it leads to the discovery of something there (Schön, 1983:144–145).

Reflection-in-action therefore makes use of exploratory experimentation to consider the consequences of various actions while one is within the process. Beard and Wilson (2002) argue that reflection-in-action (concurrent learning), as defined by Schön (1983), does not require the support of a teacher/mentor or coach, because it happens spontaneously. Over the years the individual has learnt from his professional practice how to do this kind of reflection spontaneously. However, to rely on reflection-in-action purely to develop deep learning could be dangerous. Beard and Wilson (2002) point out that, due to time pressure and various constraints, people often do not make the time to reflect on what is happening. Even Schön (1983) admits that in reality managers do reflect-in-action, but they seldom reflect on their reflection-in-action. As a result their reflection-in-action tends to remain private and not accessible to others. Hence the call for reflection-on-action (retrospective learning) by Beard and Wilson (2002), which involves the individual thinking about their previous experience, analyzing it and developing their own personal theories of action. (The differences between reflection-on-action and reflection-in-action are set

Table 10. Reflection-on-action and reflection-in-action.

Coached reflection (reflection-on-action)	Reflection-in-action
Planned intervention to support learning from experience	Spontaneous reflection that occurs as a result of a need to understand and respond to experience
Learner(s) supported by a facilitator	Learner(s) organize reflection themselves
Is planned for specific times	Can occur at any time, but usually when understanding of the circumstances is necessary and when time is available
Usually happens with learner(s) away from the immediate workplace	Usually happens in the workplace
Involves contemplation	Reflection is an active process

Source: Beard and Wilson (2002:198).

out in Table 10.) It is especially in the domain of reflection-on-action that coaching can play an important role to facilitate the development of environmental-based skills. In this respect, coaching is more aligned with the concept of **learner-centred learning**.

- (Wi). The necessary wisdom about people and things. Jaques and Clement (1997) believe that wisdom has to do with the soundness of an individual's judgements about the world and people. It is the ability to make good judgements about people and how they are likely to react in various situations. Sensitivity and empathy are central to wisdom, which expresses itself in tact. Given that this is a developmental model, wisdom is something that can develop and mature with age. This does not automatically mean that all old people are wise. What it does raise is the interesting dynamic of innovation versus wisdom. In the heyday of the dotcoms, "conventional wisdom" suggested that organizations get rid of the older, wiser members in order to make way for the young innovators. The problem was that many of these innovators did not have the wisdom (lack of experience) to manage a large complex organization through its various life cycles. The reality is that large complex organizations need both wisdom and innovation to be sustainable. Theory without practical experience is not enough. It is very true that experience is a good teacher, in that it teaches new skills and how to improve existing skills. However, when it comes to wisdom, experience on its own is not enough. Jaques and Clement (1997) point out that wisdom needs both concrete experience and abstract conceptualization. They believe that action without sound theory and concepts is unproductive, because it distorts our experience and narrows our vision. Theories and concepts determine what we see and what we learn from our own experience. Therefore the acquisition of wisdom involves Kolb's (1984) prehension dimension of experiential learning.
- T and (-T). T is the attempt to define leadership qualities and traits, and (-T) is the absence of abnormal temperamental or emotional characteristics in an individual which disrupt their ability to work with others. According to Jaques and Clement (1997:79) the focus upon personality qualities and traits is misguided:

The main point is that the particular pattern of qualities that constitutes emotional make-up has little effect upon that person's in-role leadership work, unless those qualities are at unacceptable or abnormal extremes and the individual lacks the self-control to keep them from disturbing his or her work and working relationships with others.

This is a very valuable insight which Jaques and Clement (1997) have brought into the business world. As they point out, there are over 2 500 personality variables which most people have to a greater or lesser degree. And how these variables are expressed is often dependent on the situation:

This huge range of commonly occurring characteristics combines in infinitely varied patterns to give the great richness of differences in personality make-up, all of which may be consistent with effective managerial leadership, and none of which is likely to be better or worse (Jaques and Clement, 1997:80).

Somehow we have started to believe the myth that there are certain personality traits that make better leaders than others, or—even worse—the belief that there is a correct "leadership style". As anybody with some experience knows, leadership styles come and go along with all other fads. Over the last 30 years the Gallup Organization has conducted a systematic study of excellence. This study has so far included two million of the most successful people they could find. In their study they did discover 34 prevalent themes of human talent, which is what the Clifton StrengthsFinder® is based on. The instrument helps an individual to identify their five dominant talents, where "talent" is defined as "... any recurring pattern of thought, feeling, or behaviour that can be productively applied" (Buckingham and Clifton, 2002:48).

Even though the instrument can help an individual identify their dominant talents, how those talents combine in every individual seems to be unique. Buckingham and Clifton (2002) point out that it is highly unlikely for people to have similar signature themes because there are over 33 million possible combinations of the top five talents. It is how they combine in the individual which makes the individual unique. Now imagine the permutations involved with 2 500 personality variables added to that. According to Buckingham and Clifton (2002), innate talents on their own do not lead to strengths. A strength comes into play when you combine innate talent with knowledge and skills. The latter two attributes make up the learning component of a strength.

Buckingham and Clifton suggest that two types of knowledge are required. The first is factual knowledge, which is content, concepts and theories. The second is experiential knowledge. Factual knowledge is the same as abstract conceptualization, and experiential knowledge is concrete experience, the combination of these two being Kolb's prehension dimension. A skill involves putting structure to experiential knowledge. By reflecting on what is required, all the accumulated knowledge is formalized into a sequence of steps that, if followed, will lead to performance. Buckingham and Clifton's (2002) understanding of a skill corresponds to Kolb's transformation dimension of experiential learning.

It can therefore be argued that an individual's natural strengths are a combination of their preferred learning style and their innate talents. According to Buckingham and Clifton (2002), the latter is more constant and enduring, while the former is more dynamic and changeable according to circumstances. Based on this research and on my own personal experience, I have come to the conclusion that Smuts (1973) was right when he said that

> there is a "creative Holism in Personality". And that even though my body and mental structure can have some resemblance to my parents and ancestors, my personality is indisputably mine. The personality is not inherited; it is a creative novelty in every human being that makes every person a unique individual. Hence Smuts's argument that psychology does not "materially assist" in the study of personality, since psychology deals with the average or generalized individual; and in so doing, it ignores the individual uniqueness of the personality.

Good leadership is the result of an individual using their own strengths in a given context. The message seems clear, stop messing around with people's personalities.

Sadly, many so-called "coaches" have built a practice by purely focusing and working with the (-T) factor. Unfortunately, due to pure ignorance, many individuals who sell themselves as executive coaches are in fact not coaches but psychologists still practising therapy under another name. Peltier (2001) points out that there is a difference between coaching and therapy, as summarized in Table 11. It has to be acknowledged, however, that Peltier's distinctions are not shared by all. Spinelli, E. (2008) for example, does not agree with this past-versus-future orientation. I am sure that there are numerous

Table 11. Differentiating coaching from therapy.

Therapy	*Coaching*
Focus on the past	Present and future focus
Passive orientation (listening), reflective	Action orientation
Data from client	Data is information from key others, as well as from the client
Pathology orientation	Growth or skill development orientation
Problem is intrapsychic (found in the person)	Problem is found in person-environment mix
Information is not shared with others	Information sometimes behaviour to key members of organization (with great care)
Client is clearly the person you work with	Definition of "client" unclear (may be the organization that is paying coach's fees)
Client (person) must feel enriched	Organization must feel enhanced by the coaching
Confidentiality is clear and absolute	Confidentiality is complex
50-minute sessions	Meetings of variable lengths
Work in therapist's office	Meet in executive's workplace or a "neutral" site
Rigid boundaries	Flexible boundaries, including social setting
Work through (resolve) personality issues	Work around personality issues
Client or HMO chooses therapist	Organization may choose coach

Source: Peltier (2001: xxvii).

authors and coaches who will disagree with that distinction. What I do believe is very valid, is Peltier's (2001) warning that the transition from therapy to executive coaching can be difficult and open to failure. Any therapist, in his opinion, that does not have significant knowledge of the business world, its bottom-line orientation and its assumptions, is destined to fail. M.J. Cavanagh and A.M. Grant (2006) make the same point. They point out that coaching psychologists need to develop skills and knowledge in areas that are unfamiliar to psychologists. These skills would include management, business, teaching and workplace training and learning. Executive coaching therefore calls for a wider knowledge-base. According to Cavanagh and Grant (2006), it is this wider knowledge-base, rather than its uniqueness, that is one of the critical distinctions between coaching and other forms of psychological practice.

Therapeutic issues might be raised in the coaching environment, and they can be useful. However, as Peltier (2001) points out, coaching is growth or skill development-oriented, it is not pathology-oriented. Here he is in complete agreement with Hudson:

> Coaches are quick to point out that coaching is not psychotherapy, and that is true. But coaching is therapeutic, and many of the techniques are valid instruments for coaches, as long as they serve reaching future goals rather than treating pathologies (Peltier, 1988; 12–13).

Referring to managers acting as coaches, Jaques and Clement (1997) see no problem in helping the individual smooth out some rough edges in their temperament; in their view, however, it is not the coach or the manager's role to try and change the individual's personality. If the coach is a qualified psychologist, they will be able to deal with the problem; if not, the coach has no option but to refer the client for therapy. If the coach, on the other hand, only works with (-T), it is therapy and not coaching. The emphasis in the Integrated Experiential Coaching Model is oriented towards personal growth and skills development, not working with pathology. The Model therefore leans more towards positive psychology, in that it prefers to focus on and help individuals capitalize on their strengths, and helping them discover ways to manage around their weaknesses. In this regard, the Integrated Experiential Coaching Model is in alignment with the Australian Psychological Society's Interest Group in Coaching Psychology, which:

> ... defines coaching psychology as an applied positive psychology, which draws on and develops established psychological approaches. It can be understood in terms of systematic application of behavioural science to the enhancement of life experience, work performance and well-being for individuals, groups and organizations who do not have clinically significant mental health issues or distress that could be regarded as abnormal (Lane and Corrie, 2006:150).

Jaques and Clement (1997) believe that there are five methods that can be used to facilitate managerial leadership in individuals. The five interventions are:

• Coaching, which is an important influence on values and wisdom. It can and should add to the individual's knowledge.
• Teaching imparts knowledge to the individual through lectures, practice and discussions. It is more focused on abstract conceptualization.
• Training, focused on helping the individual develop and enhance their skills through on-the-job training or simulations. It is more focused on active experimentation.
• Mentoring is usually undertaken by a manager-one-removed, and helps the individual develop sound judgement and wisdom.
• Counselling is applicable when an individual is facing some personal problems, and may at times require therapy. It is therefore more concerned with personality characteristics.

Personally, I think that Jaques and Clement have defined coaching far too narrowly; they limit it to working with V and Wi. Any executive coaching intervention should and could work with CP, V, K/S and Wi. Where I do agree with them is that coaching is different to therapy.

Intrapsychic versus person-environment mix

Peltier (2001) raises another interesting difference between therapy and coaching: that therapy assumes that the problem is intrapsychic (found in the person), whereas coaching assumes that the problem is found in the person-environment mix. This is a very important insight. When a coach is called in to work with the so-called "abnormal temperamental or emotional characteristics" of an individual, the question needs to be asked whether the manifested behaviour is really a result of a "flaw" within the individual, or whether the behaviour stems from the structural design of the organization.

An example of this dynamic occurred when I was called in to help coach an individual who had been identified as having an "abnormal temperamental issue". This executive was continually clashing with another executive in the company, and it was seen to be affecting the morale of the entire organization. As we started to work on the issue, it was discovered that these executives had actually worked together before, and that previously they had enormous respect for each other's capabilities. The problem started when the "problem" executive supported the appointment of the other executive into a new role. The symptom was that the two executives could not get along any more; in fact, there was an all-out psychological war between them. The real problem, however, was that one executive' bonus was based on just-in-time production, while the "problem" executive's bonus was based on maximum sales. To maximize his bonus at the end of the year, the production executive closed the production plant in mid-December to ensure that there was no inventory at year-end. By doing that, he maximized his bonus. The other executive could never maximize his bonus, because for the first two months of the next financial year there was no stock to sell. The problem was not with the individuals involved, but with the way the organization was designed, and in the way the reward system actually worked against the organization.

Oshry (1999) spent his whole life studying organizations and the actual behaviours that their systems produced. What Oshry (1999) found was that all organizational systems consist of three types of system, Tops, Middles and Bottoms, and that there are predictable systemic behavioural patterns associated with these three types, irrespective of the individuals involved. In this context, only the Tops and Middles will be dealt with, as executive coaching is normally only aimed at these strata. Tops are collectively responsible for the whole system, and these members are regularly confronted with complex, difficult, and unpredictable issues with long time horizons. The predictable, cognitive and affective themes of the Top system include (Oshry, 1999:59–62):

- **Fear**: They all experience some degree of fear. The question is, do they deal with it or run away?
- **Homogenization and differentiation**: They either share responsibility, information or decide together (homogenize) or they protect their own turf (differentiate).
- **Differentiation on direction**: Tops have differences with regard to what direction the whole should take. Possible behaviours associated with this dynamic are endless bickering, sabotage, avoidance and/or submergence.

These behaviours are recognized in all organizations; they are universal to executive teams. Given that most organizations are still designed according to functions instead of across business processes, it is not surprising that members of the Middle system are pulled apart from one another, out towards other individuals or groups. The predictable cognitive and affective themes of the Middle system include (Oshry, 1999:62–65):

- **Systemic dis-integration**: Ideally, members should support one another in the service of a common mission, purpose, or function. However, given the functional design structures, middles spend the bulk of their time handling their individual business and little or no time supporting one another. There is no incentive for them to support each other. Often middles are in competition with each other. Who needs to worry about external competition when we design internal competition into our own organizations?
- **Personal dis-integration**: According to Oshry (1999), if you are not confused as a Middle you are not paying attention. Middles are being pulled between two very different and conflicting systems (Tops and Bottoms), and there is legitimacy in both systems. Middles can never fully satisfy anyone, and therefore it is easy for them to internalize their dissatisfactions and consider themselves incompetent.
- **Multiplier effect**: In the absence of supportive system membership, each Middle faces these pressures, confusions, and self-doubts alone. If Middles try to stay stuck in the middle, their

mental health will suffer. They have no option but to choose sides. The question is, "Who do I support, the Tops or the Bottoms?" These are usually the most highly-stressed people in the organization.

The challenge with executive coaching will always be to work out whether one is dealing with an individual problem (intrapsychic), a systemic design problem, or a combination of both. Oshry's (1999) work has shown that a system creates its own behavioural patterns, irrespective of the individuals involved. Yes, at times the behavioural problem can be limited to the individual (intrapsychic); at the same time, however, it is possible that the behaviour results from the system and the way the organization has been designed. If that is the case, it would be more appropriate to change the system, or at the very least change our relationship to the system:

> Instead of fixing ourselves, we might do better to focus on changing the system by changing our relationship to it. Our feelings of anxiety, anger, frustration, or powerlessness are often clues to the condition of our systems. Instead of fixing or calming ourselves through therapy, drugs, or alcohol, we need to change our system by changing our relationships to them (Oshry, 1999:9).

Table 12. Key elements of the Systems and Psychodynamics Model.

Psychodynamic elements	Systems elements
Rational self (Freud's concept of ego)	System structure(s)
Instinctual self (Freud's concept of id)	System process(es)
Conscience (Freud's concept of superego)	System content(s)
Internalized self (Freud's concept of ego ideal)	Input elements
Conflict	Throughput elements
Defence	Output elements
Emotion	
Cognition	
Past relationship(s)	
Present relationship(s)	
Focal relationship(s)	

Source: Adapted from Kilburg (2000:23).

Hence, Peltier's (2001) observation that in executive coaching the problem is usually found in a person-environment mix. One coaching model that really understands this concept of person-environment mix is the Systems and Psychodynamics Model developed by Kilburg (2000). The key elements of the Systems and Psychodynamics Model are presented in Table 12.

The systems elements include the structural elements of the system, which range from tasks to be done to the roles and jobs that individuals do. For Kilburg (2000) it includes the traditional elements like hierarchy, departments, degree of centralization or decentralization, and the characteristics of the organizational environment, mission, values and culture of the organization. In his model, the key elements of the organizational processes are contained in the input-throughput-output matrix, and include things like: life cycles of products, change, resource acquisition and allocation, human resource processes, control processes, information systems, motivation, communication, goal-setting, decision-making, followership, and leadership. At the same time, it takes into account the key elements of the content of organizational systems such as: research and development, general management, transportation, engineering, manufacturing, marketing, logistics, procurement, finance, and safety. Kilburg (2000) is thus very thorough in his approach, and covers both the lower-left and lower-right quadrants of the Integrated Experiential Coaching Model. The system focus allows the coach to structure what could be almost incomprehensible, as many of these structures can either be formal or informal.

The psychodynamic aspect of the model provides complex explanations for the motivation of individuals and groups. Kilburg's (2000) model incorporates the major psychological substructures identified by Sigmund Freud. He refers to the ego as the rational self, the id as the instinctual self, the superego as the conscience, and the ego ideal as the idealized or internalized self. According to classical psychodynamic theory, these structures exist within the mind of every individual, and have different organizing principles and functions, as follows (Kilburg, 2000:27):

- The **instinctual self** is organized around the pleasure principle, and its main goals are gratification and reduction of the pressure from biologically-based drives and psychological and social needs.

- The **rational self** is organized around the reality principle, and its goal is the survival of the individual in biological, social and psychological terms. It helps the person adapt to their environment.
- The **conscience** is organized around the moral principle and its goal is to help the individual maintain social order and cohesion in their world.
- The **idealized self** contains the conscious and unconscious fantasies concerning how the individual would like to be experienced by others. It provides a model of how the individual should behave and live.

Based on the organization principles and their various goals, it is easy to see how the various internal structures can be in conflict with each other. More importantly, these conflicts can occur at the conscious or unconscious level, which adds to the complexity of any situation:

> The contents or issues of conflict can be varied and complex, ranging from external dangers to internal wishes, demands, emotions, mastery issues, achievement, attachment, separation, control, values and change. The four psychological structures, following their own goals and organizational principles, can each adopt different positions on these issues leading to major problems in the individual's efforts to manage in the external or his or her internal world (Kilburg, 2002:32).

This conscious or unconscious conflict can give rise to a host of different psychological defences, including: denial, splitting, delusional projection, fantasy, projection, passive-aggressive behaviour, dissociation, intellectualization, repression, detachment, sublimation, altruism, suppression, games, rituals, and cognitive distortions. Add to that the complex and varied patterns that are expressed in and through the different social relationships in which people are engaged on a daily basis, especially their roles and relationships at work, and you have a very complex conscious and unconscious environment of various motives for individuals and groups.

The strength of the Systems and Psychodynamics Model is that it sees the psychodynamic and systems approaches as complementary in helping to understand the personal-environment mix:

Both general systems and psychodynamic theory have strengths and weaknesses. However, in my view, they are complementary. Systems theory is useful for its abstractness, general utility and applicability, assistance in organizational and large system assessments, and allowance for prediction and control in some situations. It is not particularly useful in helping people with the content of what is happening internally, or when they find themselves in conflict or problematic situations. In my experience, psychodynamic theory picks up where systems theory leaves off. It is useful in explaining and guiding individuals' behaviour, both internally and interpersonally. It provides useful information about the human side of organizational behaviour, but it is not inclusive enough to assist a consultant or coach with the thorough assessment or diagnosis of organizational operations or human behaviour. It also lacks specificity in helping clients develop and implement new and innovative behaviours for themselves, their groups, or their organizations (Kilburg, 2000:46).

It is therefore not surprising that Kilburg (2000) believes that executive coaching is evolving as a sub-discipline of organizational development; it is not psychotherapy in the workplace.

Jaques and Clement (1997) conclude that effective managerial leadership in highly complex environments demands four basic conditions. Firstly, the individual must have the necessary level of cognitive competence to carry the required role, and they must strongly value the work and responsibility associated with that role. In a sense, this addresses the interpersonal requirements. Secondly, the individual must be free from any severely debilitating psychological traits that interfere with their ability to work with others. This is a combination of interpersonal and intrapersonal requirements. The third condition is what Jaques and Clement term organizational conditions. That is, the appropriate business processes, organizational structures and specified managerial leadership practices must be in place. These are the systemic requirements. Fourthly, each individual must be encouraged to use their own leadership style; they must be free to be themselves. There is no "magical leadership" style out there that works for everybody. Every individual is unique and every individual has their own leadership style, depending on their specific competencies and the specified role they fulfil.

Executive coaching defined

The executive coaching intervention should therefore be aimed at working with CP, V, K/S and Wi within the system in which the individual operates. In the Integrated Experiential Coaching Model, executive coaching is therefore about facilitating integrated experiential learning in individuals in order to enhance personal growth and development with the aim of improving individual and organizational performance. It is not therapy. It is integrated in that it attempts to work and think in the context of all four quadrants, and on various levels of consciousness. It is always aware that, no matter what tool or method is being used, it is only a partial truth applying to a certain quadrant or level.

This chapter has highlighted some of the complexities involved when coaching executives in corporations. Clearly, a coach with no understanding or experience of the impact of organizational design and structures on individual and group behaviour would find it very difficult to work in an integrated way with their client(s). In the absence of this knowledge and experience, the temptation according to Jaques and Clement (1977:28) will then be to "... focus upon psychological characteristics and style that leads to the unfortunate attempts within companies to change the personalities of individuals, or to maintain procedures aimed at getting a 'a correct balance' of personalities ...". As they point out, there is no way that effective leadership development is possible unless and until the organizational conditions are right, irrespective of how good the coach may be.

Summary

This chapter took the theoretical Integrated Experiential Coaching Model and added a business context to it. This was done by incorporating strategy formulation via the Balanced Scorecard of Kaplan and Norton (1996) and organizational design principles, with reference to the work of Galbraith, Downey and Kates (2002) and Rehm (1997). All of this has to happen within a world of managerial complexity which can overwhelm executives. Having set the business context, the chapter then explored the individual leadership competencies of Jaques and Clement (1997) and how those competencies could help an executive cope with managerial complexity.

What has become clear is that within the business context, coaching is not therapy. Using the work of Peltier (2001) a clear distinction was made between coaching and therapy. Lastly, referring to the work of Oshry (1999) and Kilburg (2000), it was shown that behavioural problems manifested by individuals within an organization could be intrapsychic, or due to systemic organizational design problems, or even a combination of both. Hence it is argued that an executive coaching intervention should be aimed at working with CP, V, K/S and Wi within the system that the individual operates. In the Integrated Experiential Coaching Model, executive coaching is therefore about facilitating integrated experiential learning in individuals in order to enhance personal growth and development with the aim of improving individual and organizational performance. It is not therapy.

CHAPTER FIVE

Applying and researching the Integrated Experiential Coaching Model

Introduction

At this point it is important to realize that Grof's criticism of Wilber's theory is just as relevant to the Integrated Experiential Coaching Model, namely:

> ... it is not sufficient to integrate material from many different ancient and modern sources into a system that shows inner logical cohesion. While logical consistency certainly is a valuable prerequisite, a viable theory has to have an additional property that is equally, if not more, important. It is generally accepted among scientists that a system of propositions is an acceptable theory if, and only if, its conclusions are in agreement with observable facts (Frank, 1957). ... For this reason, evaluating his ideas in the light of actual experiences and observations from ... research seems particularly important and necessary (Grof, 1998:88–89).

This chapter addresses that criticism, and covers the active experimentation of experiential learning: it briefly outlines where and how the Integrated Experiential Coaching Model was applied and researched, and summarizes the findings of my doctoral research. It then goes on to explain how the Integrated Experiential Coaching Model has strong similarities to the "Friendly Disentangling" method or Quaker Persuasion Model. The chapter then explores how the Integrated Experiential Coaching Model and my research findings relate to the five challenges identified by the Corporate Leadership Council in its 2003 report titled *Maximizing Returns on Professional Executive Coaching*. The report stemmed from research that the Council had undertaken at the request of its members into the effectiveness of executive coaching as a development intervention.

In his book *Managers Not MBAs*, Henry Mintzberg (2004) challenges the conventional notion that the MBA degree develops managers. Following on his critique of MBA programmes, Mintzberg (2004) suggests a different approach to developing managers based on eight propositions. Although he expands the propositions in the context of university training, I believe that they are applicable to coaching as well. The last part of this chapter explores Mintzberg's eight propositions, discussing whether or not the Integrated Experiential Coaching Model and its research can be related to them.

Ethical and legal considerations

I was awarded the contract to coach 17 middle and senior managers in a large IT firm for a period of six months from July 2003 to December 2003. It was agreed with the company that the coaching project be used as part of my doctoral research programme. I contracted to meet with every coachee for 12 sessions over the six-month period. The coaching sessions were usually of two-hour duration every two weeks. Experiential learning is the methodology applied in the Integrated Experiential Coaching Model, therefore participants needed the time in between sessions to experiment with and assimilate their learning.

The project involved coaching in both Cape Town and Johannesburg, South Africa. I was told that the managers concerned were chosen by the company on the basis of the belief that they would be its next generation of leaders. The company therefore wanted these managers to be coached for development and performance improvement. None of the managers for this project were selected for remedial coaching, which usually involves working with specific behavioural problems that are best addressed through therapy. So from the outset I was working with a group of people in whom the company believed. (Although as soon as I started the coaching I found out that that was not always the case. Some managers were hoping that I could change the coachees through coaching.)

The company's General Manager for Human Resources was the project sponsor, but the project received the go-ahead from the company's full Executive Committee. All costs associated with travel and accommodation were carried by the client. Due to the fact that this project involved a reasonable sum of money, the company requested that each coachee sign a contract committing themselves to the company for a period of three months after the termination of the coaching engagement. Once again, all coachees were happy to comply with this request from their company.

A confidentiality agreement was written into the project contract, in terms of which I as the coach undertook to keep confidential any information provided to me. This confidentiality agreement applied on two levels. Firstly, given that I was to coach so many people who occupied various positions within the organization, it was obvious that I would be exposed to the organization's strategic plans and operations. The company therefore had to have the assurance that this information would be kept strictly confidential. Secondly, the coachees had to know that any information they shared with me would be treated as highly confidential.

This was critical to the success of the project. This was the first time that coaching was to be undertaken within the organization, and even though the coachees were told repeatedly that they were chosen because the company saw them as its future leaders, there was a large element of scepticism and distrust about the coaching intervention. It was just as well that this agreement was written into the contract, for (as I was to find out later) a number of the coachees believed that they were put on the programme because they were being targeted as "troublemakers" within the organization.

It was therefore agreed with both the company and the coachees that all the work done within the coaching sessions would remain strictly confidential between the coach and the coachees. Notwithstanding this provision, however, all agreed that, if the coachee agreed, I could give feedback on trends to the coachee's immediate manager if they asked for that kind of feedback. If any feedback was to be given, I would first discuss it with the coachee to see if he or she was happy with what would be discussed, and would then ask them for permission to give the feedback. At times I was put under pressure by some executives and managers to give specific and detailed feedback. I refused to do this on the basis that it would compromise my position as a coach and violate the confidentiality agreement that had been agreed with each coachee and with the company as a whole.

At the start of the project I met with every coachee and gave him or her a presentation on the Integrated Experiential Coaching Model and on how I worked within that theoretical framework. Each coachee was then invited to work with me if they were happy with the content and context of the Integrated Experiential Coaching Model and the way in which I planned to coach. If not, they had the option of choosing an alternative coach. Thereafter, the coachees were asked whether they would be happy to be part of the doctoral research project. They were welcome to decline. Every member consented to be a part of the research project.

The other issue that had to be addressed was the fact that I would be an insider researcher, which could have an impact on my objectivity. To address this issue the General Manager for Human Resources (who was a registered clinical psychologist and therefore understood the importance of supervision) introduced me to Professor Frans Cilliers. Frans, a highly respected academic and practitioner in South Africa, was head of research at the Department of Industrial Psychology at the University of South Africa (UNISA), the largest university in the country. Frans had had a long-standing working relationship with the company, and was highly respected within it. The GM for HR suggested that I do some supervision with him, and even asked whether it was possible to involve Frans in the supervision of the research project. Frans indicated that he would be very willing to help with the research and coaching supervision. In addition, Professor David Lane of the University of Middlesex organized for Frans to become my academic supervisor on my DProf programme at the University. From then on Frans and I met at least once a month for academic and coaching supervision. I believe that this enabled me to stay more objective throughout the project. The GM for HR was very happy with this development.

Given the respect that Frans enjoyed within the company and his academic reputation, Frans and I agreed with the GM for HR that the research results would only be released to the company once the final project had been written-up and passed by the University of Middlesex. This made Frans and I very comfortable because we both have a reputation for only delivering high-quality work.

Implementation of the coaching process and the Integrated Experiential Coaching Model

The process that was followed is represented in Figure 22.

Stage 1 involved establishing contact with the coachees. The first sessions started in July 2003 and consisted of a one-hour meeting with each coachee, their immediate manager, the psychologist who administered the assessment centres, a representative from human resources, and the coach. The psychologist highlighted the areas that he felt were development areas. Both the coachee and their manager were free to agree or disagree with the assessment. The coachee's immediate manager was then asked to raise any development issues that they felt needed to be addressed.

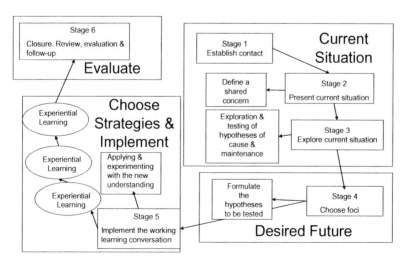

Figure 22. Stages in the coaching relationship.
Source: Adapted from Kilburg (2000:81).

From the outset, it was made very clear to all coachees that this information was to be used as input as they themselves saw fit. They were free to use this information and work with it or to disregard it, the reason being that the coachee always sets the agenda in the Integrated Experiential Coaching framework. Given that the model aims to move responsibility and accountability for personal development onto the individual being coached, they needed to realize from the beginning that it was their time and their development that was at stake. Accordingly, they chose how and when or what they wanted to work on; the coach, psychologist or their manager did not set the learning agenda, which remained the responsibility of the person being coached. At the end of this session each coachee was given a Learning Styles Inventory questionnaire, as well as a Learning Styles Inventory Interpretation. They were asked to complete the questionnaire and bring it with them to the next session.

Stage 2 involved presenting the current situation. The second coaching session was designed for the coach and coachee to get to know each other better, with the aim of arriving at a contracted piece of work based on a shared concern. It was important that both parties defined a shared concern; if no shared concern could be defined, it would have been better for me as the coach to walk away from the situation. As the coach I had to be interested in the issue at hand; if not, the coaching relationship would have been doomed from the start. More importantly, the coachee had to feel comfortable working with me. As a result, I gave each coachee a one-hour presentation on the Integrated Experiential Coaching Model and on how I work. At the end of that presentation I asked the coachee if they felt comfortable to work within that framework or not. If they did, we could continue the coaching process. If they did not they were welcome to withdraw from the process and the company would allocate them a coach they felt comfortable with. Every coachee elected to continue working with me as they felt comfortable with the coaching model.

I then asked the coachee to share their life story, from as far back as they could remember. At certain points of interest I asked some questions to further explore the particular issue. Once the coachee finished telling their story they were free to hear my life story if they so wished. Every coachee asked to hear my life story. I found that self-disclosure through storytelling did help to reduce the initial stress for both the coachee and I, in that it helped us to get things out in the open, which in turn had a cathartic effect. It helped to facilitate relationship-building between the coachee and I. It made us realize that we are all only human, and that deep down we are not as different as we often think we are. Finally, we both shared our preferred learning styles with each other, and discussed how our preferred learning styles could possibly impact the way we work together. Furthermore, it gave me an indication of how each coachee prefers to learn.

In Stages 3 and 4 the coachee and I started to explore the current situation even further. Here we tried to screen or choose possible problems, issues and/or opportunities that the coachee wanted to work on. In so doing we tried to identify a working hypothesis, i.e., something with which we could experiment and play. And I want to emphasize that it was a working hypothesis, because at the time it was the most obvious leveraged problem and/or opportunity to choose to work with. There was the realization that the hypothesis might change over time, and hence it was an open-ended experiment. Once the coachee had identified what it was that they wanted to work on in coaching, we recorded it in as much detail as possible under the "What is my Purpose?" section of a Personal Learning Contract. We then tried to define measures that would be used to assess whether we had achieved that goal at the end of the six-month period. These were recorded under the "How shall I judge and measure my success?" section of the Personal Learning Contract.

Stage 5 involved the implementation of a number of Learning Conversations (coaching sessions) for the specified contractual period. In the Integrated Experiential Coaching model, each Learning Conversation was followed by a two-week break, during which the coachee experimented with and applied what they had explored in the coaching session. Sessions generally lasted for two hours. How a typical coaching session was implemented is best illustrated by means of the case study presented at the end of Chapter three. (Interestingly enough, this is a good case example to have used, because it raised the first of a number of contradictions I was to encounter between my theoretical model and my actual practice. I had emphatically stated that this model was not about therapy, yet Logo Therapy is a form of therapy, and the coachee had found it very helpful. So obviously I could no longer be so emphatic about the model not being about therapy. These contradictions will be discussed in Chapter six.)

The final step, Stage 6, was closure and review. Here the coach and coachee reviewed the process and decided whether to renew the contract or to terminate the coaching relationship. To bring this part of the coaching relationship to closure, each coachee was asked whether or not they would like to continue participating in the coaching project as a part of my doctoral research programme. If they did want to, they were asked to write a reflective essay about what they had learnt from the coaching experience. The reason for doing this was twofold: it would later be helpful in bringing final closure to the learning experience and the coaching relationship, and it further enhanced the ability of the client to reflect on their actions and their own learning. Secondly, these essays would be used as the primary data source to conduct the actual research.

Research design

The initial idea was to develop the theoretical Integrated Experiential Coaching Model, apply it in practice, and then do empirical research to validate the model. It soon became apparent that the variables involved in the Integrated Experiential Coaching Model were far too numerous to test a hypothesis. It was even more difficult to define a hypothesis, given that it was a new theoretical model. As a result it was decided to do exploratory research, focused on the upper-left quadrant of the Integrated Experiential Coaching Model, the interior domain of the individual. Five research methodologies were researched and considered; four were found to be unacceptable for this research project. The four methodologies that were found to be unacceptable, and the reasons why they were found to be unacceptable, are presented in Table 13.

The objective of the research was to explore the individual's subjective learning experience, while being coached within the context of the Integrated Experiential Coaching Model, with the aim of using what I learnt to continuously refine or change the Model. It was about exploring and discovering, rather than measuring and explaining; exploring and discovering the meaning and essence of the learning experience while being coached. The research was about obtaining descriptions of experience through first-person accounts via the use of reflective essays. It was about exploring people's inner

Table 13. Research methodologies that were considered and rejected.

Methodology	Reason for not using the methodology
Action Research	
Action research is concerned with identifying a problem, implementing a change intervention, and then monitoring the process. Where necessary, corrective action is taken. Because it is a change initiative, it would normally involve a group of people working collectively to solve the problem.	This coaching project was not classified as a change programme. Its aim was to explore executive coaching as a means to develop managers' and leaders' ability to better manage the complexity involved in managing a large complex organization. My interest was to explore what these individuals had actually learnt during this process. The research project was therefore exploratory in nature. To start an action research project I would need to know what questions to ask. My research was aimed at generating possible questions for future research. At the start of this project we did not even know what types of question to ask.
Soft Systems Methodology	
This methodology is concerned with understanding the whole system, to understand the problem within the system, and then to implement the desirable change.	As is the case with action research, this project was not seen as a change intervention. The intervention was based on experiential learning; hence we wanted to explore what clients had actually learnt. If the research question was to explore the impact that coaching had had in the organization, then I believe this would have been the appropriate methodology. Furthermore, in soft systems

(*Continued*)

Table 13. (*Continued*)

thinking we often work with the ideal versus the real state of affairs. When we started this project we did not know what was the ideal state for coaching. My research project was exploratory, with the hope that it might enable us to start asking the questions that would enable us to do research on how things should be. In this project we wanted to generate a hypothesis that could be tested at a later stage.

Experiments

This methodology would involve manipulating one or a number of variables in order to assess the effects. It calls for a high degree of control.

The theoretical model that I had developed is highly complex, and is dependent on a number of inter-related variables. It would be virtually impossible to experiment with the model as a whole. The dependencies are far too numerous and too interrelated. For experiments to work, subsections of the model would have to be tested. Once again, I believe that my research was very exploratory in nature. The outcome of the research could be a number of hypotheses that could be tested or experimented with.

Surveys

This methodology is associated with asking people questions via interviews.

Once again, I believed that the coaching profession was (and is) in such an early stage of development that we do not even know what meaningful questions to ask. I believed that my research could help to generate questions that could be used in future surveys.

worlds or dimensions. As a result, it was qualitative in nature and hypothesis-generating, rather than hypothesis-testing. Furthermore, experiential learning and continuous growth lies at the heart of the Integrated Experiential Coaching Model. It was therefore important that the research methodology supported that philosophy and built on it. As a result, an adapted version of the transcendental phenomenological methodology of Moustakas (1994) was chosen for this study. Traditionally, this methodology involves designing questionnaires and conducting interviews, which means that interviews are the primary source of data collection. This is where I adapted the methodology; instead of gathering the data via interviews, I chose to collect the data by means of reflective essays. That was the only adaptation; apart from this change, I used the methodology as is.

The transcendental phenomenological methodology consists of four steps.

- **The Epoche process:** This is about involving oneself in a new experience in a new way. It is about setting aside our prejudgements, biases, and preconceived ideas about things. From the Epoche, we are challenged to create new ideas, new feelings, new inwardnesses and understandings. It is a way of genuine looking and experiencing that precedes reflection, forming judgements, or reaching conclusions.
- **Phenomenological reduction:** Here the task is to describe in textural language just what one sees, not only in terms of the objective reality but also in terms of the internal acts of consciousness, the relationship between the phenomenon and the self. It is called reduction because it leads us back to our own experience of the way things are. The aim is to identify individual themes, and then to develop a composite textural description from the individual themes to arrive at the experience of the group as a whole.
- **Imaginative variation:** Here the task is to derive structural themes from the textural descriptions that have been obtained through phenomenological reduction. The critical question that needed to be explored was how the experience of the relevant phenomenon came to be what it is.
- **Synthesis of meaning and essences:** The final step involved the intuitive integration of the fundamental textural and structural descriptions into a unified statement of the essence of the experience.

(For a more detailed description of the methodology refer to Chapter three, where the transcendental phenomenological methodology was integrated with the Integrated Experiential Coaching Model).

My role as researcher in terms of the design and conduct of the project

Given my extensive experience in running and managing large projects I had no doubt that I would be able to manage this research project effectively. I brought to this project years of experience in coaching people on a one-on-one basis, and felt very comfortable about that part of the research project. Another advantage that I brought to the design and conduct of this project was my strong analytical ability. This I had gained from years of analysis in companies, and it was especially developed and strengthened through the research that I did for my MBA thesis. In that thesis I had to analyze 20 years of data for the mutual fund industry. The disadvantage for this project, however, was that my skills lay in analyzing quantitative data. Prior to this project I had never done or undertaken qualitative analysis, and had absolutely no experience or knowledge of how to do qualitative research. From the time that I made the decision to do qualitative research, I knew that this could be my Achilles' heal. To compound the problem even further, I knew absolutely nothing about phenomenology. Learning about phenomenology and its associated research methodology made up the bulk of my desk research. Fortunately, I was blessed to meet Professor Frans Cilliers, who is seen as one of the foremost qualitative researchers in South Africa. I was even more fortunate when Professor David Lane organized for Frans to become my supervisor on the research project. As a result, I relied very heavily on the guidance of Professors Cilliers and Lane throughout the analysis part of the project.

Research methodology

Participants – co-researchers

The first part of the research process was to select the sample universe who could participate in the research project. In this case the sample universe was the group of coachees nominated by the company to participate in the coaching project. There were two females and 15 males involved with the project. Only two of the participants were black.

At the end of the coaching project, coachees were re-invited to become co-researchers in the research project if they wanted to. The qualifying criterion was the submission of a reflective essay. Of the initial 17 coachees, 13 opted to become co-researchers by submitting a reflective essay. Eight of the co-researchers were white Afrikaans-speaking males, three were white English-speaking males, one was a white Afrikaans-speaking female, and one was a black English-speaking male. In total, it was a response rate of 76 per cent.

Data-gathering method

During the coaching sessions I made notes of what was being discussed, and any decisions that were taken. These notes were dated and filed in a separate file created for each coachee. The amount and detail of notes taken depended on what was discussed, the depth of the conversation, and the confidentiality of the issues at hand. It was not uncommon for coachees to ask me not to record what they were speaking about. At the same time, I often used to reflect on these sessions in my own reflective journal. Here I reflected on how the session went, what worked or did not work, and how I felt about things.

From the outset, coachees were aware that they would be part of the research project. Each coachee was informed that they would be asked to write a reflective essay at the end of the coaching project, and that these essays would form the basis of the phenomenological research. As a result, each coachee was encouraged to keep a reflective journal on their experience of being coached throughout the duration of the coaching project. The Personal Learning Contract ended with the question, "What have I learnt from this exercise?" The objective of both the essay and the journal was to facilitate continuous reflection on the coaching experience.

The decision was made not to use structured interviews to collect the data for this research project. Co-researchers were asked to write a three- to four-page reflective essay on what they had learnt, by answering the question "What have I learnt from this coaching experience?" There were two reasons for doing this. Firstly, reflective essays enhanced the co-researchers' reflective abilities, thereby promoting the experiential learning process. And secondly, co-researchers could give a first-hand textural and structural description of their own experience. The assumption was that it would be a more accurate account of their experience than if the researcher had to interview them and then write up their experience through all the filters that the researcher would use to interpret the experience. These reflective essays, which can be made available on request, were the primary data source and formed the basis of the phenomenological analysis. It is important at this point to mention that every respondent was given the option to write the essay in English or Afrikaans. All respondents decided to write the essays in English, even though nine co-researchers were Afrikaans-speaking. As a result of English being the second language of these latter nine coachees, their writing was not always grammatically correct. Finally, although the co-researchers were asked to write an essay of three to four pages, the essays varied in length from one to nine pages.

Data analysis and processing

It is important to mention that the analysis and processing of the data was carried out strictly in accordance with the transcendental phenomenological methodology.

The Epoche process

This was about involving myself in a new experience in a new way. It was about setting aside my prejudgements, biases and preconceived ideas about things. From the Epoche, we are challenged to create new ideas, new feelings, new inwardnesses and understandings. It is a way of genuine looking and experiencing that precedes reflection, forming judgements or reaching conclusions.

Having received the essays, the first step was to immerse myself in the Epoche process by reading the essays for familiarization. This took about a month, during which the essays would be read, put aside for a while, and then re-read at a later stage. Interestingly enough, every time the essays were read different meanings would arise. At the same time, there was a growing awareness of my own prejudices and biases. The challenge for me was to learn to stay open.

Phenomenological reduction

Here the task was to describe in textural language just what I saw, not only in terms of the objective reality but also the internal acts of consciousness, the relationship between the phenomena and the self. The challenge was to arrive at a complete textural description of the experience of the group as a whole.

Having gained familiarity with the content of the essays, the next step involved the phenomenological reduction part of the analysis. Here the essays were content-analyzed, which involved breaking down, examining, comparing, conceptualizing and categorizing the data. The aim was to identify various themes within each individual essay.

When I started to read the essays I was initially overwhelmed by the amount of data; I did not know where to start. So I started to build mind-maps on the wall of my study. I would read an essay, see a theme developing, and create a branch under that theme supported by the data, a very labour-intensive process, especially considering that I had to do this for every essay. Eventually I began building the mind-maps on a personal computer using MindManager®, a computer package. In MindManager® I still had to create the mind maps manually, in that I would read the essay, see a theme, and then create a theme branch. The advantage, however, was that I could now just copy and paste the supporting data, from the original essay, onto that theme. This greatly enhanced the efficiency of the analysis process; with relative ease I could cut and paste data as I saw themes developing. Another advantage was that once the mind-map was completed, I could export it to MS Word®. This analysis went through a number of iterations as preliminary themes were refined even further.

Once I had content-analyzed all the essays and extracted the themes, these individual themes were collated into generalized horizons of the group as a whole. A requirement of horizontalization is that all statements are treated as equal, and the applying of hierarchies of significance should be avoided. By avoiding hierarchical assumptions, the researcher is in a better position to examine the experience with less prejudice. Similar themes from the individual essays were clustering under common horizons. The horizons that arose for the group as a whole were dependency, trusting relationship, reflection, more complex work, learning themes, self-autonomy, awareness of self in relation to others, transpersonal awareness, and self-awareness.

Having defined the horizons for the group as a whole, the next step was to develop a composite textural description to arrive at the experience of the group as a whole. Here the analysis went a step further. The first step was to refine the horizons into more coherent themes. This involved rereading all the analysis and moving some of the data where necessary to support the more refined themes. This process took about three months. Having defined the themes I shared my findings with Professors David Lane and Frans Cilliers, who pointed out that in qualitative research it was common practice to distinguish between cognitive, affective, intrapersonal and interpersonal experiences. As a result, the supporting data for every theme was then analyzed to identify interpersonal, intrapersonal and transpersonal experiences. These experiences were then analyzed even further to distinguish between cognitive and affective experiences. In so doing, the analysis was able to build a rich picture of what the group as a whole experienced as a result of their coaching experience. In total, ten themes were identified that described the experience of the group as a whole.

Imaginative variation

Having derived a composite textural description (the ten themes) of the experience of the group as a whole, the next step involved Imaginative Variation to derive a composite structural description of the group. Here the aim was to try and understand how the co-researchers as a group experienced what they experienced. The critical question to answer or explore was how did the experience of the phenomena come to be what it is? Through the utilization of imagination, varying the frames of reference, different perspective and points of views, I tried to derive a structural description of the experience and the underlying factors that account for what was being experienced. In essence, I attempted to develop an understanding or "theory" about how the experience came about.

To understand how this experience came about it was necessary to draw on the reflective essays, the coaching notes that were taken during the coaching sessions, and my reflective journals. This involved rereading the coaching notes and the reflective journal to try and understand what contributed to these experiences. By combining all three data sources, it was possible to develop a composite structural description of the group as a whole.

Synthesis of meaning and essences

The final part of the research methodology was to write up a synthesis of the meaning and essences of the experiences of the group as a whole. This was done by integrating the composite textural and composite structural descriptions of the group as a whole, which was as follows.

A number of the co-researchers started the coaching relationship deeply entrenched in patterns of dependency that included the transference of power. The transference of power was displayed in one of two dominant patterns. The first pattern was that they did not want to take responsibility for their own behaviour or the process. They felt cynical about what value the coach could add to their lives and to the business. The cynicism, moreover, stemmed from the fact that many of them were nominated by their managers as a consequence of an assessment centre they had attended about 12 months prior to the coaching programme. As a result of these assessments and their transference of power to the psychologists, they felt labelled and judged. As one co-researcher put it, "*As coaching or informal tuition was a new concept to me, my first reaction when introduced to coaching was that of uncertainty towards my abilities as line and technical manager. The assumption was that all managers not performing, [were] targeted for some kind of evaluation sessions with some outsider that would categorize the target group of managers in pre-defined blocks.*" Another expressed the following, "*This feeling was further enhanced by being interrogated, my strengths and weaknesses discussed in front of a number of people ...*" Was management serious about this process, or was it just another fad? For these co-researchers there was a strong feeling of being a victim; this was just another "thing" that was being done to them. They reluctantly got into coaching because if they did not join the programme they could receive another "label".

The second transfer pattern was the unrealistic expectations of what the coach could do for them. There was the expectation that as the "expert", the coach would be teaching them a tremendous amount. *"Secondly I was also brand-new in a new job and I needed to gain some content knowledge about the subject—fast. I was in the lucky position that my coach came from the same background. Since I had a small baby, studying was not an option at that time and I was very excited that I would be able to learn from him as I go along and draw from his experiences in similar fields."*

Again one can see the transference of power coming through: "What is the coach going to do for me?" The responsibility for success lies with the coach, not with them. Coaching is seen as a possible quick-fix or shortcut in the experiential learning process. There was even an expectation of receiving *"formal learning documentation"*, an expectation entrenched in the "training paradigm". In this paradigm the expert (the trainer, lecturer or teacher) has all the knowledge, and imparts that knowledge to the student or pupil. There was the transference of power and responsibility from coachee to coach.

At the first coaching session the co-researchers were invited to either use the feedback they had received from the assessment centres and their managers, or to ignore it. It was made clear to them that they were responsible for their own learning and development, which meant that they were free to use the feedback if they found it meaningful or to ignore it if it had no personal meaning for them. The next step was to get to know each other by getting the co-researchers to tell the coach "their" life stories, with the coach telling his life story in return. The mutual exploration of the life stories in an open enquiring and inquisitive way led to a beautiful curiosity about who and what they were. The more they experienced the ability to tell and explore their stories in a nonjudgemental open way, the more they were willing to investigate the mystery of the "self". Through the mutual exploration of their stories, defences started to drop, and a sense of vulnerability started to set in. Vulnerability in the sense that there was a realization that both coach and coachee were only human. There was a growing realization that there was no "expert", only a group of people who were on a journey of exploration. An exploration into this thing called life, and the mystery of being human and all that that entails.

Through telling, exploring and enquiring into each other's stories, a relationship started to form between the coach and the co-researchers. For the co-researchers the building of a trusting relationship was vital to the success of the coaching process. Without the establishment of such a relationship it was felt that it would not have been possible to learn. A trusting relationship was seen as the foundation of everything that was to follow.

As the trust grew, so did the willingness to enquire and reflect at various levels. One of the real dangers of the English language, and in writing up a research report, is that the process appears to be a linear progression. Nothing could be further from the truth. Given the limitations of report writing, it only appears that way. A more truthful account would be to conceive of the process as a spiral journey. There are levels of progression and regression in the spiral journey. It is not a neat linear progression, but a complex up-and-down movement along the spiral. There was movement and development up the spiral, but it was dynamic. This was particularly true when it came to reflection. The level of reflection depended on the level of trust existing at that point, and fluctuated from task-based reflection through to reflection on the higher self. The level of reflection depended on where the co-researchers found themselves on that day, how they felt, how busy they were, and their energy levels. Be that as it may, co-researchers started to appreciate the value and power of reflection. For many, reflection was a new experience and a vital new skill to learn. Given that they are so task- and output-driven, they had never afforded themselves the opportunity or "luxury" to reflect, even though they knew that they needed to. Coaching provided a disciplined and structured time and place for them to reflect.

Reflection centred on four main themes: a growing awareness of the self, the self in relation to others, the higher self and learning. The first level of reflection was around a growing awareness about the "self". There was the emergent recognition that the "self" was a belief system that had either been adopted about themselves or accepted from others. It was the dawning realization that in many instances the "self" was the product of social conditioning. This in turn led to co-researchers having to deconstruct their understanding of the "self". This deconstruction included such fundamental beliefs as my relationship to God; what is right and wrong for me; what is marriage; is it possible to love two people at the same time; what does it mean to be gay in the workplace; am I good enough; how have I become these labels that have been given to me; the continuous need to perform and succeed to prove myself; am I more than pure IQ, logic and reason; how have my failures resulted in me getting stuck with a certain self-image?

Within the context of an open, enquiring and trusting relationship, coaching provided a safe environment where the deconstruction of these fundamental beliefs could take place. More importantly, however, coaching provided the environment and support for reconstruction and experimentation with new beliefs and insights. The coach did not do the work; the coach only provided the support for the work to be done by the co-researchers. This reconstruction included creating their own belief systems about God, marriage, exploring alternative religious belief systems which was not possible before, being gay and how it contributed to leadership, and learning to forgive oneself for past failures and move on. These reconstructed beliefs of the "self" were their own, free from the labels and beliefs that other people had imposed on them. This brought with it a feeling of freedom and lightness. There was the joy of discovering a "truer self" which had more meaning for them.

The second level of reflection was around a growing awareness of the self in relation to others. Having realized how their self-concept had often been as a result of social conditioning, the co-researchers became more aware of how their own feelings, beliefs and behaviours had an impact on their teams and clients. There was the awareness that their own insecurities and need to succeed and perform, the need to be liked, fear of rejection and failure, and their own agendas, were often being projected onto their teams and management. Once again, within the context of the coaching relationship they were able to reconstruct their belief systems and explore and experiment with alternative behaviours. New behaviours included more proactive communication and interaction with management; giving their teams the opportunity to develop and learn, succeed and fail; transferring responsibility and accountability on to the teams; making people more responsible for their own development; reducing the focus on task and output; learning to coach and support teams to reflect and become more aware of things; and making use of a more facilitative approach to management. More importantly, there was the awareness that people are not labels, but individuals who are different and unique, just as they are unique. In response to this there was more of a willingness to be open to others instead of labelling them.

For a few co-researchers the level of awareness extended to the transpersonal realm. This level of awareness is closely related to the level of self-awareness as the one leads into the other and *vice versa*. Awareness of the self was intimately related to the concept of God. This is not uncommon among people who have had a strong religious upbringing. Here the tension was between what had been taught, via various institutions and belief systems, and the person's actual experience. There was a clash between the belief system and the felt experience. This led to questioning and challenging the old belief system about God, and then the creation of a new belief system via reflection, deconstruction and active experimentation. The transpersonal awareness led to the realization that self is not limited to the mind. This immediately raises the question, "well, then, who am I?" For them it is the realization that who they are is not limited to the body and the mind, there is the experiential realization that "I am". In all major spiritual traditions the "I am" is recognized as the Higher Self, the realization that God and I are one. Once again there is strong evidence that within the context of an open, enquiring and trusting coaching relationship there is the freedom to reflect (deconstruct) and to experiment (reconstruct) with beliefs, feelings and behaviours.

The fourth level of awareness centred on learning. The initial awareness was brought about by making use of the Learning Styles Inventory, which each co-researcher was asked to complete. The coach and co-researchers then worked through the scores to determine their preferred learning style. The coach in turn shared his Learning Styles profile with each of the coachees, the assumption being that if all the learning styles were made explicit, learning could be more effective. Co-researchers found it to be a meaningful exercise, and started to have a better understanding of how and why they learnt in a particular way. At the same time they had an understanding of what the coach's profile was and what his learning preference was. This created a level playing field. They knew as much about the coach as the coach knew about them. The coach was not an expert doing something to them. The coach was just a companion who could journey and explore their lives with them. By being made aware of their learning style they increased their awareness of themselves. The awareness varied from being aware of their strengths and weaknesses to realizing that they have powerful abilities, like conceptualization skills and the ability to apply those concepts in practice.

Understanding their preferred learning style and the experiential learning processes enabled co-researchers to experiment and work with Personal Learning Contracts in their day-to-day work environments. In so doing, the learning experience was made explicit. This in turn enabled co-researchers to start reflecting on how they learn. Hence, the realization for many of the co-researchers of how important reflection was for effective learning. Given the fact that the co-researchers work in an information technology company, the emphasis had always been on doing (concrete experience) and learning new technologies (abstract conceptualization). They learnt new technologies and applied them in an environment that emphasizes and rewards output. What was missing in their learning experience was the ability to reflect and to actively experiment with new thinking, beliefs, feelings and behaviours. Once again, coaching provided a safe space where co-researchers could reflect on and experiment with their own learning in an explicit way. It was this reflection and active experimentation that led to learning and personal growth. *"The learning I have experienced in this time through coaching can not be accounted for in terms of some 'desirable business or efficiency-based outcome' or some improved test score—it has been a deeply personal journey which has resulted in a more whole being and as a natural result a more focused and efficient employee. This seems counter-culture, but it's true."*

As the co-researchers became more self-aware, and aware of the self in relation to others, the Higher Self and about how they learn, they moved from dependency to more self-autonomy. As a result of the reflection, enquiry and trust, co-researchers became aware of what they believed, what they felt and why they behaved like they do. Because co-researchers came to this awareness by themselves, they started to take responsibility for their own lives. In so doing they transferred the power back from the coach to themselves. The truth suddenly dawned on them that the coach would do nothing for them except sincerely enquiring and pointing out their defences regarding their self-awareness and their underlying assumptions. Hence the movement away from "what can the coach do for me?" to "what can I do?" The first manifestation of the movement away from dependency to self-autonomy was when the co-researchers started taking responsibility for their own learning and setting their own agendas for the coaching sessions. There was even the "owning" of the fact that they should have changed the coaching approach when they realized that it was not working for them. They started to own their own projections.

As they began to take more responsibility and accountability for their own lives, the self-autonomy expanded into areas such as being more assertive, empowered and confident. Being more assertive and confident led to co-researchers becoming more focused on what is expected of them, what they have to deliver, and what their parameters are. Hence they were more able and confident to say no. Through reflection, co-researchers were able to identify what value they really added to the company, and with that came a feeling of being more empowered. This in turn gave them more confidence to break with the norm and to challenge. The rise in confidence and assertiveness, as well as the awareness of themselves in relation to others, made co-researchers more willing to delegate, and to push responsibility and accountability down to the level of where the work should be done. By delegating some of the day-to-day activities, co-researchers applied what they had learnt from coaching, and started to coach their own teams and subordinates. Applied learning is a powerful example of people becoming more self-autonomous.

As self-autonomy grew, co-researchers started to shed their victim mentality. Instead of sitting around and waiting to see what would happen in an organizational restructure, certain co-researchers started to experiment with alternative ideas of how to influence the outcome. Given the current socio-political environment in South Africa, where affirmative action is the order of the day, a white male victim mentality prevailed. For specific co-researchers the shedding of the white male victim mentality was a truly liberating experience. There was the realization that "with my training, education, skills and experience I am still very marketable even though I am white, male and over 40." The growth in self-autonomy was confirmed by the feedback from managers and peers.

Through the building of a trusting, nonjudgemental relationship, a growing ability to reflect, and the willingness to take personal responsibility for their own learning and development, the co-researchers became more willing to experiment with alternative ways of thinking and behaving. This experimentation was evident in the way they conceived and behaved towards themselves, other people, the Higher Self, and the way they learnt, which in turn led to more autonomous behaviour.

More autonomous behaviour, reflection and active experimentation was extended into more complex levels of work. As co-researchers started to question the value that they added to the organization, they started to develop more strategic levels of thinking and behaviour. The first step was to start thinking beyond their functional areas into understanding the business as a whole, to think in terms of processes instead of isolated functions. In doing that, co-researchers were able to improve their ability to distinguish between day-to-day and strategic issues. Once again, there was the realization that they could do this effectively only if they took the time to extract themselves from detailed operations and reflected on what they were doing. This in turn enabled them to align themselves with the company's strategic business objectives and themes, to reflect on the current strategy, and to take corrective action where necessary.

Despite a public acknowledgement that the company had a Balanced Scorecard in place, there was evidence that some co-researchers were starting to work with the Balanced Scorecard for the first time. When they tried to find the company's Balanced Scorecard they could not find it. Like most organizations there was a difference between the espoused theory and the theory in use. This made it difficult for them to align their functional area with that of the company. Despite this, they started to design Balanced Scorecards for their functional area of responsibility. In so doing, they experienced the difficulties involved in trying to operationalize strategic thinking and align people with those strategic thrusts. This in turn raised an awareness of the difficulties and complexities in leading large complex organizations at a more strategic level. There was a realization that action without disciplined review and reflection is a useless activity. What is the use of a strategic plan when it is not used to determine whether the business unit is on track with the desired strategy or not? At this level, review and reflection became even more critical. There was the joy of having developed a strategic vision and plan which was aligned with the company's vision, and getting the team to buy into the vision and plan.

A number of co-researchers realized that they had to put certain organizational structures and processes in place to achieve their desired strategies. Strategies are often not realizable because the appropriate structures and processes are not in place to support the strategy. Even worse is the fact that the existing structures and processes actually work against the desired strategy.

In conclusion the coaching experience is best summed up in the words of my co-researchers, "*The aims that I set out for myself for coaching did not materialize. I did not get the content I was aiming for; instead I got the me I was looking for. I can't say I would not have survived the year without coaching, or would have been divorced by now, without coaching. What I can say is that where there should have been a scar there is now thankfulness and peace.*" And "*The context of the learning that I speak about in this essay is very important. There is no doubt that the coaching experience has contributed significantly to my learning (more like development) in this period ... Coaching has been a place that has provided learning in its own right; it has also been a place where experience, opinion, problem and question find competent debate, reflection and perspective. ... The learning I have experienced in this time through coaching can not be accounted for in terms of some 'desirable business or efficiency-based outcome' or some improved test score—it has been a deeply personal journey which has resulted in a more whole being and as a natural result a more focused and efficient employee. This seems counter-culture, but it's true.*"

Research findings

For my Doctoral thesis (Chapman, 2006) I developed the Integrated Experiential Coaching Model, applied and researched the outcomes of being coached within the context of this model. The research involved a phenomenological exploration of the individual's subjective learning experience while being coached within the context of the Integrated Experiential Coaching model. Although this research project never set out to test the integrity of the Integrated Experiential Coaching Model, it is worth noting that the research evidence did support the integrity of the model. There was evidence that people explored the upper-left quadrant in some detail. They wrote about their inner feelings and cognitive insights. This reflection happened on various levels of consciousness. There was even evidence of people moving into the transpersonal level of consciousness.

There was the changing of personal behaviours which falls into the upper-right quadrant. This changed behaviour varied from being more focused, to breaking with the norm and challenging the *status quo*. There was evidence of an increased ability to delegate and an increased willingness and ability to make and take more difficult business decisions.

There was the realization that social norms and group culture, which is the domain of the lower-left quadrant, do actually have an impact on the individual. The co-researchers felt and realized how certain belief systems were inherited or taken from others. On a corporate level there was the realization of how destructive or constructive corporate politics could be. There was the development of a meaningful vision that was supported by staff and senior management. All of these are examples of activities in the lower-left quadrant.

There was the implementation of corporate structures and business processes to implement their strategies and plans. There was the designing and implementation of a Balanced Score Card as well as governance structures. These activities are evidence that the lower-right quadrant was part of the learning experience as well.

Furthermore, there was ample evidence that co-researchers were working at various levels of consciousness as well as on a cognitive, affective, emotional and spiritual level. It was therefore hypothesized that experiential learning as an exemplar of the Integrated Experiential Coaching Model can facilitate growth and development at various levels of consciousness and in all four quadrants. And in so doing, it helped to facilitate the processes in individuals to become self-organized learners. The essential characteristics of a Self-Organized Learner are:

• When an individual accepts responsibility for managing their own learning and is no longer dependent on other people's directives and initiatives. The individual gives personal meaning to the events.
• The individual becomes aware of how they learn; in other words, they start to reflect on the functional components of the learning processes. That is, they can recognize their need and translate it into a clearly-defined purpose. They develop their own strategies to achieve the purpose, and are able to recognize the quality

of the outcome they have achieved. More importantly, they can critically review the learning cycle and implement more effective learning cycles. Through the use of Personal Learning Contracts and project plans, co-researchers in this project reflected more on the functional aspects of their personal learning processes.

- The individual learns to appreciate the dynamic nature of the personal learning process, while at the same time striving for more self-organized learning. There was the realization that coaching and learning is a dynamic journey of self-discovery.

- To learn how to learn by continually challenging their existing partially developed skills. The aim being to transform these skills in order to achieve higher standards of personal competence. The research showed that there was an increased ability to recognize and trust individual feelings, intuition and experience, and use these to their advantage.

- For the individual to recognize the value of S-O-L and to practise it as a way of life regardless of the social context. Co-researchers realized that life is an integrated whole, and that learning applies to all areas of life.

- The individual redefines S-O-L in their own terms in such a way that the S-O-L expertise generates new dimensions of personal innovation and experimentation.

- Individuals constantly strive for quantum improvements in their own ability to learn. The person becomes better at learning on the job, from training courses, from experienced colleagues, and from their own and other people's mistakes. As co-researchers became more aware of how they learn, they started to expand the learning into other areas of their lives.

Based on the research findings it was hypothesized that the Integrated Experiential Coaching Model facilitated both the prehension and transformational dimensions of experiential learning in individuals. The co-researchers understood and owned some significant behavioural dynamics inside of themselves, as well as between themselves and other significant colleagues. This underlines the possibilities of coaching as a staff development intervention to facilitate self-authorization by working through one's own unconscious and dynamic behavioural issues. It is hypothesized that coaching presented from this model empowers individual employees to work towards their own cognitive insight, the experience of emotional meaningfulness and taking of responsibility for their own growth and career development.

As a result of the research findings, and the feedback that Human Resources (HR) had received from coachees and their supervisors, the HR manager responsible for organizational development and training started to ask a number of pertinent questions. Why were people so enthusiastic about the coaching intervention? As a coachee herself, and based on feedback she received, she started to ask why individuals were learning faster through coaching than traditional training methods and interventions. For years HR had tried to get employees to take responsibility and accountability for their own training and development, without any success. Yet with coaching they started to experience a growing demand for the service. People actually started to ask HR whether they could continue with coaching once the research project had stopped.

On further investigation I discovered what Dotlich and Cairo (1999) refer to as the Mass-Customization of Learning. They point out that we are seeing the de-emphasis of the one-size-fits-all type of training. In their view, this is a trend that will continue to grow as organizations start to realize and value the individuality of their leaders, customers and managers. They point out that training pro-grammes are failing to help individuals deal with change initiatives, because change impacts people differently. The point is that these programmes and training initiatives need to account for how each individual deals with change, or they will not work. Their Action Coaching model is an attempt to mass-customize training. Although the process and model does not change from person to person, it does take the individual's needs and development issues into consideration.

This is a significant insight that was critical in the development of Almaas's (1998a) enquiry methodology as well. His insight was, however, not limited to organizational training and development. He looked at teachers whose teachings are timeless and universal, like Buddha, Christ and Mohammed. He then asked himself why it is that despite the millions of people who adhere to their teachings, very few actually reach the levels of enlightenment that the founding teachers did. Traditionally the blame for this lack of enlightenment has been laid at the feet of the student, who was seen as being either too lazy or too undisciplined. Almaas disagrees, in that he sees the problem being due to teachers following a generalized teaching approach:

> We are seeing more and more that teaching cannot be done in a general way. Universal teaching, regardless of how deep and true, must be tailored to the specific needs of the particular individual. Otherwise, the teaching will be ineffective, and it is no fault of the student (Almaas, 1998b:15).

By this Almaas (1998b:13) means that the teacher must take the unique situation of the student as well as his or her level of consciousness into account:

> If the teaching is to be broadly and comprehensively effective, it must be presented in a way that is digestible to the average person, and digestible to the student. This is a matter of communication, of appropriateness, of tact, of skill, of understanding. The individual's mind and state of consciousness need to be taken into consideration for the communication to be appropriate and effective ... An effective teacher will handle a situation in a very personal way for the student, taking into consideration the unique situation of the student and his state of consciousness.

Hence Almaas's (1998b) warning that any teaching built around a particular model or a particular state of consciousness is bound to be limited. It will only be effective for people who happen to be at that level of consciousness. No model or particular state of consciousness can be universally applied to all people. Hence Smuts's (1973) call for a new science called Personology. In his view, psychology works with generalizations and ignores the uniqueness of the individual personality. The same could be said of theology. Let this be a warning for the profession of coaching. For it seems to be a pattern that as soon as a discipline or profession matures it tends to start generalizing by trying to apply certain models.

   With hindsight, there is the realization that the power of the Integrated Experiential Coaching Model is that it "mass-customized learning" for individuals. Being a multi-quadrant, multiple-level-of-consciousness model, it allowed for individuals to apply just-in-time learning. Co-researchers set their own learning agendas and used experiential learning through Learning Conversations to learn what they had to learn at a particular point. The coach did not come in with a predetermined learning/training plan or objective. People learnt what they wanted to learn, based on where they were at that particular point. This meant that the learning was very relevant and meaningful for them, and as a result they took responsibility and accountability for their own learning and development.

The Quaker Persuasion Model

In this regard the Integrated Experiential Coaching Model has strong similarities to the "Friendly Disentangling" method or persuasion model. Spears (1998) refers to the persuasion model used by the Quakers Robert Greenleaf and John Moolman. The methodology was first developed by the Philadelphia cloth merchant John Moolman to address the issue of slavery among the Quakers in the eighteenth century. He used the method with individuals and small groups, and within a period of 30 years he almost single-handedly rid the Quakers of slavery. Due to his tireless efforts, by 1770 no Quakers owned slaves. As a result, the Quakers were the first religious group in the United States to formally denounce and forbid slavery among their members. The method that he developed consisted of four principles (Spears, 1998:126–138):

- **There is good in everyone**. The basic assumption is that there is some good in all of us. This good in everyone serves as the foundation for action and learning. For him it would appear that it was better to start from what we have in common, that is the good, rather than starting with what is not so good and from how we differ. The important thing was to try and find common ground from which to build a constructive relationship. In the Integrated Experiential Coaching Model this happened through the Coach and Coachee exploring each other's personal stories.
- **Traditional customs and structures as causes of the problem**. This is the belief that individuals are in very important ways social constructions of the traditional systems and structures within which they are born and socialized. That is, individual behaviours and values are greatly influenced by the traditional system within which they are born and socialized. In this regard, it has some commonality with the post-modern perspective

as well as the Integrated Experiential Coaching Model, which recognizes that any abstract concept will be influenced by the individual's concrete experience and the cultural context in which they have developed. Secondly, the Integrated Experiential Coaching Model recognizes that a system can and is able to produce certain predictable behaviours despite the individuals involved. So, for example, Moolman found that the Quakers' children accepted slavery in part out of love for their parents and community, who in turn had become entangled in slavery and implicitly and explicitly accepted the teaching that slavery was acceptable. This was a very similar situation to what must have happened in Germany with antisemitism and apartheid in South Africa.

- **Friendly and cheerful**. For both ethical and effectiveness reasons act in a friendly and cheerful manner with those with whom you are in actual and potential conflict. For ethical reasons it is important to be friendly, because it is important to respect and care not just for those with whom you agree, but also with those who have a totally different view, values and ethical standards. Given that the Integrated Experiential Coaching Model caters for all four fields of knowledge and various levels of consciousness, it makes it easier to accommodate coachees who do have different views, values and standards because the coach is not fixated on any particular model, technique, methodology, discipline or school of thought. The coach knows that every one of these is a partial truth and not the whole truth.

- **Continuous, experimental action-learning**. John Fox, who was one of the founders of Quakerism, started his journal with the phrase "This I knew experientially". For Fox, Moolman and Greenleaf the emphasis was on experimental learning, toward action preceding learning, and toward learning through experimental action. Critical to their method was the idea that experimentation needs to be continuous. On closer inspection, however, one can soon see that they were using a form of experiential learning.

So how does the persuasion model work?

- Firstly, it is important to frame oneself in a "we" fellowship with others, and look for the source of the current problematic behaviour within the biases of an embedded tradition system, rather than solely within the behaviours and governing values of the individual. This basically means that we must look at how the prevailing culture, structures and procedures contribute to the individual's behaviour, all the time remembering that there really is some good in every individual. Basically it means accepting the person for who they are and that, for the most part, they are basically good people. At the same time recognize that some cultural or system level bias might be entangled with the individual behaviour, and we usually co-create those cultures. Once again, this is very similar to the approach adopted in the Integrated Experiential Coaching Model, where the question always asked is whether the problematic behaviour is an individual characteristic, or due to systems, structures, processes or procedures.

- Approach those involved in a friendly manner. Your approach to the people involved should be friendly and respectful, not adversarial or critical. That is why in the Integrated Experiential Coaching Model it is important to explore each other's stories in an open, inquisitive way. It is about openly exploring another person's experience, all the time remembering that any view is not "the truth" but a partial truth.

- Ask for help in disentangling a problematic behaviour from potential biases within "our" embedded tradition system. Remember that you share the situation with the individual. It is not an "I versus you" situation. Coming from a lofty position does not help; people just close up. Rather, ask for help in trying to understand where they are coming from, and which cultural biases are at play. The Integrated Experiential Coaching Model helped facilitate a similar process: "The ability to go through my life history with the mentor was a good exercise for me as it helped me realize where I had come from and where I was".

- Work with alternative behaviours and/or governing values that do not rest on the troublesome biases of the tradition system. This involves asking the other person to experiment with different behaviours or actions. This is where active experimentation comes into action. You don't ask them to do everything in a new way. All you do is ask them to experiment with a new possibility.

Moolman, for example, found it intolerable that Quakers, who have a fundamental belief that God is in every individual, could support an unjust system like slavery. That was their concrete experience. He then asked them to help him disentangle a problematic behaviour (supporting slavery) from potential biases within their embedded tradition system. What he was asking them to do was to participate in reflective observation. What they discovered through the reflective observation was that most Quakers believed that Negroes were very lazy, and that they could not work as hard as free white labourers. He then got them to reflect on this experience and assumption even further. What they hypothesized was that Negroes were actually lazy because they had nothing to work for. No matter how hard they worked, they would always be slaves; they could never improve their lot in life. Free whites, however, could become wealthier through working harder. So they hypothesized that slaves would work harder if they owned their own property. This hypothesis was their abstract conceptualization.

To test this hypothesis, Moolman asked them to perform an active experiment, which they did. He asked the Quaker farmers to free their slaves and grant them sharecropping opportunities. As a result of this experiment, the Quakers became the most profitable farmers. The remarkable thing was that Moolman did this one farmer at a time. Within 20 years, many farmers had adopted this ethical and political-economic reform, and by 1800 slavery was eliminated in Pennsylvania.

Greenleaf used exactly the same principles and approach to create and bring about equal employment opportunities for women at AT&T. Prior to employing this approach, women could not do technical work because they were not strong enough to carry 50-pound rolls of telephone wire. By going through this approach, they experimented with 25-pound rolls of wire. It was found that women could comfortably carry 25-pound rolls of wire. As a result, more women were hired to work in the technical field. Greenleaf did the same with black management development at AT&T. By using the same approach between 1955 and 1964, before the passage of the 1968 Civil Rights Act in the United States, AT&T managed to increase their black managers from about 0.5 per cent to about 4.5 per cent of total employed managers. (It might be a model worth investigating and applying in South Africa, in regard to Affirmative Action targets).

The beauty of the model is that, like the Integrated Experiential Coaching Model, it can empower the individual to work towards their own cognitive insight, the experience of emotional meaningfulness, and taking of responsibility for their own growth through experimenting with alternative cognitions and behaviours. In both cases, the knowledge is not forced on the individual. Both models actively engage the individual to explore their own assumptions, to try and understand their behaviour, to ask the individual to come up with a hypothesis of why that is the case, and then to explore and experiment with alternative assumptions and behaviours. In so doing, new cognitive and behavioural patterns are established over time.

The Corporate Leadership Council

In 2003 the Corporate Leadership Council published a report titled *Maximizing Returns on Professional Executive Coaching*. The report stemmed from research that the Council had undertaken at the request of its members into the effectiveness of executive coaching as a development intervention. The key findings of the research were as follows (Corporate Leadership Council, 2003:viii):

- **A growing trend**. Around the world organizations were getting excited about the positive impact of coaching as a leadership development intervention. From Table 14 it can be seen that executive coaching was among the top five development interventions and ranked well ahead of any other formal developmental programme. In addition, other forms of formal training were not as highly valued as coaching. The highest-ranking formal training course was people-management at number eight, followed by technical skills courses at number 16. Yet despite the strong preference for coaching, the Council found that organizations were ineffective at providing executives with coaching as an intervention.
- **A costly intervention**. Although executives have a strong preference for executive coaching, they were concerned about the cost of coaching interventions as opposed to other leadership development activities. They believe that external professional coaching is possibly the most expensive option in leadership

Table 14. Executives' preferred option for developmental intervention.

Development programme	Overall rank
Amount of decision-making authority	1
Creating leadership development plan	2
Interacting with peers	3
Meeting with an executive coach	4
Meeting with a mentor	5
Feedback	6
Turning around a struggling business	7
People-management skills course	8
Working in a new functional area	9
Working in a foreign country	10
Working in a new line of business	11
Launching a new business	12
Number of direct reports	13
Quality of direct reports	14
Off-site seminars in business skills	15
Technical skills courses	16
Business skills courses	17

Source: Adapted from Corporate Leadership Council (2003:6).

development interventions, and as a result HR departments are under increasing pressure to justify the expenditure. The demand for return on investment can be expected to grow.

• **Inconsistent implementation.** Despite the excitement around coaching interventions, organizations are not managing coaching investments in a coordinated or consistent manner.

• **Inconsistent returns.** Returns on coaching engagements varied across member organizations. The Council found that poorly implemented coaching interventions were unreliable as a driver of improvements in employee or business performance. That is, coaching engagements may not always achieve the expected positive outcome. The Council found that the presence of coaching does not guarantee performance improvement and shows variable returns on coaching at individual level, as can be seen in Figure 23.

• **Council response.** As a result of these findings the Council identified five challenges that impede the development of positive

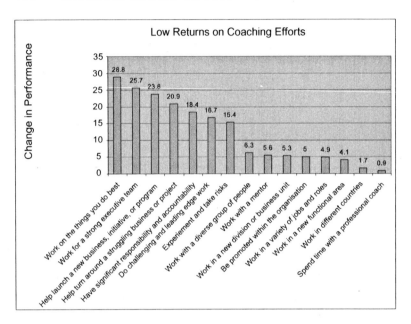

Figure 23. Low returns on coaching effort.
Source: Adapted from Corporate Leadership Council (2003:8).

coaching engagements and the linkage of these engagements to business results. The five challenges are:

- **Difficulty finding "best fit" professional coaches.** The big challenge is to identify suitable coaches, due to the abundance of coaches and the absence of coordinated coach recruitment practices. This is mainly due to the fact that the coaching market is unregulated, with coaches operating without clearly defined professional standards and accreditation. Added to that is the fact that many organizations recruit coaches on a case-by-case basis, which leads to the duplication of selection efforts and preventing the consistent and rigorous scrutiny of the coaches' credentials.
- **Unfocused coaching engagements.** Organizations do not prioritize coaching engagements properly. Often coaching is offered based on the merits of the individual's request rather

than on the business needs and requirements. The Council found that coaching is provided as a development tool for executives, without considering whether the coaching engagement is aligned with business needs.

- **Poor matching of coaching resources to executive requirements.** Effective coaching depends on a positive relationship between the executive and the coach. In fact, Council members indicated that a trusting relationship is a critical variable governing the success or failure of the coaching engagement. The Council found that few organizations are able to effectively match the coaches' experience and personality with the executives' needs and requirements.
- **Disconnect from the organization.** Coaching engagements happen "behind closed doors" which often means that coaching goals do not correspond with business or organizational requirements. Due to the high degree of confidentiality between the coach and coachee, coaching engagements run the risk of diverging from business needs. As a result, coaching fails to generate an ongoing impact on the business. For that reason, many organizations felt that although confidentiality needed to be protected, the absence of managerial reinforcement for the objectives pursued in coaching can limit the effectiveness of the engagements.

This finding opens up an interesting paradox. Schön (1983) points out that the more an organization depends for its survival on innovation and adaptation to a changing environment, the more it is dependent on learning. On the other hand, all organizations need stability and predictability. According to Schön (1983), all organizations are cooperative systems, in that individuals depend on the predictability of each other's responses. Managers need to rely on the predictable behaviours of their subordinates. Hence the need for well-established processes, procedures, roles and responsibilities, and stable outcomes. The problem is that surprise, which is essential to learning, is contrary to organizational predictability and stability. As a result, any noteworthy learning which involves a significant change in the knowledge structure and underlying values, which is essential to organizational adaptation, disrupts the

198 INTEGRATED EXPERIENTIAL COACHING

constancies on which organizational life depends. This creates a dilemma for the organization and the individual:

Reflection-in-action is both a consequence and cause of surprise. When a member of a bureaucracy embarks on a course of reflective practice, allowing himself to experience confusion and uncertainty, subjecting his frames and theories to conscious criticism and change, he may increase his capacity to contribute to significant organizational learning, but he also becomes, by the same token, a danger to the stable system of rules and procedures within which he is expected to deliver his technical expertise. Thus ordinary bureaucracies tend to resist a professional's attempt to move from technical expertise to reflective practice (Schön, 1983:328–329).

Cranton (1996) makes a similar point with regard to transformative learning. Referring to the work of Mezirow, she argues that the dogmatic insistence on learning outcomes that have been specified in advance can hinder transformative learning:

... dogmatic insistence that learning outcomes be specified in advance of the educational experience in terms of observable changes in behaviour or 'competencies' that are used as benchmarks against which to measure learning gains will result in a reductive distortion that serve merely as a device of indoctrination (Cranton, 1996:44).

- **Inconsistent delivery and quality of coaching.** Due to a wide diversity of coaching styles and approaches, organizations find it difficult to effectively implement and manage a performance standard for coaches across the organization. Hence coaching engagements can create variable outcomes across the organization.

How do the integrated Experiential Coaching Model and the research findings relate to the five identified challenges identified by the Corporate Leadership Council?

- **Difficulty finding "best fit" professional coaches.** The coaching market in South Africa is still unregulated, with coaches operating without clearly defined professional standards and accreditation.

The challenge to identify suitable coaches will be around for some time to come. The problem is compounded by the fact that currently, executive coaches are entering the market from backgrounds that vary from psychology, theology, business consulting, management training, and even personal fitness trainers, to name but a few. Even worse is the fact that there are people operating in the market that have had no professional training. The contribution that the Integrated Experiential Coaching Model brings to the profession is that for the first time an integrated executive coaching model has been developed that can be made explicit. It is integrated in that it provides a theoretical framework for human development (Wilber's Integral Model), a method that can be used (experiential learning) to facilitate the development of executive competencies (Jaques and Clement's Leadership Competency Model) within a business context (Kaplan and Norton's Balanced Scorecard). Potential buyers can be taken through the model and understand how the coaching process works and what they are buying. This enables any company to consistently and rigorously scrutinize the coach's credentials, model and way of working.

• **Unfocused coaching engagements**. The Council found that coaching is provided as a development tool for executives, without considering whether the coaching engagement is aligned with business needs. An integral part of the Integrated Experiential Coaching Model is that the coaching experience is placed firmly within the context of the company's business strategy and the operationalization of that strategy. That is why the Balanced Scorecard, especially the last two perspectives (the internal and learning and growth perspectives), are central to the coaching model. In so doing, even though other aspects of the individuals' lives are explored, the coaching stays aligned with the business need and context. Furthermore, part of the process that is followed in the Integrated Experiential Coaching Model is the active participation of the coachee's immediate boss and Human Resources in the coaching processes. They provide input into which areas they would like to see the individual develop in, and they were provided with feedback on an ongoing basis; although it was discovered that this feedback loop needs to be more formalized in future.

• **Poor matching of coaching resources to executive requirements**. Effective coaching depends on a positive relationship between the executive and the coach. In fact, Council members indicated that a trusting relationship is a critical variable governing the success or failure of the coaching engagement. This was one of the key findings of the research project; without trust and respect, learning could not take place. What the research project showed was that a trusting relationship was vital to the coaching engagement. The question has to be asked whether it is realistic to expect that organizations will be able to effectively match the coach's experience and personality with the executives' needs and requirements up-front. It is my opinion that the matching process is more an art than a science, and even with the best intentions, time is needed for a trusting relationship to be established.

• **Disconnect from the organization**. Coaching engagements happen "behind closed doors", which often means that coaching goals do not correspond with business or organizational requirements. As was mentioned above, one of the strengths of the Integrated Experiential Coaching Model is that the coaching experience is firmly grounded in the business context and strategy. The confidentiality issue in this model and research is more complex than in the case with therapy, where confidentiality is clear and absolute. Feedback is given within the organization on a regular basis, to gauge whether the process is still on track or not. Feedback would, however, be in terms of trends and not specifics. In the Integrated Experiential Coaching Model, management and human resources stay actively involved in the process. The Integrated Coaching Model therefore allows for confidentiality to be protected, and for managerial reinforcement of the objectives being pursued. However, being an integral model that works with four quadrants and multiple levels of consciousness, it still allows for the element of surprise, which is essential to learning and contrary to organizational predictability and stability. Because it is self-organized learning, where the individual takes accountability and responsibility for their own learning, the danger of indoctrination is avoided.

• **Inconsistent delivery and quality of coaching**. Based on my research, I am of the opinion that striving for consistent delivery and quality in coaching is an unrealistic illusion that should be dropped. It is an idealistic, romantic illusion based on the belief that coaching can be generalized and mass-produced. What is needed is a paradigm shift from mass-generalized learning to mass-customized learning. My research involved a number of individuals in the same company, coached by the same coach with exactly the same methodology. Although the research could identify general trends, every individual experienced the coaching differently. Within the identified general trends the learning experience was different for every single one of the 13 co-researchers. Even though general trends could be identified, the project showed that even within the same company, with the same coach and methodology, there were variable outcomes.

Coaching as a profession should heed the plea of Smuts (1973) and not fall into the same trap that psychology has, in that as a science, psychology deals with the average or generalized individual, and in so doing it ignores the individual uniqueness of the personality. Coaching which has as its very foundation a trusting relationship, is and will be a function of the individual uniqueness of the personality of the coach and the individual uniqueness of the personality of the coachee. What this study has shown is that despite the same coach and methodology within the same organization, coaching intervention outcomes do vary from individual to individual. The Integrated Experiential Coaching Model does allow for the mass-customization of learning, in that the individual is free to explore learning in any of the four quadrants of knowledge and at any level of consciousness. Furthermore, because it is such an integrated model, learning in any area or level can spill over into other areas or levels of the individual's life. In addition, given the level of complexity involved in coaching in such a complex environment, it should be clear that coaching results will be unpredictable. Cavanagh and Grant (2006:155) sum it up as follows:

> The coaching relationship is essentially a complex adaptive system that exists within, and forms part of, a network of other complex systems. This creates a dynamic system of influence which often renders the causal structure of an event unknowable except in hindsight ... What takes place at any given point in time in the coaching relationship is determined by an almost infinite causal field that is, in the final analysis, unpredictable at anything but a short-term and relatively gross level ... The unique, dynamic adaptive nature of the system formed in the coaching relationship means that coaching (along with most practical psychological interventions) is a radically unpredictable, almost

iterative process in which the next step is informed in large part by the conditions immediately preceding it. This cannot be adequately replicated in laboratory studies, or even in field trials. Each coaching intervention develops in a unique way.

Mintzberg's eight propositions

Although Mintzberg's (2004) study is not directly related to coaching as such, he does argue for a fresh approach to managerial development. Seeing that executive coaching is a relatively new approach to managerial development, I felt it worth comparing my research findings with what Mintzberg (2004) propagates in his eight propositions. Mintzberg challenges the conventional notion that the MBA degree develops managers. Following on his critique of the MBA programmes, Mintzberg (2004) suggests a different approach to develop managers based on eight propositions. Although he expands the propositions in the context of university training, the author believes that they are applicable to coaching as well. In what follows, I will explore those eight propositions (Mintzberg, 2004:243–273), and see whether or not the Integrated Experiential Coaching Model and the research can be related to the propositions.

• **Proposition 1. Management education should be restricted to practising managers.** Mintzberg (2004:242) believes that this development:

> ... begins in a very different place: that it is not 'individuals' who should be developed, but members of a social system in which leadership is embedded; that only those who already have managerial responsibility can be educated and developed as managers ...

This is a very important point of departure, as it raises the all-important question of who is the best judge of leadership potential. Mintzberg (2004) is of the opinion that the participating person cannot be the best judge of leadership potential, nor can some disconnected selection committee in a university. Neither can the coach, for that matter. The selection can only be done by those who have witnessed the individual's potential in action, those people who have worked with the nominated individuals. Management education should be a right, earned by performance as a manager. MBA programmes, on the other hand, rely on self-selection; the candidates apply and the schools select. Mintzberg (2004) believes that management development programmes are more effective when the organization selects its candidates, supports them, and pays for them. In the context of the Integrated Experiential Coaching Model, practising managers are selected for coaching by their managers and the company's Human Resources department. Coaching is aimed at the development of the individual within the context of the business, in that it facilitates integrated experiential learning in individuals in order to enhance personal growth and development with the aim of improving individual and organizational performance. The co-researchers in this project were all in various levels of management, ranging from team leaders (first level of management) to business managers (people reporting directly to the executive). They all brought some level of managerial experience into the coaching project. They were all selected by the organization (the social system) to participate in the project; they did not select themselves.

- **Proposition 2. The classroom should leverage the managers' experience in their education.** It is very important to take the experience of the managers into account, and as such the classroom learning experience must be linked to the person's job. Mintzberg (2004) advocates that managers should stay on the job and attend two-week modules every few months to allow for deep learning without undue disruption to the practice. His feeling is that too much time away from work can be very stressful, while too little time can interfere with serious learning.

    The beauty of the Integrated Experiential Coaching Model is that it does not disrupt the practice at all. The coach and client meet every two weeks for two hours to explore and reflect on the client's experience together. Between sessions, the client actively experiments with the new insights and learning. It is on-the-job experiential learning. Furthermore, Mintzberg (2004) is of the opinion that the most powerful reflection comes from reflecting on experiences that have been lived naturally. Created experiences like action learning and project work should at all times be supplementary to the learning experience and not central to it. Because the individual's natural experience is central to

the learning experience, it is important that management education should be customized for each individual.

Here, Mintzberg (2004), Dotlich and Cairo (1999) are calling for
the same thing, i.e., the mass-customization of learning or management education. The Integrated Experiential Coaching Model
empowered co-researchers to set their own learning agendas and
use experiential learning through learning conversations to learn
what they had to learn at that particular point. The coach did not
come in with a predetermined learning/training plan or objective. People learnt what they wanted to learn, based on where
they were at that particular point. Mintzberg's (2004) call is for
less teaching and more learning in management education (and
the author would add, in management development). Hence
the need for more **learner-centred** management education, as
opposed to **provider-centred** management education. The Integrated Experiential Coaching Model is more learner-centred, in
that the client and the organization set the learning agenda, not
the coach. (Although at times the coach can do some teaching.)

- **Proposition 3. Insightful theories help managers make sense of
their experience.** Mention the word "theory" to managers and
many will balk at the idea, because it is generally seen as a dirty
word. In the world of management, it is practice and not theory
that counts. The problem, however, as Mintzberg (2004) points
out, is that reality is far too complex for anybody to carry around
in their heads. It would be great if we could, and if we could make
decisions based on that knowledge. The truth, however, is that
we all carry around theories, conceptual frameworks or mental
models in our heads that help us to simplify reality and help us
to make sense of it. Hence we better have good theories or mental
models, as Jaques and Clement (1997:77) put it:

> Concepts, theories and ideas are used continuously in everyday
> life. They determine what we see and what we learn from our
> experience. Unsound theories distort our experience, narrow
> our vision, and leave us none the wiser about the effects of our
> action on others ... Action without sound theory is folly.

As Jaques and Clement (1997) have shown, it is impossible to
develop wisdom without good, sound theories. For Mintzberg

(2004), it is not a choice between practice or theory, but rather about working with different theories that inform management practice. The Integrated Experiential Coaching Model has been an attempt to develop a theoretical executive coaching model that can be applied in practice. In my doctoral research a number of theories were explored and either found useful in the learning process, or not very relevant. Some theories that were introduced were Learning Conversations and Personal Learning Contracts, the Balanced Score Card, Kolb's (1984) preferred learning styles and Transpersonal theory. An example of a theory that was explored and found not to be very helpful was the Enneagram.

- **Proposition 4. Thoughtful reflection on experience in the light of conceptual ideas is key to managerial learning**. Here Mintzberg (2004) is in complete agreement with Schön (1983) that all managers need to develop the time and capacity for reflection-in-action, which is concurrent learning. As Kolb (1984) has pointed out, it is the reflective aspect and active experimentation (transformation dimension) that leads to the discovery of meaning. So reflection is about discovering meaning. In Mintzberg's (2004) view reflection is not casual. It is difficult and messy and involves wondering, probing, analyzing, connecting and synthesizing. The importance of personal reflection was one of the learning themes that emerged from this study project. There was the realization that reflection was the first step towards changed behaviour. Although all reflection is ultimately personal, Mintzberg (2004) does believe that managers do benefit from reflecting collectively. The time away from the job, in the classroom, allows for what Beard and Wilson (2002) call reflection-on-action (retrospective learning). Management education should encourage managers to reflect collectively on their own experience. For, as Mintzberg (2004) argues, faculty members have to appreciate that managers can learn as much from each other as they can from the faculty. And for that matter, faculty can learn a tremendous amount from practising managers.

By its very nature, the Integrated Experiential Coaching Model accommodates reflection-on-action. But the reflection-on-action is limited to coach and client. I tend to agree with Mintzberg that there is enormous value to be gained by getting the managers to reflect collectively. In fact, very early in the coaching project, it was realized that enormous benefits could be gained by getting all the managers who were being coached to reflect collectively. The client and I wanted to organize dedicated day sessions where we would explore what the group was learning collectively from the coaching experience. Not only that, given the functional nature of the organization, it could facilitate the breaking-down of the existing functional silos. The idea was, however, dropped when it was pointed out that such a process could in fact corrupt the research data. The aim of the project was to explore the subjective learning experience of each individual, not to explore the collective learning experience. (Although in the end, the methodology did identify common themes from the subjective experiences.) Put differently, the research was aimed at the upper-left quadrant and not the lower-left quadrant. Collective reflection is a function of the lower-left quadrant. Be that as it may, this project did convince us that the lower-left quadrant is worth exploring, and hence my agreement with Mintzberg that collective managerial reflection can contribute enormously to managerial education and learning.

- **Proposition 5. "Sharing" their competencies raises the managers' consciousness about their practice**. This proposition ties in with Proposition 4, especially in terms of collective managerial reflection. In fact, Mintzberg (2004:261) encourages managers and educators to think of this in the spirit of reflection, in that it is about raising consciousness about competencies:

> Competency sharing is not about how a particular competency might be practised, according to some general theory, or should be practised, according to some article, but how it has been practised by those managers in the room—what has worked and not worked for them. They simply get a chance to air and compare their practices.

It does not matter whether what comes out is good or bad, profound or silly. The aim is to expose and explore alternate ways of behaving, just as alternate mental models or theories expose different ways of thinking. By doing this, managers become more aware of their own practices, so that they can continue to learn from their own experiences. Once again, I am in complete agreement with Mintzberg, and believe that it is a critical element in managerial education and learning. This is one of the weaknesses of the current Integrated Experiential Coaching Model, in that it focuses on one-on-one coaching within the business context in which the individual operates. Reflection of competencies is limited to the experience of the client and the coach. The client company and I are currently exploring ways in which we can introduce this element into their leadership development model. The current thinking is that it can be done by having dedicated days where the managers can dialogue issues and competencies collectively. As it currently stands, one-on-one coaching misses this vital element of collective learning, although it can help the individual work with and develop certain competencies. Even Mintzberg (2004:257) admits that coaching has a role to play in this domain:

> Teaching concepts is a relatively straightforward business. But developing competencies—training for skills—is not. It can be difficult and time-consuming, requiring 'learning the basic ideas, experimenting, being coached, receiving feedback' and carrying that learning on.

Teaching concepts is the domain of professors who are hired for their ability to think and do research. They are not known for their ability to teach skills. Teaching skills is the domain of coaches, mentors and of practising managers, who can learn from each other's experience.

- **Proposition 6. Beyond reflection in the classroom comes learning from impact on the organization**. The idea of sending people on programmes so that they become better-developed managers is an incorrect one. Mintzberg (2004) feels strongly that there should not be a disconnect between the learning process and the learning context. In his view, the MBA is personal learning that has resulted in a culture of self-serving managers. Instead, "Management education has to get beyond me and I, at the very least to encourage managers to go beyond themselves—in other words, to approach leadership" (Mintzberg, 2004:262). In his view every manager has to be a teacher; to coach and mentor their subordinates by sharing ideas and experiences. It is a privilege to receive formal education and development, and as such the learner should be the teacher back on the job.

Although the coaching experience was an intense personal journey for the co-researchers, raised self-awareness did help them move beyond themselves. As co-researchers became more aware of their intrapersonal issues, they became more aware of how their own feelings, beliefs and behaviours impacted on the teams they managed. There was the realization that leadership involves more self-autonomy, which enables the leader to delegate personal responsibility to others. The research showed that the Integrated Experiential Coaching Model facilitated the movement beyond the "me and I". In some cases there was even a movement into the transpersonal realms of awareness. But it did not stop there; there was ample evidence that the managers started to apply and teach their staff and teams what they had learnt. Managers even started to teach their subordinates how to use Personal Learning Contracts.

• **Proposition 7. All of the above should be blended into a process of "experienced reflection".** If you blend the previous propositions together, you get what Mintzberg (2004:264) refers to as "experienced reflection":

> ... the managers bring their experience to the classroom, where the faculty introduce various concepts, theories, models ... Reflection takes place where these meet; experience considered in the light of conceptual ideas. The resultant learning is carried back to the job, where it impacts behaviour, providing further experience for reflection on the job and back to the classroom.

Mintzberg's (2004) experienced reflection is none other than Kolb's (1984) Experiential Learning, which in turn is the injunction in the Integrated Experiential Coaching Model. The manager's experience is their concrete experience. Concepts, theories and models are abstract conceptualization. Reflecting on experience in light of conceptual ideas is reflective observation, and taking the learning back to the job to apply it is active experimentation. The only difference is that Mintzberg (2004) is applying it to groups of managers in a process that combines learning modules away from the job and at different universities around the world. The Integrated Experiential Coaching Model, on the other hand, is applying the process to individuals within the work context. I believe that management education and learning will greatly benefit from both approaches. It is not a matter of the one being better than the other, but rather a synthesis of both. Both approaches have their positives and negatives. The research showed that managers had learnt and grown tremendously through the individual coaching approach. Please note that the co-researchers did not credit coaching alone for the learning. Learning had originated in other areas as well. However, coaching had facilitated and accelerated the experiential learning process. The downside of coaching is to be found in pure economics. The one-on-one experiential learning experience is very expensive compared to group experiential learning.

- **Proposition 8. The curriculum, the architecture, and faculty should accordingly be shifted from controlled design to flexible facilitation.** For too long, management programmes have been chopped up into courses and classes, each with its own area of disassociated knowledge and skills. In other words, there is no integration or synthesis of these programmes. For this integration to happen, Mintzberg (2004) believes that there must be less control in management education and more collaboration. In that regard he sees the faculty as being the "… designers of an ongoing social process as much as the conveyers of conceptual knowledge" (Mintzberg, 2004:271). Their task is to convey interesting material to the class, but then to engage everybody with the material. This involves being a part of the learning process and introducing conceptual knowledge on a "just-in-time" basis. More importantly, it is about getting the managers involved in their own learning process. As a result of this research project, the Human Resource Department realized that they needed a more integrated approach to managerial leadership development. They wanted to move away from their current position where they controlled the management development programme, to one where they just facilitated the process. Their aim was to move accountability and responsibility for management learning down to the managers themselves.

Based on the above discussion, it is clear that the Integrated Experiential Coaching Model and the results that it produced in my doctoral research correlate very well with Mintzberg's (2004) eight propositions for managerial education.

Limitations in doing the research

The first limitation that must be considered is my subjectivity. The doctoral research took place within the context of the Integrated Experiential Coaching Model, a theoretical model I had developed. Secondly, I was the coach who applied that model in the coaching experience. Although I made every attempt to be as objective as possible, it is possible that an element of subjective bias can still be contained in the final result. It must, however, be mentioned that Cilliers (2004) analyzed the same data from a systems psychodynamic stance. His findings identified a similar movement from dependency towards more self-autonomy.

A second limitation has to be the sample bias. Firstly, the sample was restricted to one company, and I did not select the sample. The client company selected the managers they wanted to have coached in the project. The people selected were considered the future potential leaders of the company. By its very nature, this is a group of people who want to get ahead in life; they are positive and want to learn. The question has to be asked whether the same result would have been achieved if a more random sample was selected. The sample was made up of people who, in a sense, had already achieved and proven themselves within the company, and coaching could just have provided another opportunity for them to apply themselves. The other issue related to sample bias was the lack of gender and racial diversity in the group. There was only one woman and one black person; the rest were all white males. It is possible that similar themes arose because these white males are all struggling with a common issue, which is their future within the South African business context.

The third possible limitation could be due to data collection. Of the 13 participants, only three had English as their mother tongue. The rest are actually Afrikaans. At the outset of the project they were given the option of writing their reflective essays in Afrikaans, but all the participants chose to write the essays in English. This could be due to the fact that, as an international company, all official correspondence is carried out in English. As a result, I am of the opinion that some of the richness of the experience could have been lost in the process of expressing themselves in a second language. From the essays it is clear that some individuals struggled with English grammar. In such circumstances, it is very difficult for individuals to fully express how they feel. With hindsight, unstructured interviews could have been used to explore the issues or experiences even further.

The integrated experiential coaching model in a team context

On completion of the project the client company challenged me to apply the Integrated Experiential Coaching Model to team coaching. The organization wanted more people to experience the benefits and improved performance achieved by individuals who had participated in the programme. A second reason was purely economical: individual coaching was expensive, and they wanted to reap economies of scale. This model of coaching has subsequently been adopted by a major banking group in South Africa, and is being refined all the time. The application of coaching to teams moves the emphasis of the Model to the lower-right quadrant.

Given that the Integrated Experiential Coaching Model is about facilitating experiential learning in individuals, it soon became apparent that the Model could be adapted to teams with the greatest of ease. I have a working hypothesis that Kolb's genius lay in his ability to map out a very natural unconscious process. All that is needed to facilitate learning is to make it conscious and give it some structure. The entire coaching process is therefore about facilitating experiential learning. The first part of the process is highly structured, to allow the team to get to know each other better and to familiarize them with the experiential learning process. It has four simple stages: concrete experience, reflective observation, abstract conceptualization and active experimentation.

The first day usually starts with a check-in and expectations exercise. We then start the process by reviewing where the team currently is, i.e., their concrete experience.

Concrete experience

The process starts with honouring the team's personal experience. The tool that I use to facilitate this part of the process is the Six Psychological Criteria for productive workplaces. Rehm (1997) believes that there are six basic human needs that must be present for human beings to be productive; in fact, he sees them as the foundation for designing effective organizations. In an unaligned organization these six criteria will be adversely affected, or they will not be optimized, which leads to lower productivity. As outlined in Chapter four, the six psychological criteria for productive work are (Benedict Bunker and Alban, 1997:139):

- **Elbow room for decision-making**. People need to know what their parameters are. They need to feel that that they are their own bosses and that, except in exceptional circumstances, they have room to make decisions that they can call their own. On the other hand, they do not need so much elbow room that they do not know what to do.
- **Opportunity to learn on the job and keep on learning**. Learning is a basic human need, and is only possible when people are able to set goals that are reasonable, challenging for themselves, and they get feedback on results in time to correct their behaviour. Without feedback, no learning can take place.
- **Variety**. People need to vary their work to avoid extremes of fatigue and boredom. On the other hand, if people have so much variety due to too much work they become overwhelmed, which leads to high levels of stress. This is a common problem in the modern workplace, where the call is for people to continuously do more with less.
- **Mutual support and respect**. People need to get help and respect from their co-workers.

- **Meaningfulness.** Meaningfulness includes both the worth and the quality of a product, and having knowledge of the whole product and process. The more an individual can see the bigger picture or the bigger process, the more meaningful their work becomes.
- **A desirable future.** People need a job that leads them to a desirable future for themselves, not a dead-end. This desirable future is not necessarily a promotion, but a career path that will continue to allow for personal growth and an increase in skills.

Each individual is asked to rate how they are currently experiencing their job according to the following scales. The rating scale for the first three questions is: –5; –4; –3; –2; –1; 0; +1; +2; +3; +4; +5; where –5 = too little; 0 = just right; +5 = too much. The rating scale for the last three questions is: 0; 1; 2; 3; 4; 5; 6; 7; 8; 9; 10, where 0 = none, 10 = good. After they have rated themselves, they get together in the big group and share their scores. Team members are encouraged to just listen to their colleagues, and they are not allowed to respond. They are allowed to ask clarifying questions, but that is all they are allowed to do. The one rule that is applied is that nobody apologizes for their experience. The rest of the team are encouraged to honour that experience.

Reflective observation

Having completed that exercise, the team is then split into smaller groups, where they are asked to reflect on what they have just experienced, and to answer the question "What did you learn from the previous exercise?" Having explored the question in smaller groups, the big group reconvenes to discuss their learnings.

The big learning which usually arises from this exercise is the phenomenological nature of experiential learning, that two people can experience exactly the same situation of phenomena, yet experience it completely differently. It is not uncommon for structural, process, procedural and role problems to be identified this early in the process.

Abstract conceptualization

At this point I usually introduce the theory of the Integrated Experiential Coaching Model, how the experiential learning process works, and the Clifton StrengthsFinder®. The team is then asked to identify their individual preferred learning style using Kolb's (1984) Learning Styles Inventory (LSI). Based on research and clinical observation of the LSI scores, Kolb (1984) developed descriptions of the characteristics of the four learning styles. As outlined in Chapter two, the four descriptions are (Kolb, 1984:77–78):

- **The convergent learning style**. Here an individual prefers to employ abstract conceptualization and active experimentation. This approach is strong at decision-making, the practical application of ideas, and problem-solving. This learning style solves problems through hypothetical-deductive reasoning. People who prefer this style of learning prefer to deal with technical tasks and problems. Social and interpersonal issues tend to be avoided.
- **The divergent learning style**. Here the individual prefers to utilize concrete experience and reflective observation. These people tend to like working with people and are more feeling-oriented and tend to be imaginative. They love to look at things from many perspectives and tend towards observation rather than action. They are good at brainstorming because of their ability to generate alternative ideas and to think of the implications of these.
- **The assimilation learning style**. This style draws on abstract conceptualization and reflective observation. Individuals who prefer this style tend to have an ability to create theoretical models, synthesizing disparate observations into meaningful explanations using inductive reasoning. The focus is more on ideas and abstract concepts than on people. Theories are valued more for their precision and logic than for their practical value.
- **The accommodative learning style**. Here concrete experience and active experimentation are employed as the preferred learning abilities. It is action-oriented and excels at getting things done, completing tasks, and getting involved with new experiences. This style is accommodative, because it is best suited for those situations where an individual must adapt to the changing circumstances. These individuals tend to discard plans or theories when they do not suit the facts. Problems are solved in an intuitive, trial-and-error manner. These people tend to rely more on other people for information, rather than on their own analytical ability. Although they are comfortable with people, they can be seen as pushy and impatient.

Again, it must be emphasized that these are preferred learning styles. The ideal is for an individual to move through all four learning styles to optimize learning and growth. The problem, as was mentioned previously, is that individuals tend to get stuck in or concentrate on only one of the four learning abilities, and in so doing limit their own learning, development and performance.

Having identified their own individual learning style, each individual shares their preferred learning style with the others and the group maps out the team's profile. The team then goes into a discussion about what the implications of the individual styles and team profile are for the performance of the team as a whole.

It is interesting to note that Buckingham and Clifton (2002) point out that strength is a combination of an individual's preferred learning style and their natural talent. They point out that a strength needs experiential and factual knowledge (Kolb's concrete experience versus abstract conceptualization) and a skill, which is a series of steps carried out to do something. Those steps can be things you do (active experimentation) or think (reflective observation). And lastly you need talents which are naturally recurring patterns of behaviour, feelings or thoughts. Prior to the coaching intervention, each individual would have been asked to identify their natural talents using the Clifton StrengthsFinder®.

The next step of the process asks each individual team member to share their natural talents with the team. At the same time, the rest of the team is asked to validate or question these talents based on their personal experience and interaction with the individual. At the end of the two exercises, the team will have a reasonable picture of the inherent natural strengths of the team. It is my belief that, given the fast nature of change and the complexity in which large organizations operate, it is vitally important for the coach and the team to identify their natural strengths and learn to put those strengths to work as a team. The Integrated Experiential Coaching Model puts the emphasis on learning and performance, not on pathology. Philosophically, it is on a par with Buckingham and Clifton (2002) in putting the emphasis on maximizing strengths and managing weaknesses.

This usually brings the first day to an end. The day is summarized, showing the team that they have completed most of the experiential learning cycle, namely concrete experience, reflective observation and abstract conceptualization. The day is ended with a check-out process and telling the team that they will engage in another concrete experience after supper.

Storytelling

After supper the team reassembles for a session of storytelling (or for the more academic and scientifically-inclined, narrative). Personally, I am very happy with the term storytelling. I discovered the power of storytelling while I was doing my doctoral research. Storytelling was never designed to be a formal part of the Integrated Experiential Coaching Model. However, I needed something to ground people in their own concrete experience, so I asked them to tell me their life stories and I shared mine, so that we could get to know each other better before we started the coaching journey together. To my absolute surprise, the research revealed that people experienced storytelling in a nonjudgemental environment as very meaningful. We live in a world were we are continually judged and assessed to death by "professionals" who love to tell us who we are, or what we should be, or what is wrong with us. I have found that people find it very meaningful to tell their own subjective stories, because it honours their uniqueness. Storytelling to me is what Jan Smuts referred to as the discipline of "personology".

As discussed in Chapter two, Jan Smuts (1973) suggested that "Personology" should be studied by analyzing the biographies of personalities as a whole. This study should be done synthetically, and not analytically as in the case of psychology. This would enable the researcher to discover the materials that can help formulate the laws of personal evolution. Smuts (1973) called this the science of "Biography", or the story behind the uniqueness of every individual.

Accordingly, I ask team members to share their chronological life stories with each other. This is not a T group, so people share what they feel comfortable to share. In my experience as an individual and group coach, storytelling is one of the most powerful and awe-inspiring tools I have ever encountered. Personally, I am always left with a sense of awe, and it has given me an appreciation for the uniqueness of every individual. Teams normally find that in this session they learn so much about their fellow team members.

Assumptions are challenged and prejudices are shattered. We all think we know people when in reality we know so little about each other. We love to label and put each other in boxes. Storytelling, in my experience, tears open all those neat psychological boxes, leaves them in tatters and exposes a unique human being, a mystery that will never be fully known or classified. It gives us the freedom to explore our own unique journey.

Active experimentation

On the second day I usually contract with the team about an issue they want to explore in coaching. Once the contracting has been done, we get to work exploring the issue using the experiential learning process. What is the issue we want to work on? (Concrete experience). Why is it an issue? Why is it manifesting? (Reflective observation). What are our options? What are the different scenarios? (Abstract conceptualization). This is where we formulate our own theory of the problem, and how we are going to fix it. At the same time, the team is reminded of what they had learned and experienced about each other on the previous day. So one option is to consider how we are best going to use each other's strengths as a team to deal with the issue at hand. Who is the best person to do what? How can we compensate for any glaring weaknesses that are inherent in the team around the issue at hand? Lastly, we come up with an action plan for the way forward, the next steps, with roles and responsibilities and timelines attached. (Active experimentation).

The second day is concluded by contracting a follow-up coaching session and date (or to conclude the coaching intervention). The final part is a check-out.

Follow-on coaching interventions

Any follow-up intervention will start with a review of how the plan (active experimentation) actually materialized (concrete experience), and a review of where the team is at (reflective observation). The process will then start all over again, by contracting the issue at hand to be explored. It is a process of ongoing experiential learning.

Conclusion

At this point it is worth returning to Figure 23 in Chapter five and revisiting the results of the research undertaken by the Corporate Leadership Council (2003). You will remember that their research showed that spending time with a professional coach led to 0.9 per cent change in performance for the individuals being coached. Compare that to the 28.8 per cent change in performance brought about by an individual being able to work on the things they do best. Further, compare it with the 25.7 per cent change brought about by working for a strong executive team (which, in turn, is possible only if the individuals in that team are allowed to work on the things they do best).

The research speaks for itself: it is better to focus on strengths, rather than on what is wrong. Having significant responsibility and accountability, which ties in with Rehm's elbow room for decision-making, yielded an 18.4 per cent change. And meaningfulness, which is having challenging and leading-edge work, yielded a 16.7 per cent change. I also find it interesting that experimentation and taking risks, which are integral parts of this team coaching methodology, were found to bring about a change in performance of 15.4 per cent.

In conclusion, team coaching using the Integrated Experiential Coaching Model is about facilitating experiential learning within the context in which the team finds itself. Its major assumptions are that we are all unique, with inherent strengths and weaknesses, and that we can all learn effectively. Experiential learning is a natural process that we all identify with once it has been made explicit. Combined with our natural talents, it yields strengths that should be harnessed with the greatest of ease to improve team performance. And it does so by consciously making a choice to identify strengths and to use them. It is about harnessing the natural potential of individuals and teams, rather than focusing on what is wrong.

CHAPTER SEVEN

The impact of stress on learning

Lloyd Chapman and Sunny Stout Rostron

Stress and the management of complexity – by Lloyd Chapman

I now want to turn my attention to the upper-right quadrant. One area that continuously worried me while developing and researching the Integrated Experiential Coaching Model was the impact that stress could and does have on a manager's ability to manage complexity. To do that, I need to recap slightly on stratified systems theory and complexity. Complexity was defined as "... a function of the number of variables operating in a situation, the ambiguity of these variables, the rate at which they are changing, and the extent to which they are interwoven so that they have to be unravelled in order to be seen" (Jaques and Clement, 1997:xvii). We know that these variables can be numerous and very elusive; there can be hundreds if not thousands of variables that contribute to the success or failure of an organization. Given that these variables interact in both observable and non-observable ways, "true prediction and control are elusive". In short, the reason that executives sometimes find it difficult to implement their designed strategies is because they become overwhelmed by the complexity involved with modern managerial leadership.

According to Jaques and Clement (1997), Cognitive Power is one of five individual competencies required to effectively manage the levels of complexity involved:

- **(CP):** Cognitive power (CP) is the potential strength of cognitive processes in an individual and is, therefore, the maximum level of task complexity that the individual can handle at any given point in his or her development. CP is the maximum number, ambiguity, rate of change, and interweaving of variables that an individual can process in a given period of time. CP is the necessary level of cognitive complexity required to manage the level of task complexity of the specific managerial role. Underpinning CP are the cognitive processes by means of which an individual is able to analyze, organize and synthesize information to make it available for doing work. Jaques and Cason's (1994) research found that there are only four mental patterns or types of mental processes that individuals use:
  - **Declarative processing**: The individual explains their position by using a number of separate reasons. Each reason is seen as separate, and no attempt is made to connect the reasons. They stand alone and independent of each other. This processing has a declarative quality.
  - **Cumulative processing**: The individual explains their position by bringing together a number of ideas. The individual ideas are insufficient to make the case, but taken together, they do. This processing has a pulling-together quality.
  - **Serial processing**: Here the individual builds up an argument through a sequence of reasons, each reason building on the other. Ultimately, the result is a chain of linked reasons.
  - **Parallel processing**: Using serial processing, the individual explains their position by examining a number of other possible positions as well. The lines of thought are held in parallel, and can be linked to each other. It involves working with various scenarios at the same time. This kind of processing has a conditional quality. Not only do the various scenarios link with each other, but they can condition each other.

By combining these observable thinking patterns with the observable levels of information complexity (concrete order, symbolic order, abstract conceptual order, and universal order), Jaques and Clement (1997) were able to develop their categories of complexity of mental processing. Using these categories of mental processing they were able to define an individual's current potential capability (CPC) by observing and analyzing the mental processes being used. They showed that it is possible to identify the amount of complexity any individual could handle, at that point of their development, by observing and analyzing their thinking processes. They concluded that there are categories of complexity of mental processes, and that they mature over time. Individuals become completely overwhelmed by complexity when their cognitive power does not match the level of task complexity demanded of them. This could be due to the individual not having matured into the required cognitive complexity, or they simply do not have what it takes. However, although cognitive power is the most critical requirement to handle organizational complexity, it is not the only criteria for success.

Stress and biofeedback

In my experience as a coach, I have found that, despite having the potential to manage complexity, many executives and senior managers were still overwhelmed by it. The natural question was why it was happening, particularly to people who had the potential and experience to manage complexity. Over time I became more and more convinced that stress was a major factor. As a result, I started to research the impact of stress on cognition. At first I tried to see what academic research had been done in psychology. I soon found that a number of psychological research projects had been undertaken in this area, with one major problem: most of the research had been done on rats. Needless to say, it was a bit disappointing to find that the research was limited to rats. I work with people, not rats.

It was while working with Team Shosholoza (the South African entry) in the 2007 America's Cup Challenge that I became interested in biofeedback and its potential implications for coaching. I turned my research efforts to the field of biofeedback to see if any research had been done on the impact of stress on cognition. I stumbled onto research that the Institute of HeartMath (2001) had been doing in this domain. Theirs is a very novel approach, which I briefly discuss below.

Their research looks at how stress impacts heart rate variability, and how heart rate variability in turn impacts cognition. Heart Rate Variability (HRV), as measured with an electrocardiogram (ECG), measures the beat-to-beat changes in heart rate. Many of us have become so used to wearing heart rate monitors when we exercise that we mistakenly assume the heart beats monotonously and regularly. In reality, the rhythm of a healthy heart under resting conditions is surprisingly **irregular**. These moment-to-moment variations in heart rate are easily overlooked when average heart rate is calculated with a heart rate monitor. The normal variability in heart rate is due to the synergistic action of the two branches of the autonomic nervous system (ANS), the parasympathetic (vagus) nerves, which slow heart rate, and the sympathetic nerves, which accelerate it:

> The mathematical transformation (Fast Fourier Transform) of HRV data into power spectral density (PSD) is used to discriminate and quantify sympathetic and parasympathetic activity and total autonomic nervous system activity. Power spectral analysis reduces the HRV signal into its constituent frequency components and quantifies the relative power of these components. The power spectrum is divided into three main frequency ranges. The very-low-frequency range (VLF) (0.0033 to 0.04 Hz), representing slower changes in heart rate, is an index of sympathetic activity, while power in the high-frequency range (HF) (0.15 to 0.4 Hz), representing quicker changes in heart rate, is primarily due to parasympathetic activity. The frequency range around the 0.1 Hz region is called the low-frequency (LF) band and is also often referred to as the baroreceptor band, because it reflects the blood pressure feedback signals sent from the heart back to the brain, which also affect the HRV waveform. The LF band is more complex, as it can reflect a mixture of sympathetic and parasympathetic activity (Institute of HeartMath, 2001:13–14).

HeartMath research has shown that during mental or emotional stress there is an increase in sympathetic activity which releases the hormone cortisol into the body and increases fibrillation. Figure 24 is an example of an erratic and chaotic heart rate variability pattern

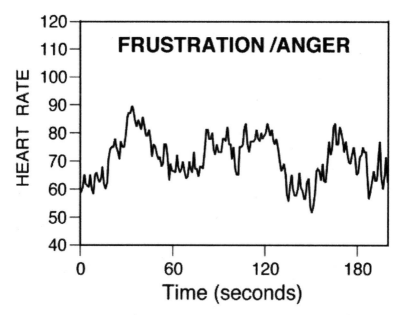

Figure 24. Heart rate variability pattern showing frustration or anger.
Source: The Institute of HeartMath (2001:18).

produced by a negative emotion like anger and/or frustration. Under conditions of severe or prolonged stress an individual will have a similar heart rate variability pattern.

HeartMath (2001) research shows that a chaotic heart rate variability pattern has a negative impact on cognition and leads to what is known as cortical inhibition, and as a result an individual is inclined to experience:

• less ability to think clearly;
• less efficiency in decision-making;
• less ability to communicate effectively;
• reduced physical co-ordination;
• higher risk of heart disease; and
• higher risk of blood pressure.

Most of us know this process from our own experience. A good example is when you walk down a dark alley. There is no danger, but you believe there is potential danger. Physiologically you get anxious; your hands start to sweat, you begin to breathe shallowly, your heart rate speeds up, and your imagination runs away with you. You imagine more and more dangerous things. This is a clear example of how illogical your thinking becomes.

I often see this process being fired-off in the IT clients with whom I work. I have tested this with a number of IT departments in other companies, and the experience seems to be the same. Just imagine the scene: a major IT system has gone down, and the line of business that is affected is "throwing its toys out of the cot". All hell breaks loose, and an emergency meeting is called. If you ask people to tell you what those meetings are like, they are usually very emotional, and it is not uncommon to try to find some person to blame. There is finger-pointing and arguing. In the heat of such emotional turmoil, decisions are often made that later have to be reversed. That is the best-case scenario. In the worst-case scenario, the decisions taken can lead to even bigger problems, because it is actually physiologically impossible to think clearly in such a situation. The group has fallen victim to cortical inhibition: their heart rate variability is not coherent, and as a result they cannot think clearly.

When there is large increase in power in the low-frequency (LF) band (typically around 0.1 Hz) and a decrease in the power in the very-low-frequency (VLF) and high-frequency (HF) bands, heart rhythm coherence develops—a stable, sine-wave-like pattern in the heart rate variability waveform, as shown in Figure 25. Positive emotions (especially love and appreciation), and better stress management, create harmony and coherence in the heart's rhythms and improve balance in the nervous system. The fastest way to get into this frequency or state is to practice deep abdominal breathing and to feel appreciation. More importantly, high HRV coherence has also been found to lead to increased synchronization between the heartbeat and alpha rhythms, as measured by the electroencephalogram (EEG). HRV coherence therefore leads to cortical facilitation, which means that the cortex operates at its optimal level. The more relaxed you are, the easier it is to get into this state.

This coherent pattern leads to:

- improved mental performance and achievement;
- more creativity and problem-solving;

- better decision-making;
- more flexibility in the way we think;
- improved memory; and
- improved immunity to disease.

Having read through the excellent research that the Institute for HeartMath has produced, I began to experiment with various bio-feedback instruments in my coaching sessions. At first I used the Institute of HeartMath's EMwave PC-based system and Wildivine Healing Rhythms. I was pleasantly surprised to see how well managers and executives responded to the biofeedback system, and their desire to work with the systems. The system actually enabled them to measure their stress levels and to see how stress and negative emotions were affecting their heart rate variability. Being a scientist, and being curious by nature, I wanted to start collecting data to enable analysis of the data and to explore what was happening. As a result, I worked with Thought Technology Ltd's Procomt Infiniti equipment, using it extensively in my coaching sessions. I found that

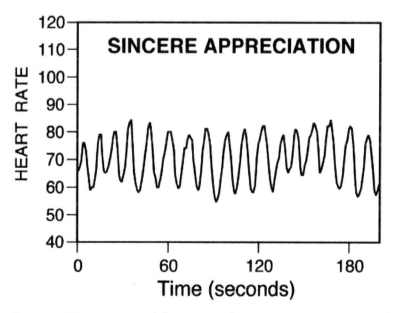

Figure 25. Heart rate variability pattern showing sincere appreciation.
Source: Adapted from the Institute of HeartMath (2001:18).

by allowing the client to spend 20 minutes on the Procomt Infiniti system, during which time they learned to control their heart rate variability, they relaxed very quickly and were ready to engage in the coaching conversation.

Previously, my experience was that people needed quite some time to vent and rid themselves of all their frustration before they could engage effectively and meaningfully in the coaching session. Deep breathing and controlling HRV seems to short-circuit that process. For the first time, I was actually starting to work on an integral level, as opposed to just talking about it. Physiologically we could explore what was happening to the individual and how that was impacting their learning. As a result, my experience has shown that individuals who learn to get into a more coherent heart rate variability pattern, through effective stress management, are able to significantly improve their experiential learning in coaching. The more relaxed an individual is, the more effectively they learn, which in turn increases their ability to manage managerial complexity. More importantly, given the research I have read, and based on my own experience with my clients, I personally carry a portable biofeedback instrument with me at all times. It is very rare for me to start a coaching session now, either with individuals or groups, without first getting myself into a coherent heart rate state. I find that it centres me in the present moment, increasing my mental clarity. My post-doctoral research interest is focused within this domain, as I believe it can make a very valuable contribution to the developing profession of coaching.

The following section on the Ten Components of the Thinking Environment® is kindly authored by my colleague, Dr Sunny Stout Rostron, who has had extensive experience working with Nancy Kline and in facilitating the Thinking Environment® coaching process with individuals and teams.

The Ten Components of a Thinking Environment® – by Sunny Stout Rostron

Heart rate variability training is a very powerful tool to improve performance for individuals, but how do you apply it in a group or team coaching context? In the team context one does not often have the luxury or the time to train every individual in a team. One of the areas that I am currently exploring within the team context, is the work underpinned by Nancy Kline's Thinking Environment® methodology, particularly the Ten Components. It is our working hypothesis (which still needs to be scientifically researched) that if a team coach can effectively create the right conditions for a thinking environment, working proactively with the ten components, it is possible to create the same physiological state within each individual team member as represented in Figure 25. This is a discussion that Lloyd and I have started with Nancy Kline and it is an intriguing possibility.

I first met Nancy Kline in Cape Town, South Africa when I began my practitioner training for the Thinking Environment® coaching and consulting programme. Previously, I had read *Time to Think* and completed a four-day Thinking Environment® programme with two colleagues, Margaret Legum and Dorrian Aiken, who had both been responsible for promoting the methodology in South Africa for a number of years.

As I work from an existential stance in my coaching practice, I have found the underlying premise of Nancy Kline's thinking skills to be in alignment with the way in which I coach, i.e., the individual thinker is best able to do their own thinking, and all clients have the internal mental resources they need to learn or think for themselves. The basis of the Nancy Kline thinking process is one of uncovering limiting assumptions and creating positive liberating alternatives.

Several of my doctoral colleagues had been introduced to the six stages of the Thinking Partnership®, and kept telling me that the process was the perfect fit to both my individual and team coaching processes. It has proven to be so, as a thinking environment is based on three key factors: positive philosophical choice, the Ten Components, and uncovering limiting assumptions that either hold back the individual or limit their thinking.

I had already worked for a number of years with the Best Year Yet® team and individual coaching processes; these move through ten stages to identify limiting assumptions—ultimately creating a new empowering paradigm from which the client can clarify values and set new goals. More importantly, my own evolving coaching model works with identifying and replacing limiting paradigms, assumptions or worldviews in order to help the client move forward.

As human beings, we have trained ourselves to jump to conclusions. That is how we view the world; from our assumptions and the conclusions we have deduced as a result. In coaching sessions, I hear it again and again with clients; they jump to certain conclusions in order to figure out how to do their working day. This is because our thinking and behaviour is based on assumptions (limiting and liberating), and our conclusions are a result of those assumptions. In the Thinking Environment®, the real block to people's thinking is considered to be an untrue limiting assumption. There are three criteria which help to determine the truth of the assumption: **positive philosophical choice, information** and **logic** (Nancy Kline, 2005:19).

Also, because of the way our brains are hard-wired (thinking cortex over limbic emotional brain) we cannot think without emotion. And when we consider our reaction and interpretation of everyday encounters, there is nothing that doesn't have emotional impact. More importantly, as coaches we need to constantly challenge our own assumptions as we intervene in the client's narrative or story. As Siegel explains in his book, *The Developing Mind: How Relationships and the Brain Interact To Shape Who We Are* (1999:4–7), "Interpersonal experiences directly influence how we mentally construct reality ... Patterns of relationship and emotional communication directly affect the development of the brain ... and one way in which the mind attempts to integrate these varied representations and mental models is within the narrative process ... the way the mind establishes meaning—the way it places value or significance on experience—is closely linked to social interactions ... the mind's creation of representations provides us with insight into how reality is shaped by emotional and interpersonal processes ... Emotions can thus be seen as an integrating process that links the internal and interpersonal worlds of the human mind".

Nancy Kline's Thinking Environment® methodology is based on positive philosophical choice, incisive questions to remove limiting assumptions, and ten thinking components or behaviours, one of which is "feelings". These Ten Components are considered to be essential to create the external and internal space for the client (Kline, 2003:35). Positive Philosophical Choice is based on the "chosen philosophical view that human beings are by nature good: intelligent, loving, powerful, multi-talented, emotional, assertive, able to think through anything, imaginative and logical"; Kline says that "behaviour to the contrary is seen as the result of assumptions generated over a lifetime by events, conditions and attitudes in a person's environment" (Kline, 2005:4). In the Thinking Environment®, the crucial work is to identify and replace limiting assumptions with a more powerful worldview by choosing one core limiting assumption at a time that is relevant to the presenting issue.

According to Nancy Kline (1999/2004:100–1), team effectiveness depends on the calibre of thinking the team can do. Yet most teams do not operate within a Thinking Environment® with the ten components necessary to enhance quality thinking and decision making. Teams are the most strategic place to begin organizational change, but the limiting assumptions of each team member and the limiting assumptions of the group as a whole need to be identified and replaced with empowering assumptions.

The Ten Components of a Thinking Environment® are:

1. **Attention** (listening with interest and without interruption);
2. **Equality** (treating the other as a thinking peer; keeping agreements and boundaries);
3. **Ease** (offering freedom from internal rush or urgency);
4. **Appreciation** (a 5:1 ratio of appreciation to criticism);
5. **Encouragement** (moving beyond internal competition);
6. **Feelings** (allowing sufficient emotional release to restore thinking);
7. **Information** (supplying facts; managing organizational denial);
8. **Diversity** (welcoming divergent thinking and diverse group identities);
9. **Incisive questions** (removing assumptions that limit ideas); and
10. **Place** (creating a physical environment that says to the other, "You matter").

Based on the research of the Institute of HeartMath (2001), positive feelings allow for optimal thinking. From both individual and team coaching studies, indications are that people experience the Ten Components very positively and that they help to facilitate an experiential learning process. It is worth exploring the ten components in more detail.

Attention

The first component is **Attention**: the thinking environment cannot be created without attention. The **definition of attention** is listening with "respect, interest and fascination" (Kline, 1999:35). Attention helps people to do their own thinking; and it is important to understand that attention is not a technique: it is a way of being with the thinker, or the other person. It is an attitude that is driven by a number of assumptions. Several of these assumptions are that the thinker is inherently intelligent and "if you set up the right conditions, people **will** think for themselves" (Kline, 1999:20). The thinker is able to come up with ideas that are better than the thinking partner— particularly when the issue is the thinker's own specific issue. A second assumption is that the thinker is inherently worth your time, and a third assumption is that the thinker is inherently good, compassionate and able to figure things out. The thinker is able to cope, and deserves the best in terms of outcomes and attention.

A second aspect of attention is that the thinking environment is based on the interest and giving of undivided attention from the thinking partner. The listener, i.e., the partner, does not have to have an interest in the thinker's topic, but the listener does have to be truly interested in the thinker's process of thinking. Notice how this ties in with observable thinking patterns and observable levels of information complexity (concrete order, symbolic order, abstract conceptual order, and universal order) identified by Jaques and Clement (1997). In fact, there is really nothing more complex in our lives today, or perhaps more inexplicable or valuable, than the simple phenomenon that the listener is focused and fascinated and truly interested in the thinker's thinking. This is undeniably "catalytic" for the thinker (Kline, 2005).

In the context of the coaching conversation, the ability for the client to speak clearly, articulately and with quality depends very much on the quality of the attention that is given by the coach, or by the facilitator in a team coaching process. The reason for this is that the thinker, or in this case, the client, knows that they will not be interrupted in their thinking. You, the reader, will have experienced having been interrupted and put off your stride when you were thinking. To know you will not be interrupted "allows the mind to truly think for itself". In Nancy Kline's words to "know that you will not be interrupted or stopped" allows you to "venture into your finest and most courageous thinking" (Kline, 1999/2004).

Another important aspect of attention is that, by giving the thinker focused and undeniable attention, a rapport emerges in the internal and external mental space that allows the listener, whether silent or speaking, to explore the depths of their imagination. Attention means giving the thinker space when silent because the silent thinker is still busy thinking. To be interrupted when you are silent is as derailing as to be interrupted while you are talking. Some of our most original ideas occur to us when we are silent, and it is so important that the listener does not interpret silence as a signal for rescue. In silence reside reflection, thoughtfulness, productivity and creativity.

Another important characteristic of attention is that the listener must be willing for the thinker to take their thoughts or feelings in their own direction. It is so important that the listener does not register alarm or fright at the thinker's ideas, or think it important to correct the thinker if it differs from the partner's point of view. This is challenging as we are used to correcting others and inserting our point of view in normal conversation or dialogue.

This can also be challenging if the thinker's issues are close to the heart of the thinking partner—this quality of attention means that the thinker lets go of all their own assumptions, biases and ideas and pays close attention to the issues of the thinker. And finally, the listener needs to be drivingly interested in what the thinker may think next (Kline, 1999/2004).

The final characteristic of attention is "physically" showing attention; this is not to be confused with technique. What the thinking partner does with their eyes, face and body while they are listening shows fully focused and concentrated attention. To be physically present, showing interest and respect, the listener keeps their eyes on the eyes of the thinker. The thinker may look away, but the listener does not, unless the culture of the thinker requires the partner to look elsewhere, or to be seated in such a way that the physical environment supports the thinker without interfering with cultural values and norms. To keep your eyes focused on the thinker only works in cultures where eye contact is an affirming action. Also, if the thinker has requested an active thinking session to take place when walking, driving or even while talking on the telephone, attention must be physically focused without eye contact. The face and/or voice of the listener will say that "I am interested, relaxed, and am glad to be here listening to you". The face of worry or fear or judgement will not create that positive, affirming attention.

Even just giving each other a few minutes of undivided listening attention can be catalytic for the thinker to think through, uninterrupted, a problem or issue that needs solving.

Equality

The second component of the thinking environment is **Equality**. Equality can be defined reassuringly as "You get a turn too". In a coaching environment, the professional coach listens to the client; in the thinking environment between peers both people have a turn to listen and to speak. When coaching, it is the client who gets the attention, but in a thinking environment (particularly in team coaching) each person matters as much as the next and each person will have a chance to think equally. It is considerate to discuss some type of time boundary to ensure that both individuals are aware of time constraints and so that both have an approximately equal amount of time.

In a thinking environment, equality means that each person's thinking is as important as the other's; both individuals have a turn to think and to be the thinking partner. One of the assumptions underpinning this component is that, even in an organization with a hierarchy, each individual can be treated as an equal thinker no matter what their position. A second assumption is that the listener's thinking improves as they concentrate, listen and focus on the other with equal respect no matter what their role in the organizational ladder.

Another definition of equality is that if "treated as an equal, each individual can think with quality" and another is that "some of the best ideas come from the people at the lower end of the hierarchy", i.e., the people with their feet and ears to the ground, who live at the coal face of the organization facing clients, customers and suppliers. The people who live day in and day out with a problem are most often the best ones to find the solution to the problem.

In a thinking environment, equality means respecting boundaries and agreements. With each new level of attention and with genuine, communicated respect the thinker can refine the quality of his/her thinking and the two individuals, both thinker and listener, can begin to understand each other at a more profound level.

We are naturally drawn to the other person's warmth, intelligence and values. We are thus able to collaborate at a different level, creating trust and rapport. The feelings generated for another human being with similar concerns, issues, emotions and values can emerge when our communication is not constrained by our standard way of rushing, interrupting each other, or not giving each other equal time due to hierarchies. These constraints impose limiting assumptions that separate us, and cause us to hurt each other, thus creating resistance and a lack of trust and resistance.

A real sense of trust and respect are rare for most people in their daily life experiences. This is because most individuals do not experience a thinking partnership with a contract for equality. Hence the ten components are an essential as part of an individual or team coaching contract.

Ease

The third component of a thinking environment is **ease**. The definition of ease is "offering freedom from internal rush or urgency" (Kline, 1999/2004:35). This is to be distinguished from eliminating the rush and the urgency in our own individual external environments.

It would be greatly beneficial to us to alleviate rush from our lives; but it is difficult to do so with the pace at which the world and society operates. If we aren't able to slow down our lives or our pace at work, we can at least develop internal ease with others; in particular we can create our own internal ease in order to think and listen to one another.

The key characteristic of ease in the thinking environment is that ease is always achievable. Ease is inside the listener and the listener therefore has control over his or her own ease. There may be chaos or behaviour that creates urgency around us, or we may have only a few minutes to listen to the individual who has entered our office— or rung us up out of the blue. However, in that short amount of time, even in the midst of chaos, we can be equally present and without the sense of anxiety the speaker may be suffering from. If you create ease for the thinker, it will be in the presence of that ease that the thinker can think quickly, clearly and "without stress" to arrive at a solution. That is why both Lloyd and I personally always try to get into a coherent heart rate state before we work with an individual or group.

Something of which most of us are unconsciously aware, but don't necessarily take the time to notice, is that rushing takes up much more time than being at ease. Rushing "seems counter intuitive because it seems we are gaining on time if we are in a hurry"; urgency is actually destructive physically and mentally; ease is creative. As Kline indicates, urgency is "counter cultural and counter experience" (Kline, 1999/2004:67–70).

We leave behind chaos as we proceed through life in a whirlwind, leaving havoc and destruction behind us in terms of hurt feelings, lack of awareness and lack of consciousness of the needs of others. And the faster we go, the slower we go. Think about what happens to you when you lose your car or house keys when you are in a hurry. You turn your house and office upside down, becoming quite stressed and impatient, possibly beginning to deal with others in a fury. This is because you have created a chaotic heart rate pattern, as represented in Figure 24, which inhibits your cortex from working at its optimal level. Yet if you slowed down and walked quietly through the events that led to the loss of your keys, your intuition or rational thinking would more often than not come to your rescue. You would create a more stable, sine-wave-like pattern in the heart rate variability waveform, as shown in Figure 25, which leads to optimal thinking. It will save time if you sit back and enjoy your time with the thinker even if for just a few minutes to let them think through their present concern.

If you have only three minutes, set the boundary of three minutes with the thinker and be at peace that you can give your complete undivided attention for that span of time. You will then be free to move on with the rest of your day, or to suggest meeting at another time for an extended period. Knowing there are only three minutes of your intense concentrated attention will free the thinker to think freely and fluidly and with the greatest of ease. Your ease will make it easier for the thinker to get past their own tension and into realms of thought of which they had no apparent awareness. Like attention, ease is "catalytic". The focus of the listener will help the thinker to stay on track with their own thinking no matter how challenging for the listener.

Appreciation

The fourth component of a thinking environment is **appreciation. We think this is the most important component, and combined with deep abdominal breathing it is the fastest way to get the heart into a coherent sine wave.** The key definition of appreciation is "practising a 5 to 1 (5:1) ratio of appreciation to criticism" (Kline, 1999/2004:62). The most important feature of appreciation is that it needs to be a genuine appreciation of a particular quality in the thinker, and it needs to be communicated authentically. This links in with The Institute of HeartMath research which shows that the heart only moves into a coherent state when the individual actually feels appreciation as opposed to thinking about appreciation.

To develop the coaching relationship effectively, the principles and concepts of the Rogerian, person-centred approach are useful to us. This is a relationship-oriented experiential approach, requiring the practitioner to listen with acceptance and without judgement if clients are going to be able to change (Rogers, 1961:33–35). The quality of your appreciation for the thinker will come not only through your words, but from your tone of voice, the look in your eyes, the position and stance of your facial and body language, the attitude conveyed by all of the above, and finally by the enthusiasm and sincerity of your appreciation. Appreciation is one of the most critical components of the thinking environment—because it ultimately makes the thinker feel good about themselves. Most importantly, the human mind seems to work best with a full picture of reality, and that realistic picture is completed with the positive, appreciative comments of the listener; that appreciation need not be long, perhaps fifteen words or so which will enhance the thinking of the thinker the next time.

What is interesting about the concept of appreciation is that we usually expect to hear only "bad news" from others. It is rare that human beings really truly appreciate each other on a regular basis. We are used to hearing where we have failed, messed up, created chaos or uncertainty—in other words it is not our personal accomplishments for which we gain recognition, but for our mistakes or where things have gone wrong. **This, as we now know, leads to an erratic and chaotic heart rate variability pattern.** For some reason it is the negative side of life that seems to be considered to be reality.

The positive successes, the joy we create, the fine qualities of our being are not characteristics with which we typically recognize each other explicitly, or characteristics that we even consider to be "real". When you hear someone say to you, "I just need to give you some real honest feedback", you don't expect that they will be telling you something positive; you'll be expecting negative feedback. You will expect to hear, not how wonderful you are, but something more along the lines of a personal criticism.

Human beings are more drawn to criticize each other rather than to praise each other. Criticism is much easier to do, e.g., how many individuals do you know that when given a compliment actually say, "Thanks that makes me feel great!" Usually, they push back the compliment and protest to its lack of truth. So much for encouraging someone to praise us; we actually create an environment where it is difficult to praise us. We are more comfortable in saying what is wrong, not what is right or positive.

Encouragement

The fifth component of the thinking environment that positively impacts on HRV and stress is **encouragement**. Within the thinking environment, the definition of encouragement is "moving beyond internal competition". In the thinking environment, encouragement helps give people the courage to go past the normal boundaries of their thinking, to be creative, to think of ideas never thought of before, to look at the things they would not usually dare to see. Encouragement helps the thinker go to places within their mental space where they would not usually go to, that may even be beyond the scope of the status quo. Encouragement will help the thinker to be more creative than they ever dreamed, and to move past the usual rewards or incentives in the working environment to come up with something new and innovative.

Competition is rife in the working environment to create, not just good ideas, but the best ideas. Often cutting-edge ideas are neither thought of nor voiced due to the fear of competition or discouragement from peers, or from those senior to us. When frightened or fearful it is not possible for the thinker to think creatively, innovatively or outside of the box. If new ideas are frowned upon, not recognized or even stolen by others inside the working environment, individuals will never be encouraged to think for themselves. If creative or innovative thinking is not encouraged we may feel frightened or vulnerable.

Winning is the name of the game in business, and what if our idea is silly, boring or downright unworkable? We are frightened of losing, and losers are positively discouraged in the working environment. Some of the key intrinsic drivers for people at work are achievement, recognition, making a difference and financial security. If it's necessary to win in order to be admired, it may be too risky to come up with cutting edge ideas; and it certainly isn't possible in a fearful, constrictive or constrained environment.

Feelings

The sixth component of the thinking environment is **feelings**. The definition of feelings within the thinking environment is to "allow sufficient emotional release or expression of feeling to restore thinking" (Kline 1999/2004:35).

Feelings are a part of the thinking process, and we really mean to say that the thinking (and coaching) environment is essentially a "thinking and feeling" environment. Contrary to the standard wisdom of society, feelings are considered to be an inhibitor to thinking, and to be potentially destabilizing within the working environment.

Even good feelings are worrying when it comes to thinking. If feelings need to be released, the underlying current of thinking is "please release them elsewhere!" It can be said that good feelings may help us to think, but if they are extreme in any way they scare people at work and at home.

In the thinking environment the expression of feelings is encouraged and is okay. If by releasing these feelings it helps us to regain our balance then they are probably useful feelings. Perhaps shedding a tear is helpful during a thinking session, and by releasing the tears it lessens the hold or block on the thinker's fluidity in thinking.

Even bad feelings can be expressed in a thinking session, because one of the key foundation stones of the thinking environment is that the listener never comments judgementally on the content or subject matter of the thinker.

Siegel's description of the brain is helpful to us here. "The brain is a complex system of interconnected parts: The 'lower structures' include those circuits of the brainstem deep within the skull that mediate basic elements of energy flow ... the 'higher structures', such as the neocortex at the top of the brain, mediate 'more complex' information-processing functions such as perception, thinking, and reasoning ... The centrally located 'limbic system' coordinates the activity of higher and lower brain structures" ... and the "limbic regions are thought to mediate emotion, motivation, and goal-directed behaviour" (Siegel, 1999:10).

The limbic brain (which lies underneath the neo-cortex or higher thinking brain) is an important part of cognitive thinking. Research shows that we cannot think without emotions, they are part of the filters through which we analyze our thoughts and experiences. The release of feelings allows the thinker to think more intelligently (provided they are positive emotions; strong negative emotions actually inhibit thinking), and the thinking environment not only allows people to think with emotions, it positively encourages the thinker to do so in order to think clearly, fluidly, logically and coherently.

The thinking environment is not encouraging an individual to break down or fall apart; it is just that emotions are another aspect of the fuller picture of reality. It is important for the thinking partner to stay nonjudgemental and be focused on the thinker when feelings are released, whether those of sadness or joy. And the thinking environment is not a form of therapy, the listener does just that—listens with focus, intensity and compassion.

It is important that the listener not be frightened if the thinker actually does cry or laugh excessively. The expression of feelings is considered to be a normal part of thinking—allowing the thinker to stay at ease. What is crucial is that the listener keeps giving attention, no matter what negative feelings are being expressed, because in the process, the thinking environment allows the thinker to move to where the thinker needs to uncover any limiting assumptions that may be holding back their thinking. And the best thinking will only take place once those negative feelings have been expressed.

The expression of feelings can actually refine a person's thinking even if it feels tough in the moment; even if they think they sound incoherent, some of the real jewels of their thinking emerge in the release or expression of feelings.

This is a very difficult concept to grasp because, on the whole, society prefers that we repress not just feelings but big and bold ideas that interfere with obedience, hierarchy or the status quo. Nancy Kline talks about the development of "isms" such as terrorism and fundamentalism that emerge with cultural abuse (Kline, 1999/2004:87–96). What we are actually suggesting within the thinking environment is that the ability to express feelings responsibly and respectfully is important if we are to develop finer and finer thinking, and to manage our emotions, anxiety and stresses positively and effectively.

Although society does allow for some expression of feelings, society is uncomfortable with extreme or exhaustive levels of expression; this includes laughter of the belly-aching kind. That kind of laughter is considered to be exclusive, out of order and at the extreme end of behaviour. That's the kind of laughter that leads to tears and everyone wonders what has just happened; first you're laughing then you're crying.

Even with bereavement we are expected to keep our feelings under control and not bring up our feelings in relation to the lost loved one. People worry that you might go too far, and that they won't know how to handle you or the emotions you are expressing. What I am really saying here is how little emotion society actually condones for us to express.

Information

The seventh component of a thinking environment is **information**, and there are two definitions of information within the thinking environment context. One is about "supplying the facts" and the other is about "dismantling denial". Information is a difficult component as the listener has to decide when and whether to supply the facts that have been requested by the thinker.

There is an appropriate moment when the supplying of information will not derail the thinker. If the thinking partner enters too soon with information for the thinker, the partner may be offering information that the thinker later manages to discover for themselves. Also, the information the listener was asked to provide may actually become irrelevant as the thinker continues in the thinking process. The key is for the listener to be alert to any signals from the thinker when it may be appropriate to give information or facts.

To dismantle denial is different to supplying facts. Dismantling denial means to face the facts. This refers back to my earlier point that human beings think best "in the presence of the fullest picture of reality," and facing what is real takes immense courage. Organizations are notorious for denying what is not in their favour—especially if there is a knock-on effect on profitability or it interferes with share holder income.

It is almost impossible to think clearly when we deny what is true. What is staring us straight in the face is sometimes hard to see, yet it is in the thinking environment where the thinker is allowed to face what is right in front of them. Coaches work with question frameworks to help clients see what is staring right at them, but generally it is more important to create a container of safety in which the thinker can face the facts or the information at hand. Safe within the thinking environment means that the thinker has a chance to "think it through" and to come up with plausible solutions and to find a way forward. It is the thinking environment that makes it possible to dismantle denial.

Within the Thinking Environment® two questions can help to dismantle denial (Kline, 1999/2004:83):

1. What do you know now that you are going to find out in a year?
2. What is in front of your face that you are not facing?

Therefore, the component of information is not just about supplying information or hard facts; it is related to facing up to what is real or staring you in the face that you are not facing.

Diversity

The eighth component is **diversity.** Diversity is about difference: in equality, power, and worldview. In the business environment, the coach needs to become aware of and manage their own responses to questions of diversity, before they can begin to coach a client on similar issues (Stout Rostron, 2009:256).

Having worked for many years with Nancy Kline in the Thinking Environment®, I have come to understand how important it is for us as business coaches to first help ourselves, then our clients, by exploring the roots of our own discriminatory attitudes and behaviours. We do this by starting to examine "untrue" limiting assumptions that society and organizations make about people on the basis of their "group" identities and their place in the hierarchy of work and society (Kline, 1999:88–89). On an individual level, many problems are also fuelled by our own self-limiting assumptions. We see through the filters of our own worldview, as we are all products of our personal histories, language, culture, experience, education, gender and social conditioning (Stout Rostron, 2009:141).

Although people live and work in a diverse world, we have become suspicious and mistrusting of our differences. In so doing we discriminate against, and disempower others on the basis of their difference, rather than welcoming these differences and encompassing other worldviews to enhance our own. When working with a client in the coaching conversation, it is useful to help them learn to remove the limiting assumptions they hold about themselves, others and the systems in which they live and work. We actually need diversity in order to approach difficult situations with fresh thinking and ease. Only true, liberating assumptions can free individuals and groups and help them to reclaim their self-esteem and influence. This of course means developing an awareness of our own prejudices, biases, limiting thinking and life conditioning.

Nancy Kline defines diversity as "difference and equality" (Kline, 1999:87). To truly honour diversity requires genuinely diverse thinking with an appreciation for difference, an elimination of punishment for difference, and crucially highlights authority issues (who has the power?) and the fundamental issue of individuals being encouraged and permitted to think for themselves (Stout Rostron, 2009:141).

In working with teams in the thinking environment we often ask, "do we think better if there is an amount of diversity, safety and openness; and if so, why?" (Kline, 2005:30). One answer is that diversity simply gives us a more complete picture of reality. Another question is, "if the norm is power in organizational teams and in societal groups, how can we create 'safety' to help people to think clearly" (Kline, 2005:30)? An answer to this question is that, "we think best in the midst of diversity" (Kline, 1999:87). To appreciate the power of diversity, however, we need to operate from a foundation of really believing that people are created equal. We all need to work on developing an **internal ease** in the world of difference that we face everyday. (Stout Rostron, 2009:141).

There are two kinds of thinking environments: one provided externally by the coach or person giving attention to the thinker; the other is provided internally, residing in the mind of the thinker, provided by positive assumptions about the self as a thinker. Both kinds of environments are affected by society's limiting assumptions about people's group identities (Kline, 2005:30). Kline talks about group identities as they link to worldviews. She reaffirms that prejudice against people is driven by untrue limiting assumptions about their group identities. The core limiting assumption is that you, inherently, cannot think as well as the people outside your group. When this assumption (and the assumption that the dominant group will have to think for you) becomes internalized by members of the group, the group agrees to stay disempowered (Kline, 2005:30).

On an individual level, many problems are fuelled by our own self-limiting assumptions. We see through the filters of our own worldview, as we are all products of our personal histories, language, culture, experience, education, gender and social conditioning (Stout Rostron, 2009:140). When working with a client in the coaching conversation, it is useful to help them learn to remove the limiting assumptions they hold about themselves, others and the systems in which they live and work.

A feature of diversity is that people will only think for themselves when they know that they will be treated with interest and respect even if their ideas diverge from the norm, and that they will not experience reprisal from some sort of authority if they deviate from what is considered normal. Most people will not think for themselves if their thinking is going to get them into trouble, and more importantly, we may not take the risk of diverging from our group and thinking for ourselves. Thinking environments need to be created so that individuals, teams and groups of any kind can be encouraged to think creatively or differently and to generate new ideas and feel safe if they are suggesting something against the status quo.

Homogeneity, or sameness, is not necessarily beneficial or healthy. The reality within society today is that it is rich with difference—differences of people, cultures, language, education, politics, faith, thinking and behaviour. Yet most societies are intent on controlling those they consider as inferior.

People think at their best when they are respected; if they belong to a marginalized group it may be hard for them to think clearly and lucidly as they may be fearful of speaking up within their family, organization or society. Within the thinking environment, diversity recognizes that oppression and stereotyping people for their thinking, behaviour and cultures is underpinned by untrue limiting assumptions. These untrue limiting assumptions are not "inherent in the human being" (Nancy Kline, 2005).

The entire premise of the component of diversity within the thinking process is that these assumptions can be identified, analyzed and replaced with more empowering assumptions. This is done by asking a question such as: **What does society assume about our group that is limiting its voice, its power and its wellbeing in the world? Or, what are we as a group already assuming about each other that is limiting the way we listen to one another?**

These types of questions are excellent when the coach is working with a merger or acquisition of some kind, or when an organization is restructuring or downsizing. It means there will be a newly formed group with many untrue limiting assumptions driving their behaviour. These assumptions will limit the amount of attention each group pays to the other, and may interfere with the degree of respect that they accord one another.

Within a thinking environment, the two groups can explore their disempowering assumptions and examine them and replace them with a new way of thinking that will empower them to deal with their organizational changes. This is important as the limiting assumptions people make about each other in relation to their own group identities need to be replaced with true liberating assumptions about both groups.

This will free up everyone's thinking and will lead to new attitudes, new behaviour and new policies, and finally to better thinking and decision making. Diversity in terms of divergent ideas and diverse group identities is a crucial component and creates **ease** in the thinking environment, leading to clear, independent thinking and the possibility of accepting achievement and excellence from all no matter which group they maintain membership in.

Incisive questions

The ninth component is the **Incisive Question**. Incisive questions are undoubtedly one of the core components in the thinking environment. The key is that, when properly constructed, the incisive question contains all ten components within it. The definition of the incisive question is that it removes assumptions that limit thinking (Kline, 1999/2004:54). The untrue limiting assumption is what blocks the thinker; a true liberating assumption replaces an untrue limiting assumption and thus empowers and frees the thinker.

Incisive questions are constructed entirely of the thinker's own words, and are linked to the thinker's personal session goal. Incisive questions also work because they align an assumption (that the thinker considers to be true) to three criteria: **logic, facts** and **positive philosophical choice** (Kline, 2005:4).

The liberating true alternative is often based on positive philosophical choice. It is not just the thinker's personal view of the world; it is choosing to see human nature and life in a particular way. Another feature of the incisive question is that it is intentional; an incisive question is constructed as a hypothesis, or as a possibility and usually begins with a phrase that is in the subjunctive or hypothetical tense: "if you knew that" (insert liberating alternative); "how would you feel ... accomplish ... what would you do, feel" and so on. "So if you knew, how would you" are in the subjunctive.

The incisive question invites the thinker to look at a new empowering possibility (or truth) in alignment with the thinker's three criteria. The part of the incisive question which is called the "true liberating assumption" is in the present tense to emphasize what is true. With positive philosophical choice, the thinker is intelligent and worthy. The incisive question is made up of three parts:

1. Hypothetical tense.
2. Present tense.
3. Hypothetical tense.

For example, "if you **knew** that you **are** good enough **how would you** accomplish your next task?" Kline insists that what lies right inside the incisive question is true human liberation. The existentialists would love this. Liberation from our own internalized untrue limiting assumptions about ourselves, or about how life works that holds us back, keeps us victimized or stopped in our tracks. Incisive questions are in the thinker's words, and incisive questions actually liberate the thinker.

Place

The final, tenth component of the thinking environment is **Place**. Place is composed of two definitions: The first is creating a physical environment, i.e., it says to people that "You matter"; the second definition is treating your body as if it matters (Kline, 1999/2004:84–86).

What is important about the component of "place" is that people think their best when they know that they matter. The assumption that they don't matter can cause stress, blocking original thinking, feeling and the generation of ideas.

The first definition of physical environment requires that we suitably arrange the physical environment in which we plan to do our thinking; this shows that we are of importance. The rearrangement or re-creation of the physical environment can range from moving chairs, to filling the room with flowers, to turning on the under-floor heating in winter. In this way we begin to create a sense of presence, an ambiance in the room that is personally suited to coach and client.

Existentialism and the thinking environment

Similar to Lloyd, my approach is from an existential as well as a phenomenological viewpoint. My clients ultimately wish to talk about their "purpose in life" and the anxiety they experience in trying to "be" who they are and to "do" what they need to do within the complexity of the systems within which they work. Existentialism says there is no subjective or objective frame of reference; there is only the process of thinking about it. From my own doctoral research, I have learned that coaching helps the client to reconstruct their own reality and to interpret how they construct meaning of their reality (Stout Rostron, 2006:145).

In other words we share a lot of experiences as human beings, but ultimately each individual's experience of the world is unique. Each of my clients is unique in the way they think, in the way they see the world, in the way they interpret events. In my research, the key concern for investigation is "existence as experienced by man as an individual" (Spinelli, 1989:105). This is in perfect alignment with the basic premises of the thinking environment.

Here existential phenomenology is related to the thinking environment, where openness and an attitude of wonder mean that "we are free—free to choose the meanings in our lives, free to construct our interpretations of experience, free to reassess and alter them if we choose to" (Spinelli, 1989:116). My research into the coaching intervention is based on this existential phenomenological approach, where themes and patterns emerge in the context of the coaching conversation, but the coach needs to remain as free as possible from personal assumptions, bias and pre-judgement about the significances and meanings for the client within that coaching conversation.

Learning from experience and emotional literacy

There are two key sources of influence in learning, i.e., past experience and the role of others in the present that support our learning. And different kinds of learning occur depending on whether the context is perceived as positive or negative. "The way in which we interpret experience is intimately connected with how we view ourselves," (Boud, Cohen & Walker, 1996:15–16). This determines how we develop confidence and self-esteem which are necessary to learn from experience

"As human beings we can respond to the world through our emotions, but we can also through our emotions and our ability to reflect on them, come to grasp things in a new way" (van Deurzen-Smith, 1988). Understanding discloses the potential of our being, and shows us what we are capable of.

Working with the coaching client in an individual or team coaching conversation, from this point of view, is about coming to a new way of understanding the self and one's interaction with the world. It also means the coach needs to work with emotional literacy. Also known as emotional intelligence, this is the ability to read accurately and respond appropriately to the emotional reality of the other; in this instance the client.

Kline's interpretation of emotional literacy is that "intellect and emotion are inextricably enmeshed ... to be alert to the clues of a person's emotional state, to be able to listen deeply to the emotional component of a person's issues, to know what kinds of questions to ask in order to help a person express feelings and integrate them effectively with ideas and **to be aware of one's own feelings** is to promote highest standards of clear thinking, measurable outcomes and business results" (Kline, 2005:8).

Although neither Nancy Kline nor Carl Rogers (founder of humanistic psychology) are existentialists, this is in alignment with Rogers' (1980) client-centred approach and person-centred prophecy in *A Way of Being*, where he predicts a future changing in the direction of more humaneness. His research demonstrated the psychological conditions for allowing open communication and empowering individuals to achieve their full potential.

Moving away from traditional psychoanalysis, Rogers developed client-centred psychotherapy, which recognizes that each client has within him or herself the vast resources for self-understanding, for altering his or her self-concept, attitudes, and "self-directed" behaviour—and that these resources can be tapped by providing a definable climate of facilitative attitudes (Natalie Rogers, 2005). In conclusion, these ten components, or essential ten behaviours, need to exist for a Thinking Environment® to flourish.

Conclusion – by Lloyd Chapman

In conclusion, I believe that biofeedback, and especially the work done by the Institute of HeartMath, is now a vital component of the Integrated Experiential Coaching Model, in that it helps to create a positive, if not optimal, physiological state for the facilitation of learning. More intriguing is the idea that a coach can create the same physiological state by creating an environment in which the Ten Components of the Thinking Environment® can be applied.

It is far cheaper and easier to implant the Ten Components rather than biofeedback. This is done by simply teaching the team the Ten Components and continuously raising their awareness when the situation necessitates it. In my experience, both heart rate variability training and practising the Ten Components seem to enhance the experiential learning process undertaken in coaching.

CHAPTER EIGHT

Personal reflections and implications of the coaching journey

Implications of the coaching journey for me as a person

The design, application, research and continuous refinement of the Integrated Experiential Coaching Model was, and continues to be, an intense experiential learning journey for me. By far the most challenging and difficult part of the journey was the abstract conceptualization, which involved the development of the Integrated Experiential Coaching Model's theoretical framework. It is a synthesis of 20 years of concrete experience and 14 years of reading and research. The biggest challenge was to decide what to include and what to exclude, and to what depth I should explore. The work of Wilber and Almaas is enough to keep anyone busy for years.

It is a natural tendency for any researcher to feel that there is so much more that could and should be incorporated into the literature study and the theoretical model. Hence, I am left with the feeling that all that has been developed is the skeleton of the theory. In the end, however, every model has to have a cut-off point. Pure economics necessitates being practical, rather than being more idealistic. The exciting thing, however, is that the current theoretical model is not the end, but the beginning of a journey. There is the realization that the research work has only laid the foundations for a lifetime's work of applied research: it is the start of a lifelong journey to become a reflective practitioner. Most books on executive coaching seem to have either a psychological or business consulting bias. This model adds a third theoretical alternative to the profession, an integrated experiential learning approach.

On the practical side, the research project greatly contributed to me becoming a better coach. For example, prior to starting the project I had not heard of phenomenology. At first, phenomenology was seen purely as a research methodology, but the more I worked with the methodology, the more I realized that it, in itself, is actually a coaching methodology. In a sense, it taught me to be more open, and to stop using various models as a filter through which to listen to other people. It also made me realize that all models, including the Integrated Experiential Coaching Model, are only models; and models are limited ways of seeing reality. Transcendental phenomenology taught me to be more open and more present to my clients, to listen to what they say, and to be inquisitive about where the current experience was taking them.

The application of any model involves the danger of wanting to steer people down a certain path. The danger of the Integrated Experiential Coaching Model is to think that higher levels of development are more important or better, and then to try and steer the client to those levels. Transcendental phenomenology has helped me to become more open, and to stay or go with the client where they want to go. It has also made me aware of just how little I actually do know. At its core, human life, and what makes each of us tick, is still a big mystery. My ongoing work has left me with a sense of mystery and awe about what it means to be human.

I am more convinced than ever that there are levels of consciousness, and that experiential learning can facilitate human growth and development. However, I am left with an absolute respect and appreciation for the uniqueness of every individual with whom I am privileged to work. Every single person is unique. We all have our very own unique stories to tell, and every single one of us is a unique expression of the Divine. No one model works for everybody. Certainly, my research showed that general themes could be extracted from the experience of the group as a whole, but how they experienced these themes was unique to every individual. Same coach, same model, yet every person experienced it very differently. The meaning extracted from the experience was unique to the individuals. When I re-read the group's reflective essays, I am amazed and feel blessed that I could have been part of the process, but I am left wondering why we have to do this kind of research anyway. I feel that I have taken something away from the individual experience by trying to discover the essence of the experience of the group. Is it not good enough to have had people express their experience, and to leave it there? It was their experience, and it had an existential meaning for them.

Having just read another book about Jan Smuts, I cannot help but feel that my work has validated Smut's idea of Holism. I quoted Wilber extensively in this project, yet the true genius of Wilber's work is to be found in Smuts. I am of the opinion that Wilber has not given Smuts the credit that is due to him. My research has left me with a real sense of admiration for Smuts; I agree with him that every individual is unique, and that each one of us is a creative expression of evolution. Maybe that is why I am left feeling that I have done every individual a disservice by trying to extract their collective experience. But then again, that is where academia is at the moment. The real challenge for me is to go back and read Smuts again to try and study his method of arriving at the science of Personology. I am convinced that Smuts saw a greater vision than most of us see, and that it is worth pursuing. Be that as it may, somehow every person that participated in the research project had become a little more self-aware, and hence matured a little more. If that is all I have achieved with Smuts's work, then I am more than satisfied that I have made some small contribution to making the world a little more aware.

I am convinced that what the world needs is mass-customized learning, and that experiential learning is a wonderful process to facilitate this kind of learning. With hindsight, the more I reflect on this research experience, the clearer it becomes to me that the real essence of what can be done within the Integrated Experiential Coaching Model is to facilitate experiential learning on a one-on-one basis. In essence, that is all I work with; everything else is just a tool to be used, as and when I need it. So, for example, storytelling, narrative, 360-degree feedback and shadowing are tools used to facilitate a better understanding of the person's concrete experience. Personal learning contracts, journaling and meditation, for example, are tools that help to facilitate reflective observation. Systems thinking and stratified systems thinking facilitate abstract conceptualization.

It has dawned on me that the world is filled with tools which we often mistakenly believe to be the answer or the truth. In the end, they are just tools which facilitate an aspect of experiential learning. This realization has brought with it a tremendous sense of freedom. All tools have their place, and can make a valuable contribution in the experiential learning process. The art is to learn which aspects they facilitate, and when it is best to use or not use them. There is no need to defend a tool or model; they all have a relevant part to play. No single tool is the answer or the "silver bullet". Human life is far too complex to be captured or explained by a single model or tool. I therefore completed the development of the Model having learnt a tremendous amount. Yet at the same time, I am starting afresh, knowing that there is so little I know, and I am very excited to realize that there is still such a huge mystery to explore.

Lastly, having carried out both qualitative and quantitative research, I can honestly say that I much prefer qualitative research. It is more difficult and exciting than quantitative research. Throughout my research project, I was excited and completely involved in what I was doing; the project was one of being in the flow. For my masters degree, I analyzed 20 years' worth of data, doing multiple correlations and advanced statistical analysis. In the end, doing correlations made me a technical expert, but it did not leave me with the same sense of wonder and excitement as my doctoral research. In my years of experience, especially when working with mergers, I noticed that correlations and financial data do not excite people. What gives people meaning through the difficult times of mergers and acquisitions is not the logical, rational, or financial explanations; it is the human stories that they tell each other; it is the discovering of their own personal meaning within that experience. Quantitative research, so highly prized by academia and the business community, cannot capture that kind of essence.

In the end, organizations are made up of the human beings who manage and operate within them, and it is qualitative research that can help give us better insights into the inner working of the person. This project has convinced me that we need to have both kinds of research within organizations. Unfortunately, there is still a tendency to rate qualitative research not as "real" research, while quantitative research is "real" and "scientific". Hopefully the results of my research, and the development of the Integrated Experiential Coaching Model, can start to change that perception in some small way. Qualitative research can be and is exciting research to do, and in my case led to immense personal growth and development.

Final reflections on learning

The first thing that strikes me as I reflect on the development, application and research of the model is the seemingly open contradictions and differences between what happened in practice and the theoretical Integrated Experiential Coaching Model. The first contradiction is that in the Model it was emphasized that coaching is not about therapy but about facilitating experiential learning in order to facilitate growth and development. It was and is about improving performance. Yet the data show that some co-researchers found it meaningful to work on defining their purpose in life. Others found it meaningful to work on certain spiritual beliefs. These types of issue are existential in nature, and the co-researchers found working through such issues to be therapeutic. This raises the question whether this Model is not about therapy. I think it must be pointed out that the Model does not deny that therapeutic moments can and do occur. Nor does it deny that therapy or therapeutic techniques can be used as a coaching model.

I do, however, believe that only certified psychologists should practice therapy. Given that I am not a psychologist, I am not qualified to work in that domain. In my training for the ministry we were taught how to identify issues that should be referred to qualified professionals as and when this was required. In the Model I make it very clear that I do not work with any pathology; when it is recognized, I immediately refer the client to a psychologist or psychiatrist, and am happy to work with that therapist. The emphasis in the Model is not on therapeutic moments or issues, but on experiential learning and what the individual can learn from the experience whatever it may be. Going into the future, I do not see myself changing my view on this position. I think it is unethical for me as a coach to work in the domain of therapy if I am not a qualified professional.

The second difference involved the use of the Personal Learning Contract (PLC). In the theoretical Model, the PLC was seen as the means by which experiential learning would be recorded and analyzed in order to make the learning experience explicit. I started with the assumption that it would be a very useful learning tool, that everybody would find easy to use and to work with. In reality, that was not the case. Some co-researchers refused to use it after a few sessions; they saw it as being too much like homework. When I started the project, I was hoping to use the PLCs as secondary data sources for the research. Halfway through the coaching sessions I realized that not every coachee was using the PLC on a regular basis, and that it would not be possible to use it as a data source. What I learnt is that the PLC works very well with people who like the coaching sessions to be more structured. Others, however, preferred a more unstructured approach to the coaching sessions, and for them the PLC was a hindrance and an obstacle to learning. In fact, I soon learnt that the PLC, when enforced, could actually perpetuate certain problems.

Early in the coaching project I recognized a very interesting trend developing. Coachees would start the coaching session by apologizing for the fact that they had not filled in the PLC. I noticed that they saw the PLC as something that they had to do to satisfy me. It was not about their learning, but a chore they had to do to keep me happy. Even worse, some coachees were working on issues of nondelivery. They did not have enough time to deliver. So by not completing the PLC they were starting to feel even guiltier about their nondelivery. Here was just another thing or area in which they could not deliver. When I picked up this trend I immediately stopped emphasizing the use of the PLC. I carried on using it only with those coachees who found it meaningful. As a result, I now see and use the PLC as just another tool which can be used by some coachees if they find it to be meaningful. Learning Conversations are still central to my Model, but the PLC is not as important in practice as was indicated in the theoretical Model. The big learning for me was that even the most well-intended tools can, in fact, perpetuate certain underlying problems. The lesson for me was very clear, that as a coach I must always be open and not get attached to any technique or model—even my own Model. Reality is far too complex to be described by any model. Any model is only a tool that should be used with the greatest of care. The person is always more important than any model or technique.

The third contradiction, which is almost too embarrassing to mention, is how I contradicted my own Model in the way that I wrote up the original research. I started the theoretical Model by arguing very passionately for the inclusion of the left-hand quadrants of the Model. My argument was, and still is, that the business world and academia should recognize and take cognizance of the inner world or domain of the individual and the communal. Yet, in writing up the research, I completely ignored my own inner experience, by not bringing it into the project. I wrote the research project up as if it was a completely right-hand quadrant activity. I even went as far as to write in the third person. When my examiners, Dr Armsby and Dr Garvey, asked me in my doctoral *viva voce* examination why I had written in the third person, I responded that this was an academic exercise. Whereupon I was politely challenged to question my own assumptions about what academia is. So here I was passionately challenging the purely empirical scientific method, but in practice perpetuating the very system that I was so passionately criticizing—rather embarrassing to have this pointed out to you by your external examiners.

On the upside, however, this point does validate my argument in the Model that coaching is a good medium to facilitate reflection-on-action. My own experience, which I have just mentioned, as well as my experience of coaching others, has shown me how easy it is for all of us to become trapped in a particular way of thinking and doing. It is the coach as an objective outsider, with no emotional attachments, who can help facilitate this reflection-on-action. The data in the research project supported this observation, as did my *viva voce* experience. Drs Armsby and Garvey had no emotional attachment to my work, so they were able to facilitate that reflection-on-action for me. I found the *viva voce* experience very valuable in facilitating my reflection-on-action. This whole experience helped me to validate that part of the Model even further.

Another aspect of the Model that was highlighted in the research was that of storytelling. The co-researchers found it meaningful to tell their story in a nonjudgemental environment. I suppose that like everybody I was disappointed that I had to make revisions and amendments to the project; I just wanted to get it finished and get on with my life. At first I felt overwhelmed by the feedback. I especially battled with one examiner's point that he did not see my personal signature on the work. How could that be? This was my model that I developed; I did the work and the research, and I wrote it up. It was my work, so how could he say it missed my personal signature? As I reread the feedback over and over and reflected on it, I eventually realized that what was missing for the examiners was my story. All the feedback was pointing to the story behind how the work was done and my role in that. They were asking me to validate my own experience. This has been an ongoing issue for me as a person and coach. I sometimes think that is a hangover from the South African apartheid era. I was born in apartheid South Africa, and grew up in a society that was despised by the world. Maybe deep down inside that was part of the issue (this feeling of not being good enough— a second-class citizen of the world). Professor David Lane has continuously challenged me to honour my own experience. Sadly, I thought I had made major advancements in this area, but this experience highlighted the fact that it is an area that I continuously need to work on.

I realized that I tend to shy away from honouring my own experience; it is a false sense of humility. Yet as I started to amend the project work and add in my own experience by telling the story behind the story, I found that I was actually starting to enjoy it. I found it liberating and energizing to tell my story within this context. By asking me to tell my story, the examiners gave me permission to validate my story and my experience. I found it to be an empowering experience.

Secondly, I think the experience gave me a better understanding or insight into why my co-researchers found storytelling to be such an empowering experience. There is something meaningful and powerful in validating who we are by being allowed to tell our own story. As a result I am using storytelling more and more in my coaching. My experience has, however, taught me that as a coach, I need to listen to people's stories with a healthy dose of scepticism. We all have blind spots and there can be a certain amount of exaggeration. It is the coach's role to challenge the story and the perceived blind spots in a nonjudgemental way. I think it has, however, made me realize that people are tired of being told what is wrong with them.

By telling their story they actually start to recognize and validate what is right with them. This has led me to explore positive psychology further, and I am experimenting with the Clifton Strengths-Finder® in my coaching. The aim of this tool is to help individuals discover their five biggest strengths and use them optimally; the idea being that if every individual maximizes their strengths and manages their weaknesses, they will be successful. The emphasis moves to developing strengths rather than trying to eradicate weaknesses, which ties in very well with Jaques and Clement's (1997) leadership competencies. This further enhances the idea that my Model is closer to Peltier's (2001) definition of coaching (i.e., as being aimed at working with growth and development as opposed to having a therapy-based approach, where therapy is defined as working with pathological behaviour). My Model tries to identify what is good about people and maximize those aspects. It does not mean that I deny the need to work on weaknesses; in my Model the aim is to manage those weaknesses, but not to eradicate them. The emphasis is on what is right, as opposed to what is wrong.

Natural questions which arose at the end of the Doctoral programme were whether it was worthwhile, and whether I would do it again. I started the programme because, on one level, I felt inadequate as a coach. I knew I had the business experience and some experience in working with people from my days in the ministry. But somehow I felt I needed to obtain some professional qualification. The further I stepped into the programme, the more I realized just how much experience I had. All that was needed was for me to integrate years of experience and theory. What this programme did was to help me make all my assumptions and thinking explicit, and to test them in an open forum. The emphasis on experiential learning and personal construct psychology strongly facilitated the process of making my thinking explicit. Some of the theoretical input on the programme I found disappointing. It was at that time that I realized just how much experience I actually had.

I started off being incredibly idealistic, my aim being to develop the ultimate coaching model. The more the Model developed, and the more I used it in practice, the more I realized that it is not the model that is important, but who I am as a person. Who I am is more important than any model. The Model worked for me because it is who I am; it is my thinking and my way of doing the work.

The question that keeps going around in my mind, is whether the results are due to the Model, or to me just being me, or to a combination of the two. I think that the building of the theoretical Model and the practical application of it taught me that a good coach is more about being than doing. The more I stopped trying to be a good coach, the more the relationship developed. But then again, this is a real chicken-and-egg situation: was I relaxing because I had this insight, or because I had made my model and process explicit and as a result felt very comfortable within the framework I had developed? At this point, I cannot honestly answer that question.

If being is more important than doing, then I have to ask myself whether I would not have grown more as a person if I had put the same amount of money, time and energy into some inner disciplines like meditation and yoga. This in turn would have led me to be a better coach today. Somehow I am left with the feeling that the latter is true. Coaching is not about how good or academically correct your model is, it is about how comfortable you as a coach are with yourself. The more I can accept myself and the more comfortable I am with myself, the easier it is for me to allow others to be themselves. The less likely I am to project my issues, fantasies and ideals on to the coachee. And if that is the case, more intense inner work would have been more worthwhile. But then again, it is easy to write this with the benefit of hindsight.

The other idea I started with was that maybe one day I could enter academia. My experience on the doctoral research programme shattered that ideal. I have spent the last 20 years working in business, a large part of which has involved improving organizational effectiveness and efficiencies. In order to survive, organizations have to adapt to constant changes in the environment. I have always found that exciting about business. An endless irritation has been the lack of effectiveness and efficiency of the university programme. An immense amount of time was wasted as a result of having to rework assignments due to incorrect information and instructions. Due to the high level of frustration, I even tried to change to a university in South Africa. That was even more disastrous. My Model was too interdisciplinary for their liking. The business schools had no understanding of phenomenological research; they could not get past the question of which variable I was testing. The concept of hypothesis generation versus hypothesis testing was just too foreign for them to comprehend. I journaled all these experiences, and later spent some time reflecting on them. The common theme was that I had found interaction with universities drained my energy. Universities tend to be more set in their ways than business. Coaching and business, on the other hand, energized me. As a result, I now know that I prefer working in the business environment. I must, however, mention that within the university context, like most organizations, I did have the joy of working with individuals who were highly professional in what they did. I am very thankful that I had the opportunity to work with Professors Frans Cilliers and David Lane. Like good coaches, both were able to challenge me to bring out my best. Frans kept sending me back when I was doing the analysis, challenging me to do more with the data, moving into higher and higher levels of abstraction. David, on the other hand, continuously challenged me to honour my own experience.

In conclusion, then, I became a better coach as a result of the doctoral research programme and the development of the Integrated Experiential Coaching Model. It helped me to honour my own experience, to take that experience and develop the Model, and to test and research the Model in practice. As a result, it has given me more confidence to go and sell my services in the market. I can market myself much more effectively because I can make my work and my model explicit, and show that it has been researched and examined. In the end I am thankful that I did it through the National Centre for Work-Based Learning, because it enabled me to become a better practitioner through continuously challenging me to reflect on my experience, my work and my model. In so doing, it kept me grounded in practice, when it would have been so easy to escape into an academic ivory tower. At the same time, it highlighted the fact that being is more important than doing. It thereby emphasized my areas of continuous professional development: meditation and yoga.

From an ongoing professional development standpoint, I am really excited about the potential of biofeedback as a tool to enhance the capabilities of my coaching and to help facilitate learning. My post-doctoral research interests are now focused on stress and the implications this has for an executive's ability to think clearly. I look forward in anticipation to wherever the journey will lead me.

CHAPTER NINE

Conclusion

This book was a response to the *Dublin Declaration on Coaching*, which noted the importance of research to the professionalization of coaching, and that coaches are responsible for doing research in their own practitioners (GCC, 2008:11). The lack of books on or examples of how a coach could develop their own practice and coaching model within the scientist-practitioner framework was the idea behind writing this book. This has been a personal account and example of how I developed and researched my own coaching model and practice within the scientist-practitioner framework, which ultimately led to the first Doctorate in Professional Studies in Executive Coaching completed through the National Centre for Workbased Learning at Middlesex University, London. This book was not an attempt to present the definitive model on coaching, but rather the sharing of a structured thought process, which I hoped would enable you, the reader, to get a better idea of how you can develop your own coaching model and practice within the scientist-practitioner framework. At the very least, the book will give you an example of how to go about being a scientist-practitioner as a coach.

As I reflect on my own journey as a coach, and the phenomenal growth that we have seen in coaching globally, I keep asking myself why coaching has become so popular—what is driving this trend? My current working hypothesis is that it is an evolutionary response to the ongoing development of the human spirit. Could it be that coaching is the new profession of "Personology", to which Smuts (1973) alluded as early as 1924—in that it is a more integrative approach to dealing with the human being? I find it interesting that most of the coaches I respect did not plan to become coaches; they evolved into coaches after they found their own disciplines too limiting to be able to understand and work with individuals. It seems to be a characteristic of the human spirit to defy generalizations and dogma.

Let us take a step back, and reflect on the bigger picture for a moment. For centuries, religion was the mechanism which facilitated growth and development in individuals. In the West, this occurred predominantly through Christianity. With the Reformation, however, Christianity experienced a move away from the concrete experience of the individual as being primary, to abstract conceptualization as primary. And with that shift came religious dogma. The dogmatic belief system became primary, which brought with it the suppression of personal concrete experience. But the evolving human spirit defies dogma, and a few centuries later it finds expression in a new developing field: psychology. And the human spirit flourished within this new eclectic discipline; it was open, inquisitive and explorative. The human spirit had broken free of the shackles of religious dogma. Soon there were a number of schools in psychology.

However, in an attempt to find or define the "ultimate" or "the" school of psychology, psychology, too, became dogmatic. While religion took a few centuries to become dogmatic, psychology did it in less than a century. I believe coaching has evolved as the next discipline which is a result of the human spirit's continuous ability to defy dogma. My concern with coaching at the moment is the big rush to try and find and define the "ultimate coaching model". Do we not run the danger of simply becoming dogmatic faster than any other discipline that has gone before? And let us not forget that it is on the shoulders of those disciplines that we are building the discipline of coaching. Coaching, in my opinion, is the next synthesis.

That is why in the beginning of this book I emphasized that this is not an attempt to outline the definitive model on coaching, but rather to share a model which evolved out of my personal concrete experience. Hence, the model is part art and part science. It is an integration of Wilber's left-hand and right-hand quadrants. Can I claim that it is 100 per cent scientifically correct? Of course not. However, it has been scientifically researched, and it did meet what Wilber (1998b:155–160) calls the "three aspects of scientific inquiry" or the "three strands of all valid knowing":

- **Instrumental injunction**. This is the actual practice of doing the methodology or inquiry. It is an injunction, an experiment, a paradigm. According to Wilber (1998b) it always takes the form "If you want to know, do this". In the Integrated Experiential Coaching methodology the injunction is experiential learning and the research methodology is transpersonal phenomenology.
- **Direct apprehension**. This is the direct experience or the apprehension of data that is brought about by the injunction. In Kolb's (1984) language, this is grasping the data via direct apprehension as a result of active experimentation. This is the data of direct and immediate experience that is collected, analyzed and synthesized.
- **Communal confirmation (or rejection)**. This is where the data or experiences are checked by a community of people who have completed the injunction and the apprehensive strands. In a sense, this is a combination of reflective observation and abstract conceptualization. Having had the experience and collected the data, an individual will reflect on it, and via comprehension share it with a community who will either validate or invalidate the data. In my case, the data were written up and presented to the National Centre for Work-Based Learning at the University of Middlesex, and found to meet the requirements for the Doctorate in Professional Studies (Executive Coaching).

I am certainly not suggesting that every coach should do a doctorate. My call is for each of you to develop your own model. Remember that my thinking is very much aligned with the suggestion of Smuts (1973) that every individual is a unique expression of evolution— there will never be another you. And if you take that concept seriously, then you should immediately realize that your coaching model/ approach/methodology will be as unique as you are. Coaching is a synthesis of who we are. It is my honest belief that if your coaching methodology or approach is an expression of who you are, you will be coaching with integrity. However, if we want to develop coaching as a profession, then it is imperative for us to at least make our work explicit to our clients and to the coaching community for critical reflection and communal confirmation or rejection.

So how can you go about developing your own model, and holding it up for critical reflection? I would suggest Smuts's idea that "Personology" should be studied by analyzing the biographies of personalities as a whole. However, in this case it is your personal biography that should be studied. This study should be done synthetically, and not analytically as in the case of psychology. This would enable you, the researcher, to discover the materials that can help formulate the laws of your personal evolution as a person and coach. Smuts (1973:262) called this the science of "Biography", and he believed that it would form the basis of a "new Ethic and Metaphysic" which would have a truer spiritual outlook on personality.

I am not the first person to recommend this approach. Dr Ira Progoff wrote his doctoral dissertation on the psychology of C.G. Jung. When Jung read the dissertation, he invited Progoff to come and study with him in Switzerland, which he did in 1952, 1953 and 1955. Then Progoff had a turning point in his life; he read Smut's *Holism and Evolution*, which had a profound effect on him. He took Smuts seriously, and as a result developed the intensive journaling method and a whole new theory of depth psychology based on holism:

> In its goals and its procedures, depth psychology is the very opposite of an analytic, segmental approach to man. Its subject matter is the human being, but depth psychology does not desire to become another one of the specialized sciences of man. It deliberately refrains from dissecting man and marking him off into compartments. It desires rather to comprehend man in his wholeness and so, when it studies the depth process of personality, it maintains the perspective of man as a unity that is ever in the process of growth. Depth psychology is now, at least in the conception of it that we shall present in this volume, holistic in the profound, integrative meaning that Jan Christian Smuts gave the term (Progoff, 1973:4).

I am not going to go into Progoff's work here, because it is beyond the scope of this book. (I would, however, highly recommend that any coach who is serious about their own development should study Progoff's (1992) intensive journaling method.) I simply want to draw your attention to the fact that Smut's idea of using a journal to study your own biography is a very powerful tool, as Progoff's (1992) work has shown. It is a very holistic and structured way to journal in order to explore your own evolutionary development. For our purpose, however, I would recommend a simpler, yet very powerful, approach: the four steps of Kolb's Experiential Learning Cycle. The first step is to actively start journaling as a discipline. As you journal over time, you will start to notice your own threads of development. Find a journaling method that works for you: some people like to journal on their PC, while others prefer to have a collection of loose papers. What works for me personally is a hardcover journal and a pen; I find something very cathartic in writing. You might experience the same by typing, or even by using a voice recorder.

Concrete experience

Start by recording a chronological timeline of your life. Try record the period as holistically as you possibly can. Describe both the inner and outer events that come to your mind as you reflect on your life. Try to be as objective as you can, and stay open to the experience as you record the events. Like the Epoche process in transpersonal phenomenology, don't judge. Remember that *Epoche* is a Greek word which means to abstain, stay away from, or refrain from judgement. In our day-to-day lives we tend to hold knowledge judgementally; that is, we are biased due to our expectations and assumptions. The Epoche requires that we bracket as far as possible our biases, understandings, knowing and assumptions, and look at things in a new and fresh way. Journal whatever comes to mind. And following Progoff's (1992) advice, limit the entries to factual descriptions of your experience. Tell your own story and record it. So, what were the major events in your life that had an impact on you? Moving to a new city; the death of a friend or family member; studying or ending your studies; friends or relatives who had a major impact on you; being retrenched or fired? Write the story of how you got into coaching. Try to keep the events as brief as possible, and try and write down as many as possible. The danger here is concentrating on the outer events; remember to record the inner events as well.

Reflective observation

This is the ability to reflect and to observe your experience from many perspectives. The aim is for you to reflect, reflect again, and then describe the experience in terms of textural qualities, varying intensities, special qualities and time references. As you reflect on the chronological events that you have recorded, turn inward in reflection and describe whatever shines forth in consciousness. Include individual memories, judgements and perceptions, as they are integral to the process. The process will allow you to return to the self, in that the world is experienced from the vantage point of self-reflection, self-awareness and self-knowledge. The more you reflect, the more exact the phenomenon will become. Whatever stands out and is meaningful for you is explored and reflected on. Reflect in particular on those events that you think contributed towards you becoming a coach.

Was it due to an external event like being fired or retrenched? Was it an internal process of dissatisfaction about your own life? Were you looking for a change in your life? Was the interest in coaching brought about due to research or through reading? Was it through being coached, or due to a significant person who you respected? Was it because you had reached the limits of your current profession? It could be anything. Record those events and describe them in as much detail as possible. More importantly, keep asking yourself why why this event, or person, or circumstance? The more you reflect and describe, the richer the picture will become.

More importantly, try and reflect on the theories, practices, processes and toolsets that you have used in your coaching practice. Why do you use them and not others? What are the strengths and limitations of the theories, processes and toolsets that you use?

It is important to remember, however, that reflection is never-ending. You might reach a point where you consciously stop the reflective process, but the potential for reflection and discovery remains unlimited. In phenomenological reduction this is known as "horizontalization". No matter how many times you reconsider or reflect on the experience, the experience can never be exhausted, because horizons are unlimited. Even the final textural description, although completed in a point of time, remains open to further reflection. In my experience, you could find yourself returning many more times to reflect some more. And with every iteration the picture gets even richer. So it does not matter whether you do it in one or many sittings. In fact, the more the better.

Abstract conceptualization

This is the ability to create concepts and to build logically sound theories from your observations. Through the utilization of your imagination, varying your frames of reference, different perspectives and points of views, try to derive a structural description of the experience and the underlying factors that account for what is being experienced. Write it up in your journal. The aim is to understand the "how" that brought about the "what" of the experience. The question that needs to be explored is: how did the experience come to be what it is? This is the point where you try to make what you do in coaching explicit. What are you trying to achieve with your coaching? What is its purpose? Are you a life, business, executive, wellness, fitness or financial coach? More importantly, in what context do you or do you not coach? In which niche do you coach?

Next, you need to define what Lane and Corrie (2006:48) refer to as the "perspective" of your model. It is your ability to define what you as a coach bring to the encounter. This would include all the models, values, beliefs, knowledge and philosophies, as well as a sense of their competence limitations. What philosophy and theory underpins the approach? What is your theory about coaching? What makes it so unique? This is where you synthesize all your concrete experience with the conceptual knowledge that you have gained over the years, to develop your own theory and practice about coaching. Describe the philosophy and theories that underpin your work.

Having defined the purpose and perspectives that underpin the work, it becomes possible to structure a process to undertake the work. So what methods or tools can be used to help achieve the desired purpose within the constraints of the specified perspective? Why do you use the processes, methods and toolsets that you do? What is the process that you follow when you coach? Why do you use that approach? What are the limitations of the process, methods or tools? I, for example, do not undertake any remedial coaching at all. My model does not cater for it, and I personally am of the opinion that a psychologist-coach would be better at this.

Active experimentation

This is the ability to use the constructed theories to make decisions and experiment with new behaviours and thoughts. This is where you go and apply your model and then continuously reflect on what you are doing. It is here that journaling becomes even more critical. Wherever possible I try to journal every day. Once again, just as in the experiential learning cycle: what was the concrete experience of the day's coaching? Try to explain what you experienced in the coaching sessions. Simply describe it. Then reflect on the experience. Did you stick to your process or methodology? Did you deviate? What worked or did not work? Did you learn anything new? Where you surprised by anything? Are there still some unanswered questions or issues worrying you?

Having done that, try to understand how it happened. Explore various angles and possible explanations. Write down your working hypothesis of what is going on and why it is happening. And then think about what you are going to experiment with in the next session. What will you stop doing, continue doing, or try to do differently? Write it down. It will help you to distinguish between the espoused theories and the actual theory.

Conclusion

Journaling is a very powerful tool to make your thinking explicit and to develop your critical reflective ability. I have been asked on numerous occasions how it was possible for me to develop such an integrated theory and practice of coaching. The answer is very simple: I just reread my journals. My experience and thinking have developed over a number of years, but I was fortunate enough to have recorded them in my journals. I have a record of my unfolding journey. For that I am indebted to the Reverend Tom Cunningham, my lecturer in Pastoral Psychology. On the day that I completed my theological degree I went to greet Tom. His parting words to me were, "Lloyd, do you want to continue growing and developing as a human being?"—to which I responded "Yes". Tom then said to me, "In that case, keep a journal from tomorrow for as long as you can"—the best advice I have ever been given. I still journal, and my model continues to evolve. You can do the same. Good luck with the journey.

BIBLIOGRAPHY

Almaas, A.H. (1998a). *Essence with The Elixir of Enlightenment*. Boston, MA: Weiser Books.

Almaas, A.H. (1998b). *The Elixir of Enlightenment*. Boston, MA: Weiser Books.

Almaas, A.H. (1998c). *Facets of Unity: The Enneagram of Holy Ideas*. Berkley, CA: Diamond Books.

Almaas, A.H. (1998d). *The Pearl Beyond Price—Integration of Personality into Being: An Object Relations Approach*. Berkley, CA: Diamond Books.

Almaas, A.H. (2002). *Spacecruiser Inquiry: True Guidance for the Inner Journey*. Boston, MA: Shambhala.

Beard, C. and Wilson, J.P. (2002). *The Power of Experiential Learning: A Handbook for Trainers and Educators*. London: Kogan Page.

Beck, D.E. and Cowan, C. (2000). *Spiral Dynamics: Mastering Values, Leadership, and Change*. Malden: Blackwell Business.

Benedict Bunker, B. and Alban, B.T. (1997). *Large Group Interventions: Engaging the Whole System for Rapid Change*. San Francisco, CA: Jossey-Bass.

Boar, B.H. (1994). *Practical Steps for Aligning Information Technology with Business Strategies: How to Achieve a Competitive Advantage.* New York, NY: Wiley.

Brooks-Harris, J.E. and Stock-Ward, S.R. (1999). *Workshops: Designing and Facilitating Experiential Learning.* Thousand Oaks, CA: Sage.

Bruch, M. and Bond, F.W. (1998). *Beyond Diagnosis: Case Formulation Approaches in CBT.* New York, NY: Wiley.

Buckingham, M. and Clifton, D.O. (2002). *Now Discover Your Strengths: How to Develop Your Talent and Those People You Manage.* London: Simon and Schuster.

Cavanagh, M.J. and Grant, A.M. (2006). Coaching psychology and the scientist-practitioner model. In: Lane and Corrie (Eds.), *The Modern Scientist-Practitioner: A Guide to Practice in Psychology* (pp. 146–157). Hove: Routledge.

Chapman, L.A. (2005). An integrated experiential coaching approach to executive coaching. Paper presented at *1st Annual Consulting Psychology Conference*, Pretoria, November.

Chapman, L.A. (2006). *An Exploration of Executive Coaching as an Experiential Learning Process Within the Context of the Integrated Experiential Coaching Model.* Unpublished dissertation for Doctorate in Professional Studies (Executive Coaching). London: Middlesex University.

Corporate Leadership Council (2003). *Maximizing Returns on Professional Executive Coaching.* Washington, DC: Corporate Executive Board.

Cranton, P. (1996). *Professional Development as Transformative Learning. New Perspectives for Teachers of Adults.* San Francisco, CA: Jossey-Bass.

De Mello, A. (1990). *Awareness.* Grand Rapids, MI: Zondervan.

De Quincey, C. (2005). *Radical Knowing. Understanding Consciousness through Relationship.* Rochester, VT: Park Street Press.

Dotlich, D.L. and Cairo, P.C. (1999). *Action Coaching: How to Leverage Individual Performance for Company Success.* San Francisco, CA: Jossey-Bass.

Egan, G. (2002). *The Skilled Helper: A Problem-Management and Opportunity-Development Approach to Helping.* Pacific Grove, CA: Brooks/Cole.

Galbraith, J., Downey, D. and Kates, A. (2002). *Designing Dynamic Organizations: A Hands-On Guide for Leaders at all Levels.* New York, NY: Amacom.

Global Convention on Coaching (GCC). (2008). *Dublin Declaration on Coaching Including Appendices.* Global Convention on Coaching. Dublin, August. Webpage: www.coachingconvention.org

Goldratt, E.M. (1990). *What is This Thing Called the Theory of Constraints and How Should it be Implemented?* Great Barrington, MA: North River Press.

Goldsmith, M., Lyons, L. and Freas, A. (Eds.). (2000). *Coaching for Leadership: How the World's Greatest Coaches Help Leaders Learn.* San Francisco, CA: Jossey-Bass/Pfeiffer.

Greenleaf, R.K. (1977). *Servant Leadership: A Journey Into the Legitimate Power and Greatness.* New York, NY: Paulist Press.

Grof, S. (1998). Ken Wilber's Spectrum Psychology: Observations from clinical consciousness research. In: Rothberg, D., and Kelly, S. (Eds.), *Ken Wilber in Dialogue: Conversations with Leading Transpersonal Thinkers* (pp. 85–116). Wheaton, IL: Quest.

Hammer, M.M. and Champy, J.A. (1993). *Reengineering the Corporation: A Manifesto for Business Revolution.* New York, NY: Harpercollins.

Harri-Augstein, E.S. and Webb, M. (1995). *Learning to Change: A Resource for Trainers, Managers and Learners Based on Self-Organized Learning.* London: McGraw-Hill.

Harri-Augstein, E.S. and Thomas, L.F. (1991). *Learning Conversations, Self-Organized Learning: The Way to Personal and Organizational Growth.* London: Routledge.

Institute of HeartMath (2001). *Science of the Heart: Exploring the Role of the Heart in Human Performance.* An overview of research conducted by the Institute of HeartMath. Webpage: www.heartmath.org/research/science-of-the-heart-variability.html

Jaques, E. and Cason, K. (1994). *Human Capability: A Study of Individual Potential and its Application.* Arlington, VA: Carson Hall.

Jaques, E. and Clement, S.D. (1997). *Executive Leadership: A Practical Guide to Managing Complexity.* Arlington, VA: Carson Hall.

Kaplan, R.S. and Norton, D.P. (1996). *The Balanced Scorecard: Translating Strategy into Action.* Boston, MA: Harvard Business School Press.

Kilburg, R.R. (2000). *Executive Coaching: Developing Managerial Wisdom in a World of Chaos.* Washington, DC: American Psychological Association.

Kline, N. (2003). *Time to Think: Listening to Ignite the Human Mind.* London: Cassell Illustrated.

Kline, N. (2004). Keynote Address, in *Coaching in a Thinking Environment.* Wallingford: Time to Think.

Kline, N. (2005). *The Thinking Partnership programme: Consultant's guide.* Wallingford: Time to Think.

Koestenbaum, P. (1991). *Leadership: The Inner Side of Greatness*. San Francisco, CA: Jossey-Bass.

Kolb, D.A. (1984). *Experiential Learning: Experience as the Source of Learning and Development*. Englewood Cliffs, NJ: Prentice Hall.

Lane, D.A. (1990). *The Impossible Child*, Stoke on Trent: Trentham.

Lane, D.A. and Corrie, S. (2006). *The Modern Scientist-Practitioner: A Guide to Practice in Psychology*. Hove: Routledge.

Leonard, G. (1992). *Mastery: The Keys to Success and Long-Term Fulfilment*. New York, NY: Plume.

Leonard, G. and Murphy, M. (1995). *The Life We Are Given: A Long Term Program for Realizing the Potential of Body, Mind, Heart and Soul*. New York, NY: Archer and Putman.

Levine, M. (2002). *A Mind at a Time: How Every Child Can Succeed*. London: Simon and Schuster.

Lewin, R. and Regine, B. (1999). *The Soul at Work: Unleashing the Power of Complexity Science for Business Success*. London: Orion.

Mintzberg, H. (2004). *Managers not MBAs: A Hard Look at the Soft Practice of Management Development*. San Francisco, CA: Berrett-Koehler.

Moustakas, C. (1994). *Phenomenological Research Methods*. Thousand Oaks, CA: Sage Publications.

Mouton, J. (2001). *How to Succeed in your Master's and Doctoral Studies*. Pretoria: Van Schaik.

Oshry, B. (1999). *Leading Systems: Lessons from the Powerlab*. San Francisco, CA: Berrett-Koehler.

Peltier, B. (2001). *The Psychology of Executive Coaching: Theory and Application*. New York, NY: Brunner-Routledge.

Pennington, B.M. (1996). *Thomas Merton, My Brother: His Journey to Freedom, Compassion, and Final Integration*. New York, NY: New City.

Perry, L.T., Stott, R.G. and Smallwood, W.N. (1993). *Real-Time Strategy: Improving Team-Based Planning for a Fast-Changing World*. New York, NY: Wiley.

Progoff, I. (1973). *Depth Psychology and Modern Man*. New York, NY: McGraw-Hill.

Progoff, I. (1992). *At a Journal Workshop. Writing to Access the Power of the Unconscious and Evoke Creative Ability*. New York, NY: Tarcher/Putman.

Rehm, R. (1997). *Participative Design*. Unpublished paper.

Roberts, B. (1993). *The Experience of No-Self: A Contemplative Journey*. Albany, NY: State University of New York.

Rothberg, D. and Kelly, S. (Eds.). (1998). *Ken Wilber in Dialogue. Conversations with Leading Transpersonal Thinkers*. Wheaton, IL: Quest.

Schön, D.A. (1983). *The Reflective Practitioner: How Professionals Think in Action*. New York, NY: Basic Books.

Schumacher, E.F. (1978). *A Guide for the Perplexed*. New York, NY: Harper and Row.

Schumacher, E.F. (1989). *Small is Beautiful: Economics as if People Mattered*. New York, NY: HarperPerennial.

Senge, P. (1990). *The Fifth Discipline: The Art and Practice of the Learning Organization*. New York, NY: Doubleday.

Senge, P., Ross, R., Smith, B., Roberts, C. and Kleiner, A. (1994). *The Fifth Discipline Fieldbook: Strategies and Tools for Building a Learning Organization*. London: Nicholas Brealey.

Smuts, J.C. (1973). *Holism and Evolution*. Westport, CT: Greenwood.

Spears, L.C. (Ed.). (1998). *Insights on Leadership: Service, Stewardship, Spirit and Servant-Leadership*. New York, NY: Wiley.

Spinelli, E. (1998). *The Interpreted World: An Introduction to Phenomenological Psychology*. London: Sage.

Spinelli, E. (2008). Coaching and therapy: Similarities and differences. *International Coaching Psychology Review*, 3(3): 241–249.

Vardey, L. (1995). *Mother Theresa: A Simple Path*. London: Random House.

Visser, F. (2003). *Ken Wilber: Thought as Passion*. New York, NY: State University of New York.

Washburn, M. (1995). *The Ego and the Dynamic Ground: A Transpersonal Theory of Human Development*. New York, NY: State University of New York.

Whitworth, L., Kimsey-House, H. and Sandahl, P. (1998). *Co-Active Coaching: New Skills for Coaching People Toward Success in Work and Life*. Palo Alto, CA: Davies-Black.

Wilber, K. (1995). *Sex, Ecology, Spirituality: The Spirit of Evolution*. Boston, MA: Shambhala.

Wilber, K. (1996). *A Brief History of Everything*. Boston, MA: Shambhala.

Wilber, K. (1998a). *The Eye of Spirit: An Integral Vision for a World Gone Slightly Mad*. Boston, MA: Shambhala.

Wilber, K. (1998b). *The Marriage of Sense and Soul: Integrating Science and Religion*. New York, NY: Random House.

Wilber, K. (2000a). *Integral Psychology: Consciousness, Spirit, Psychology, Therapy*. Boston, MA: Shambhala.

Wilber, K. (2000b). *One Taste: Daily Reflections on Integral Spirituality*. Boston, MA: Shambhala.

Wilber, K. (2001). *No Boundary: Eastern and Western Approaches to Personal Growth*. Boston, MA: Shambhala.

Wilber, K. (2003). Foreword. In: Visser, F., *Ken Wilber: Thought as Passion* (pp. xi–xv). New York, NY: State University of New York.

Zohar, D. (1997). *Rewiring the Corporate Brain: Using the New Science to Rethink How We Structure and Lead Organizations*. San Francisco, CA: Berrett-Koehler.

INDEX

abstract conceptualization – see
  adaptive learning modes
accommodative knowledge
  67–68
accommodative learning style –
  see *learning styles*
active experimentation – see
  adaptive learning modes
adaptive learning modes (Kolb):
  abstract conceptualization
  3, 13, 64–65, 67, 69–70,
  79, 87, 93–94, 102, 104,
  122, 129, 142, 146, 148,
  151, 182, 193, 208,
  212–215, 217, 249, 252,
  262–263, 267
  active experimentation 64–65,
  67, 69–70, 79, 87, 93–94, 101,
  104–105, 109, 122, 144, 151,
  161, 181–182, 184, 192, 205,
  208, 212, 214–215, 217,
  263, 268

concrete experience 13, 63, 65,
  69, 70, 79, 83, 87, 89–91, 94,
  104–105, 121, 129, 141–142,
  146, 148, 182, 191, 193, 208,
  212, 214–217, 249, 262, 265,
  267–268
  reflective observation 64–65, 67,
  69, 70, 79, 87, 91, 94, 102, 121,
  144, 193, 208, 212–215, 217,
  252, 263, 266
Almaas, A.H. (A-Hameed Ali) 15,
  61–64, 66–67, 80, 94–95, 101,
  114, 188–189, 249
applying coaching skills – see
  coaching skills
assimilation learning style – see
  learning styles
assimilative knowledge 67–68

Balanced Scorecard (Kaplan and
  Norton) 7, 11, 58, 120, 127–131,
  136, 158, 184, 199

275

biofeedback 221, 225–226,
247–248, 259
business processes 4, 10, 11, 58,
101, 128–131, 134, 136–138,
153, 157, 186

Category B–1 task complexity 29,
32, 63
Category B–2 task complexity 29
Category B–3 task complexity
29, 134
Category B–4 task complexity 29
Category C–1 task complexity 29, 32
Category C–2 task complexity
29, 134
Category C–3 task complexity 30, 63
coaching skills:
applying coaching skills
107–109
engaging coaching skills
107–110
informing coaching skills
107–109
involving coaching skills
107–109
Co-Active Coaching Model
(Whitworth, Kimsey-House
and Sandal) 110
cognitive complexity 7, 28–30, 134,
139, 141, 220–221
cognitive power (Jaques and
Clement) 7, 11–12, 28, 30, 139,
141, 220–221
communal confirmation,
communal rejection 102,
263, 264
complexity of information (Jaques
and Clement) 34–36, 42, 140,
221, 230
concrete experience – see *adaptive
learning modes*
convergent knowledge 67–68

convergent learning style – see
learning styles
co-researchers 172–174, 177–187,
189, 201, 203–204, 207, 209,
253–256
Corporate Leadership Council 162,
194–202, 218

developmental hierarchy 26, 75
divergent knowledge 67–68
divergent learning style – see
learning styles
dynamic ground (Washburn)
53–55
dynamic-dialectical 55–56
dysfunctional hierarchies 28, 30,
133–134

engaging coaching skills – see
coaching skills
Epoche process – see
*transcendental phenomenology
methodology*
evolution 2, 16–19, 23–26, 31–34,
36, 49–51, 59, 75, 136, 142, 157,
216, 227, 251, 262, 265, 268
experiential learning 3, 7–8, 10,
13, 15, 63–65, 67, 73–75, 77,
79–82, 85, 87, 93, 95–96, 99–103,
105, 107, 109–110, 114–115, 121–
123, 125, 129, 142, 144, 146, 148,
158–159, 161–162, 165, 169, 171,
174, 178, 182, 186–187, 190–191,
199, 203–204, 208–209, 211–213,
215, 217–218, 226, 248–254, 257,
263, 265, 268
extension (Kolb) 64, 66–68, 79–80,
85, 87, 94

four fields of knowledge
(Schumacher) 10, 19–20, 23, 80,
81, 87, 114, 123, 191

four-quadrant Integral Model
(Wilber) 10, 20–24, 58, 77, 79–80,
81, 114, 123, 199–200

Grof, Stanislav 53, 57, 59, 60, 161

Harri-Augstein, Sheila 10, 81,
103–108, 110–114, 123
heart rate variability 222–226, 234,
236, 248
heterarchy 26–28, 30, 44, 133
hierarchy 26–28, 30–31, 39–40, 43–44,
53, 55, 57, 74–75, 92, 133–134,
155, 175, 232–233, 239, 241
holarchy, holarchically 26, 28, 33,
44, 47–48
holism 16, 18, 148, 251, 264
holons 24–35, 75

imaginative variation – see
transcendental phenomenology
methodology
individual competencies 58,
139–151, 187, 220
informing coaching skills – see
coaching skills
Institute of HeartMath 221–223,
225, 229, 235, 247
instrumental injunction 100–101, 263
Integral Model (Wilber) – see
four-quadrant Integral Model
(Wilber)
Integrated Experiential Coaching
Model 10, 12–13, 15, 79–81, 93–96,
99, 104–105, 107–108, 113–114,
117–120, 123, 125, 150, 155,
158–159, 161–162, 164–168,
171–172, 185–187, 189–192,
194, 198–206, 208–209, 211, 213,
215–219, 247, 249–251, 253, 259
integrating 20, 77, 81, 83, 93, 123,
177, 228

intension (Kolb) 64, 66–68, 79,
85, 94
intentionality (Husserl) 84–86,
94, 114
intrapsychic 149, 151–152, 154, 159
involving coaching skills – see
coaching skills

Jaques, Elliott 7, 11–12, 28–30,
32, 34–36, 42, 44, 50, 52, 58,
63, 76, 83, 132–141, 146–147,
150–151, 157–158, 199, 204,
219–221, 230, 257
Clement, Stephen D. 7, 11–12,
28–30, 32, 34–36, 42, 44, 50, 52,
63, 77, 83, 132–141, 146–147,
150–151, 157–158, 199, 204,
219–221, 230, 257

Kaplan, Robert S. 7, 127–128, 130,
158, 199
Kolb, David A. 10, 15, 58, 63–83,
85–86, 89–91, 93–95, 101, 114,
123, 134, 137, 142, 144, 146, 148,
205, 208, 211, 214–215, 263, 265

leadership competencies (Jaques
and Clement) 11–12, 58,
158, 257
learner-centred 106–107, 142–143,
146, 204
learning conversations (Harri-
Augstein and Thomas) 10, 81,
103–114, 119, 123, 167, 190,
204–205, 254
learning styles (Kolb):
accommodative learning style
70, 72, 108–109, 214
assimilation learning style
70–72, 107–108, 214
convergent learning style
70–73, 108–109, 214

divergent learning style 70–72,
107–108, 214
lower-left quadrant – see
quadrants
lower-right quadrant – see
quadrants

managerial complexity 5, 7, 9–10,
35, 121, 138–139, 141, 158, 169,
215, 219–226, 245
mastery curve (Leonard) 97
Washburn, Michael 40, 53–57
Mintzberg, Henry 162, 202–209
Moustakas, Clark 81, 83–84, 87–89,
92–93, 123, 171

noematic 84–86
noetic 84–86
Norton, David P. 7, 127–128, 130,
158, 199

organizational design 9, 11, 58, 131,
136–158, 159
organizational structure 10–11,
131–132, 136–158, 184

personal – see *phases of individual
development*
personal learning contract 103–105,
109, 118, 122, 167, 173, 182, 187,
205, 208, 252, 254
personal learning myths 111–113
person-environment mix 149,
151–157
Personology (Smuts) 17–18, 189,
216, 251, 262, 264
phases of individual development
(Wilber):
personal 10, 36–37, 41–44, 48,
52, 57, 77, 80–81, 95, 114, 123
prepersonal 36–37, 40–41, 44,
48, 61

transpersonal 10, 36–37, 40,
42–48, 51–53, 57, 60–61, 77,
80–81, 94–96, 114, 119, 120,
122–123, 176, 181, 185, 205,
208, 263, 265
phenomenological reduction – see
*transcendental phenomenology
methodology*
phenomenology 22, 81–96, 114, 123,
172, 246, 250, 263, 265
physicodynamic pole 53–55
prehension dimension 63–65, 68,
86, 142, 146, 148, 187
prepersonal – see *phases of
individual development*
provider-centred 107,
142–143, 204
quadrants (Integral Model,
Integrated Experiential
Coaching Model):
lower-left quadrant 22–23, 59,
74, 155, 186, 206
lower-right quadrant 21, 23, 59,
74, 120–121, 125, 155, 211
upper-left quadrant 21, 23,
58, 74, 120–121, 123, 168,
185, 206
upper-right quadrant 21, 23, 59,
74, 120–121, 123, 186, 219

Quakers 43, 162, 190–191, 193
Quaker Persuasion Model 162,
190–194

reflection-in-action, reflect-in-
action 106, 144–145, 197, 205
reflection-on-action, reflect-on-
action 104, 106, 145–146,
205, 255
reflective observation – see
adaptive learning modes
research methodologies 168–170

Schumacher, Ernst F. 10, 16–17,
19–21, 23–24, 31, 36, 43, 80–81,
87, 114, 123
scientist-practitioner xxi–xxv
1, 261
self-organized learner 105–106,
109, 186
servant leadership 43, 58–59
Smuts, Field Marshal Jan C. 16–21,
23, 36, 43, 148, 189, 201, 216,
251, 262–264
Spinelli, Ernesto 82, 84–86,
90, 149, 246
stages of development (Kolb)
75–78, 94
stages of individual development
(Wilber) 36–52, 54–57, 78, 94
strategy 4–7, 9, 39, 59, 63, 104–105,
109, 120, 126–132, 136, 138, 158,
184–185, 199–200
stratified systems theory (Jaques
and Clement) 7, 28, 34–36, 42,
58, 138, 219, 252
stress 116, 135, 154, 166, 203, 212,
219–226, 234, 236, 239, 245, 259
structural-hierarchical model/
paradigm 53, 55, 57
structures of consciousness
(Wilber) 37–39, 56
synthesis of meaning and
essences – see transcendental
phenomenology methodology
Systems and Psychodynamics
Model (Kilburg) 154–156
systems thinking 5, 7, 21, 58, 98,
126, 252

task complexity (Jaques and
Clement) 11, 28–30, 32, 35–36,

51, 63, 133–134, 137, 139–141,
156, 158, 169, 215, 219–221, 226
Ten Components of a Thinking
Environment® (Kline) 226–245
Thinking Environment® (Kline)
226–247
Thomas, Laurie 10, 81, 103–106,
110, 114, 123
three worlds framework for
research (Mouton) xxiii–xxiv 1
transcendental phenomenology
(Moustakas) 81, 88, 93–95, 114,
123, 250
transcendental phenomenology
methodology:
Epoche process 83, 88–90, 94,
171, 174, 265
imaginative variation 88, 92, 94,
171, 176
phenomenological reduction
88, 90–91, 171, 175–176, 266
synthesis of meaning and
essences 93–94, 171,
177–185
transformation dimension 64,
66–67, 69, 86, 144, 148, 205
transpersonal – see phases of
individual development

upper-left quadrant – see
quadrants
upper-right quadrant – see
quadrants

Wilber, Ken 7, 10, 15, 20–61, 66,
73–75, 77–81, 87, 94, 100–102,
114, 123, 126, 133, 161, 199, 249,
251, 263